Amazing Words

PRAISE FOR *AMAZING WORDS*

"I am awed by Phil Cousineau's scholarship and the overall view he has of inner matters. He has a genius for the soulful dimensions of words, and a rare intelligence for communicating the numinous dimension of language. *Amazing Words* will grace the lives of all who read it, and inspire them to respect, even revere words as much as its author does."

—Robert A. Johnson, author of *He, She,* and *Slender Threads*

"Phil Cousineau's *Amazing Words* is a wonderful meditation on words that can be read from beginning to end if you are obsessed with speech, greedy for mountain air, and into enlightened verbal play. Not a dry lexical listing, each word Cousineau chooses sings with cellos, vagabonds through tongues and history, and bounces like a balloon on the moon, and as high as his quirky imagination takes us. Compelled reading for residence in the ancient synagogue of the word."

—Willis Barnstone, author of *The Restored New Testament* and *Ancient Greek Lyrics*

Amazing Words

A Journey into the World of Weird and Wonderful Words

Phil Cousineau

Illustrations by
Greg Chadwick

JAICO PUBLISHING HOUSE

Ahmedabad Bangalore Bhopal Bhubaneswar Chennai
Delhi Hyderabad Kolkata Lucknow Mumbai

Published by Jaico Publishing House
A-2 Jash Chambers, 7-A Sir Phirozshah Mehta Road
Fort, Mumbai - 400 001
jaicopub@jaicobooks.com
www.jaicobooks.com

Published in arrangement with
Start Midnight, LLC
101 Hudson St, 37th Floor, Suite 3705
Jersey City, NJ 07302, USA

AMAZING WORDS
ISBN 978-93-88423-61-8

Original English language edition published by
VIVA Editions, an imprint of Start Midnight, LLC as
Wordcatcher

First Jaico Impression: 2019

Printed by
Thomson Press (India) Limited, New Delhi

This book is dedicated to
Gregg Chadwick,
friend, companion,
fellow believer in the
power of the painted word

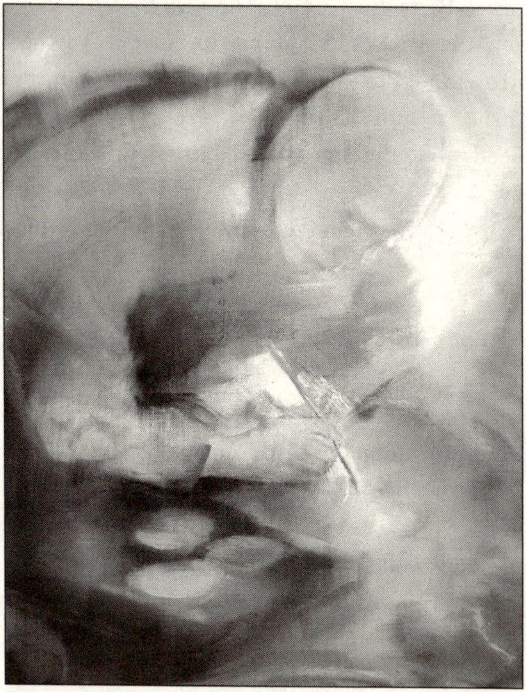

The Korean Brush

In Eric Partridge's book *The Gentle Art of Lexicography,* there is a story about an elder lady who, on borrowing a dictionary from her municipal library, returned it with the comment, "A very unusual book indeed—but the stories are extremely short, aren't they?"

—Henry Hitchings, *Johnson's Dictionary*

I am not yet so lost in lexicography, as to forget that words are the daughters of the earth, and that things are the sons of heaven.

—Dr. Samuel Johnson, preface to the *Dictionary*

You know well that, for a thousand years, the form of speech has changed, and words that then had certain meanings now seem wondrously foolish and odd to us. And yet people really spoke like that, and they succeeded as well in love as men do now.

—Geoffrey Chaucer, *Troilus and Criseyde*, 1372

ACKNOWLEDGMENTS

n. 1594. *Act of acknowledging influences; a token of due recognition or appreciation; a favorable notice; an expression of thanks.* Its roots reach back to the Medieval English *aknow*, from the Old English *oncnawan*, to understand, recognize, know, and the old verb *knowlechen*, to admit, especially the truth.

If asked how long this book took to write I would have to say it's been in the works all my life, so my first acknowledgment goes to my parents, Stanley and Rosemary Cousineau, who imbued in me the discipline of consulting ***dictionaries***[1] and ***encyclopedias*** whenever I had trouble with my boyhood studies. For better or worse, I've been in thrall to words ever since. While still in my teens I was blessed with an offer to work at my hometown newspaper, the *Wayne Dispatch*, where I'd appear every Thursday night to "put the paper to bed," and it's to Roger

[1] Words in ***italicized bold*** are "headwords" that are defined, described, and derived later in the book.

Turner, my first newspaper editor, I'd like to offer a token of recognition for that blazing red pencil that sent me scurrying to the dictionary. A nod of deep appreciation is also in order to the late Judy Serrin, my journalism teacher at the University of Detroit. Writing this book revived a dormant memory of how she began the first class each year with two simple questions: "Who reads the Op-Ed pages?" "Who reads the dictionary?" After seeing all the blank stares, she would ask, "How else are you going to learn to think for yourself?"

As sure as heliotropic plants turn to the sun for light, so does the *logotropic* soul turn to words for illumination. In that light I would like to acknowledge with a raft of favorable notices my early *lorefathers*, the mentors who reminded me of the love of learning, the ***animateurs***, Joseph Campbell, Huston Smith, and Robert A. Johnson, all of whom contributed words to my vocabulary, such as ***metaphor, cornucopia,*** and ***numinous***. I would also like to ***broadcast*** my thanks to Ernie Harwell, the Detroit Tigers Hall of Fame broadcaster, who illuminated for me the origins of ***boondocks,*** a word I learned from his home run calls on WJR, the sound of the Motor City. Thanks to Jeanne and Michael Adams for their offer of the use of Ansel's cabin in Yosemite, where I found the rest and respite to finish a large portion of the book, and discovered the wonderful citations for ***beauty, camera,*** and ***scootch*** in Ansel's well-thumbed library. Others who have shown special *fellowfeel* for this project over the years include County Clare's own favorite son, P. J. Curtis, who helped clarify several of the euphonious entries from Ireland, such as ***cant*** and ***cahoots***, and my logodaedalus Dublin friend Jaz Lynch, whose use of the old term ***kibosh*** caught my attention at McDaid's Pub in Dublin many years and many pints ago. The versatile wordmonger R. B. Morris supplied me with the marvelous Tennessee riff on "help" and "hope" and true ***companionship*** over the years as we discussed the imponderabilia of language in bars from Knoxville to North Beach. To the late Frank McCourt, I want to acknowledge the ***craic*** we shared while we lectured together on the Silversea *Silver Shadow*. I'll never forget how he described over lunch one day his introduction to the ***beauty*** of words in his first reading of Shakespeare, which he said felt like jewels in his mouth.

I would also like to extend a susurrus of thanks to the librarians at the San Francisco Public Library, the Detroit Public Library, and the New York Public Library, where I discovered much of the research for this book, as well as a round of ***accolades*** to the Two Kevins, the chrestomathic owners of Green Apple Books, in San Francisco, and George Whitman, at Shakespeare and Company, Paris, for years of serendipitous inspiration.

To my fellow bibliomancer Brenda Knight, I offer profuse thanks for thinking of that simple request that I look in my rolltop desk for any old manuscripts, or notebooks with book ideas, which is how this book was born. Thanks to copyeditor Mark Rhynsburger for his perspicacious help, Elena Granik for her marketing savvy, Frank Wiedemann for his elegant book design, Scott Idleman for his cover design, and to my publisher Frédérique Delacoste, who gave the green light to this project. Profuse thanks to my agent, Amy Rennert, for her graceful efforts in turning the idea into a reality and fighting for the best possible artifact. And I would like to ***enthusiastically*** offer a palette of colorful thanks to Gregg Chadwick for his ***gorgeous*** illustrations, and even more, his doughty dedication to the cause of "the painted word," which helps bring poets and painters together. Final acknowledgments, in the third sense of the word, understanding the truth of something, are due to my family, Jo Beaton and Jack Cousineau, who gracefully dealt with my long disappearances into my writing studio and distant libraries, as I rode my hobbyhorse of word fascination.

May all who read this book learn to love the riffling of pages in their favorite dictionaries.

INTRODUCTION

> Every word, without exception, is an enchantment, a wonder, a marvel, aphorisms compressed to single words, sometimes single phonemes.
>
> —Lewis Thomas

Every Friday night of my boyhood my father pulled out the plug of the old Philco television and pulled down one of his favorite books from the oak bookshelves in the living room. After asking my mother to pour him his nightly shot of Jack Daniel's, he asked her to join my younger brother and sister and me around his favorite leather reading chair. There he would lead us, one page at a time, through the classics that he loved, Homer, Mark Twain, Edgar Allan Poe, Herman Melville, Robert Louis Stevenson, or *Tales from the Arabian Nights.*

Naturally, there were a few words in those difficult but powerful books that we kids didn't understand. But my parents encouraged us to admit when we were stumped and to ask questions. To this day I can recall being enchanted, as Lewis Thomas writes above, but stymied by such unusual words as ***shanghaied*** in *The Sea Wolf;* ***mentor*** in *The Odyssey*; *rapscallion* in *Huckleberry Finn*; *or bohemian* in Van Gogh's letters. Tentatively, I would ask my father, whose knowledge of words was ***encyclopedic***, the meaning of the ones I didn't understand. But rather than give me an easy answer, he would point to our hefty edition of *The Random House* ***Dictionary,*** whose covers were always open like the wings of a giant bird, on the ottoman next to his chair.

"Look it up, Philip," he'd say. "That's why I bought the ***damned*** thing."

But his pedagogic tricks didn't end there.

When I started playing baseball he gave me a subscription to the *Sporting News*. One day he noticed that I was reading Ray Bradbury so he signed me up for a science-fiction book club. Saturday mornings were dedicated to sharing breakfast together at Brownie's, the old diner in town, where we would try to solve the crossword puzzles in the *Detroit Free Press*. If he took me to the Henry Ford Museum he couldn't resist telling me the story behind the names of famous cars like *Mercury*, inspired by the Greek god of speed, *Maverick,* after a cattle rustler, *Dusenberg*, which gave us the word *doozy*, or *Cadillac*, after the French explorer who founded Detroit.

"Someday you're going to thank me for this," my dad would say.

And then there were the road trips. We must have been the only family in America to actually carry a dictionary in the car with us when we went on vacations. When we made the pilgrimage to Edgar Allan Poe's home, in Philadelphia, I heard our guide pronounce the sonically thrilling *tintinnabulation*—and of course had to look it up back in the car. On a visit to a Matisse exhibit in Toledo, Ohio, I read in an art catalog the French word for a quick sketch, ***pochade***. When my parents drove us up to Stratford, Ontario, to see a performance of *A Midsummer Night's Dream*, the word ***seeksorrow*** leapt out at me from the stage, and I've loved it ever since.

This is also how my life as a wordcatcher began. Word by word, book by book, play by play, movie by movie, road by road, café by café, pub by pub, conversation by conversation, dictionary by dictionary.

In this spirit, the words that have fascinated me most have also compelled me to follow them back as far as my dictionaries and lexicons will take me, as if I were following in the wake of my French-Canadian *voyageur* ancestors up a surging river to its distant source. This is, in every sense of the word, the very meaning of *derivation*, from *de*, from, *rivus*, stream. Originally, it referred to the act of following a current of water to its source, and eventually came to mean, as the great Dr. Johnson defined it, "the tracing of a word from its origin."

Together, we find that to *derive* a word is to explore it, track it back to its earliest reference, story, or citation, the place from which it *flows*, a place full of immense energy, history, and mystery.

As the African proverb says, "Every river runs to its mama."

The River of Words

When the great J. R. R. Tolkien listened to a lecture by his son Christopher, Tolkien the elder was moved to see himself and his life's work in an entirely new light.

"I suddenly realized that I am a *pure* philologist. I like history, and am moved by it," he later wrote to his son, "but its finest moments for me are those in which it throws light on words and names."

My own fascinations often feel boundless, from history to literature, ***travel*** to sports, architecture to music, but my deepest passion runs like whitewater rapids when the words and names in those worlds rise to meet me. For the last thirty-five years—I know the exact date and place I began to write them down: April 10, 1975, when I moved into a matchbox-sized room in Kilburn, London—I have filled virtually hundreds of journals and notebooks with my favorite word lists. And now all these years later I have condensed and compressed those entries into this one volume, *Amazing Words*, in the hope of passing them on to other avid word hounds.

To create my own "word-hoard," in Tolkien's utterly gorgeous description, I have used a simple standard. Each and every "headword" that is explored here evoked in me an "Aha!" when I first encountered it.

Often while compiling this collection I have thought of the twice-told tale of the time the English poet W. H. Auden was asked to teach a class in poetry. Two hundred students applied to study with him, but there was room for only twenty in the classroom. When asked how he chose them, he said he picked the ones who actually ***loved*** words, which means he was seeking other *logophiles*, other word lovers.

That, too, has been my standard. But I have also tried to set *Amazing Words* apart from the scores of other wonderful word books. Not to be orchidaceous, but perspicacious; not ostentatious about the use of words, but keenly discerning, shrewdly knowledgeable.

To do so, I have included a few innovations. First, all of these words have surprising derivations, like ***baffle***, an old Scottish word to describe a disgraced knight. Second, each word here is either fun to say, such as ***bamboozle***, or mellifluous to hear, such as ***swaff***. Third, I've included "***companion*** words" at the end of each word story, in the spirit of those close friends who enjoy dining out together, a practice which honors a lifelong practice of mine of meandering from one word to another in my myriad dictionaries. Seeing how ***desultory***, *consultant*, and *result* are all related to the old Roman word for the trick rider who leapt from horse to horse makes our language, well, *jump* off the page. Fourth, I've introduced a few common words in uncommon ways, coming at them from a different angle to help us see them in fresh, even startling ways. For example, the everyday word *story* is so recognizable it is almost impossible to appreciate its lapidary meanings. So I introduce it within the ***story poles***, an ancient term for marking the ground for a building about to go up, which also serves as a vivid ***metaphor*** for laying the foundation of our lives with narratives. Likewise with *myth*, a word so common and so abused I have revived ***mythosphere***, a brilliant coinage by essayist and mythologist Alexander Eliot, to describe the "atmosphere" of sacred stories that surrounds us at all times. Fifth, I have tried to offer a great range of citations, from Mae West to the Marx Brothers, to illustrate how the words are actually used.

In a word, this book of weird, wonderful and wild word stories is a game of catch. When I throw a baseball around with my son Jack it's a game of give and take, each of us throwing the ball so the other can catch it. It's an ordinary activity, but also a profound metaphor for life and for my relationship to words. If I see an amazing word thrown to me in a book, magazine, or movie—***chicanery***, ***bedswerver***, *lucubrate*—I am ***thrilled***, and I want to keep the game of language going by looking it up, writing it down, using it in a story, poem, script, or conversation. Call it the sport of a wordcatcher, playing catch with the ball of language that's been thrown to me by all the writers and storytellers who came before me.

Finally, it is my fervent hope that by exploring the delightful backstories of the 250 or so words that compose this book you will be inspired to develop the delightful habit of running to your own dictionary, whether on your bookshelf or on your laptop, every time you're frustrated, intrigued, or *tantalized* by a curious word. Not necessarily for the purposes of self-improvement, or to *loftify* your social status, but to feel that throb in the heart that inspires us to follow a word home and learn about it, then maybe even use it in your own conversations and stories. I believe that if we trust that natural instinct, there is a strong chance we will be surprised by the joy often lurking inside the words that lured us forward.

No one captured this joyous jolt better than Shakespeare when he wrote in *King John:* "*Zounds!* I've never been so bethumped by words before!"

Zounds!—what an expression! *Bethump*—what a verb! What a marvelous use of exclamation points!

The first time I read that line my face broke out in a wild wall-to-wall grin, a ***flizzen***, as they said in the Bard's day. Then I raced to my family's old *Random House Dictionary*, which now graces my writing studio, and flipped to the back of the tattered old dictionary to find out where such words came from—*zounds*, God's wounds! and *bethumped*, knocked over backward.

And feeling once more the ***thrill*** of the chase I carried the old dictionary upstairs and carefully placed it in the corner of the living room of my own house, so my own son can discover for himself in the years to come the utter joy of wordcatching.

Phil Cousineau
April 2010
San Francisco

A

ABRACADABRA

An incantation, a charm, a magician's mantra, a healing formula to rid a person of disease or illness. A word so old hair is growing on it. *Abracadabra* is said to consist of the first letters of the Hebrew words *Ab* (Father), *Ben* (Son), and *Ruach ACadsch* (Holy Spirit), and when combined was believed to cure afflictions ranging from ague to toothaches. Traditionally, *The American Heritage Dictionary* says, the word *abracadabra* was worn as an amulet, furtively "arranged in an inverted pyramid" on a piece of paper that was suspended by a linen thread around the neck. As one letter disappeared in each line, so too was the malady of the patient supposed to disappear. Beyond its cult symbolism the word gained popularity when it was adopted in magic shows, circuses, and theater acts of the mystical persuasion. In the indispensable *Devil's Dictionary* Ambrose Bierce defined it: "By *Abracadabra* we signify an infinite number of things. 'Tis the answer to What? And How? And Why? And Whence? And Whither?—a word whereby The Truth (with the comfort it brings) is open to all who grope in night, Crying for Wisdom's holy light." Speaking of which, Ezra Pound, who wrote that a book should be like a ball of light in your hand, also said, "Mass ought to be in Latin, unless you could do it in Greek or Chinese. In fact, any *abracadabra* that no bloody member of the public or half-educated ape of a clargimint could think he understood." Companion words include the hypnotic *abracadabrant*, marvelous or stunning.

ABRACADABRA
ABRACADABR
ABRACADAB
ABRACADA
ABRACAD
ABRACA
ABRAC
ABRA
ABR
AB
A

ABSURD

Ridiculous, incongruous, contrary to reason. Unbelievable because inaudible. Yet its roots in the Latin *ab-surdus*, deaf, stupid, reveal that *absurd* really does mean "not-hearing," or as Merriam-Webster suggests, "unsound," which sounds just right. By the 16th century, its meaning had worn down to "silly or folly," then took on its secondary meaning of "having no rational or orderly relationship to human life." Figuratively, it suggests life is strange because you haven't been listening very closely. Everything sounds discordant, seems inharmonious, out of tune; life has lost its melody. You're deaf to the truth. "The Theater of the Absurd," based on the writings of Albert Camus, Samuel Beckett, and Eugène Ionesco, plays up this sinking feeling that there is no ultimate meaning or purpose in the universe, as if to say even God isn't listening—or there is no God at all to listen to our woes. It's *absurd* we don't better appreciate the depths of this word, although it has been stretched by the *Absurdists* to also suggest that human beings are ultimately free because nothing is fated. In that light, consider Lily Tomlin's sly observation: "You cannot achieve the impossible without attempting the *absurd*." The great poet Louis Simpson writes in "An Impasse," "To say, 'The news is good' / in French would be bad ***grammar***, and *absurd*, which is worse."

ACADEMY

A school to teach specialized skills or thought; a body of established opinion widely accepted as authoritative; a society for the advancement of art or science. The term comes from the Grove of Akademos, where Plato taught, in honor of Akademos, a mythic ***hero*** in the Trojan War, said to live on a farm "six *stadia* outside Athens," and who gave refuge to Castor and Pollux after their search for their kidnapped sister, Helen of Sparta. The word has held on to this sense of respite from the real world. By the 16th century, it had taken on figurative significance as any center of training, and by the mid-19th century "the academy" had come to mean the extended world of education and scholarship. However, *academic* has devolved into an embattled term far afield from Plato's school. On one hand, it suggests rigorous intellectualism; on the other, scholars hopelessly lost in clouds of thought. Camille Paglia said, in an interview with Shane Berry of Three Monkeys Online, "[A]s the decades passed and poststructuralism, postmodernism, and New Historicism took root in the *academy*, I began to realize how many of my skills as a commentator on art and culture came from my early training in the New Criticism." Synchronistically, I recently found this note I took from a conversation with my friend mythologist Joseph Campbell, in which he said, rather impishly: "I'm with those philosophers in the academy—until their feet leave the ground." Companion terms include *the groves of Academe,* a reference to Horace's *silvas Academi*; the venerable *Académie Française*;

and the *Academy Award*, alluding to the romantic notion of an idyllic life dedicated to thinking, research, or creativity, whether on a bucolic campus, amid the privileged halls of Paris, or behind the walled gardens of Hollywood.

ACCOLADE

Praise, laurel, award. A laudatory word worthy of honors. Imagine, if you will, as Rod Serling would intone, a ritual for conferring knighthood, featuring an all-night vigil for the candidate, a ceremonial embrace, and a light tap on the shoulders with the flat side of a sword, capped off, if we can trust the movies, with the immortal phrase "I dub thee Sir Lancelot, or "Sir Loin," as the case may be. That's your *accolata*, the name of the ceremony, whether it takes place in a cathedral, a castle, or on the battlefield. The ennobled word derives from *ad,* to, and *collum*, the neck or collar, from Latin *accolare*, to embrace, and French *accoler*, which the *Random House Dictionary* warmly defines as "to hug round the neck." Webster's adds a concise secondary meaning of "a mark of acknowledgement," and a third, the vivid musical usage "a brace or line used in music to join two or more staffs carrying simultaneous parts." Notes joined at the neck, you might say. In his poem "Memorial Day," Joyce Kilmer wrote, "May we, their grateful children, learn / Their strength, who lie beneath this sod, / Who went through fire and death to earn / At last the *accolade* of God." More recently, actor Morgan Freeman said upon receiving his ***Academy*** Award, "Getting a standing ovation was kind of humbling. ... So many people are so happy that I have been named for this award. A lot of people say you're due—maybe you are, maybe you aren't—it's an *accolade.*" Thus, an *accolade* is an honor or praise that feels like a warm embrace, or a tap of approval on the shoulder from a favorite uncle or coach or book critic.

ADUMBRATE

To prefigure, render a sketchy outline, disclose a bit of what you know, give warning. Not just another "inkhorn word" but a useful verb, since so much of our life is in and out of the dark. Like many light-and-dark words, it comes from the Latin *ad*, to or fore, and *umbra*, shadow, thus *adumbratus*, meaning "to lightly foreshadow." If you look it up, you'll discover a shadow theater of silhouetted words: *umbrage*, *shadowbox*, and *skiamachy*, or "shadow-fighting," a favorite practice of boxers, familiar to anyone battling imaginary enemies. My own earliest recollection of the word was in my first college film class, at the University of Detroit, in 1974, where we studied the use of foreshadowing. One morning the professor wrote in white chalk caps on the blackboard: THE ART OF ADUMBRATING IN HITCHCOCK. That lecture changed the way I viewed movies, teaching me how to look for signs and symbols. Writing of Hitchcock's *Odd Man Out*, Thomas M. Letich says, "[He] has made it fun to watch the revelation of Alicia's character by involving her in a promisingly dangerous situation while *adumbrating* the danger with such authority and wit that following the continuity provides the same perverse pleasures as identifying Hannay's char and the body she discovers in *The 39 Steps*." Companion words that *shadow forth* include *skiascope*, an optometrist's tool for determining the "refractive condition of the eye" by following the movement of "retinal lights and shadows," and *chiaroscuro*, an art born of light and shadow, like moonlight on castle ruins, or the gold-haunted portraits of Rembrandt, the feverdream movies of Terrence Malick, the shadow-strewn architecture of Tadao Ando.

Adumbrate (Shadow Boxing)

Aftermath

AFTERMATH

Consequences. Today we speak of the *aftermath* of something as its long-lasting results. But this has nothing to do with your old math classes, which still haunt some of us who suffer the odd nightmare about receiving high school transcripts that say we failed our tenth grade math class and have to take it over. No, thankfully, *aftermath* has been harvested from *after*, following, and *math*, from *mæð*, Old English dialect meaning "to mow, cut hay," and originally referred to the second crop of hay grown in the same season after the first had been scythed. By the 18th century, the agricultural term took on its modern figurative meaning of reaping what we sowed. Now the only question is: What's the word for that head-spinning smell released from all that cut grass that I mowed for $5 a lawn when I was kid? Companion words include *polymath*, from *poly*, much, and *mathein*, learner, and so someone who simply loves to learn. And speaking of math, *algebra* derives from the *al-jabr*, a book by its inventor, Muhammad al-Khwarizmi. *An afterword* for *aftermath* reveals a distant cousin, *afterclap*, which refers to the ... sudden silence ... after the applause dies away—a word well worthy of revival because it names the currently nameless trauma suffered by ex-***athletes***, actors, and politicians who desperately miss the applause after they retire.

AGONY

Pain, conflict, struggle. Ancient Greece teemed with competition. There were upward of 300 ***gymnasiums***, stadiums, and hippodromes, which regularly held a thrilling range of contests, from wrestling and chariot racing to sculpture and drama. Collectively, these were called the *agonia*, the struggle for victory in the games, from the earlier verb *agein*, to drive, to lead, to celebrate, and *agon*, or contest. So fierce were all contests in ancient Greece that the winners were celebrated, even apotheosized, while the losers slunk away ignominiously. The visceral memory of those fierce competitions comes down to us in our word *agony*, which by the 14th century stretched out to mean wrestling against the fierce opponents of mental anguish, physical torment, even the suffering before death. In the

International Journal of Lexicography, John Considine writes that the earliest recorded use in English, in Wycliffe's Bible, is the description of Christ "in *agonye*" in the Garden of Gethsemane. Companion words include *protagonist* and *antagonist*, the two ***characters*** pitted against each other in any drama, whether essentially an arena or theater; and *antagonize*, which means to put someone else in *agony*. Figuratively, *agony* is the heart of all drama; encountering, confronting, then triumphing over it. "There is no greater *agony* than bearing an untold story inside you," writes Maya Angelou. Seamus Heaney expanded on this aspect after translating a certain 9th-century Anglo-Saxon epic: "One way of reading *Beowulf* is to think of it as three *agons* in the hero's life." Curiously, an *agonist* is a drug that activates cell molecules in a way that replicates their natural processes. In China, the ***writhing*** of tea leaves in the bottom of a teacup when hot water is poured in is called "the *agony* of the leaf." On *Star Trek* "*agonizers*" were red-glowing weapons used on those who had committed minor offenses, while those who were guilty of major ones were sent to the "*agony* booth."

ALLEGORY

A long **metaphor;** *a story with an inner and outer meaning; a narrative with symbolic significance.* An *allegory* is a description in which a place, object, or action is personified or holds moral, social, religious, or political importance. To fully appreciate the magnitude of this word, think of an average day in classical Athens. An indignant citizen walks down to the agora, the marketplace under the Acropolis, and delivers a heated *allegoria*, a veiled but critical speech designed to expose the actions of a politician he vehemently disagrees with. We've been speaking and writing that way ever since. *Allegories* abound in novels, songs, movies. Jonathan Swift's *Gulliver's Travels* is an audacious adventure story, but its deeper power is as an *allegorical* satire on 17th-century English mores. Francis Coppola's *Apocalypse Now* and Katherine Bigelow's *The Hurt Locker* aren't only movies about the Vietnam and Iraq wars, but *allegories* about the insanity of all wars in all times. What I find stirring is that the word picture still shines through. Our English word derives from 14th century French *allégorie*, via the Greek *allegoria*, from *allos,* another, different, plus *agoreuein*, to speak openly in the agora. Thus, to be *allegorical* means to express yourself openly but differently, figuratively, metaphorically, symbolically, sometimes furtively. Plato's "*Allegory* of the Cave" was to the ancient world what Maya Lin's *Confluence* is to ours. John Keats wrote of one who employed it most ingeniously, "Shakespeare led a life of allegory; his works are the comments on it." "The Allegory of Painting" (1665-67) by Vermeer features a drawn-back curtain that reveals the artist himself painting a model dressed as Clio, the muse of history; it was considered his own favorite painting. More recently, in *Men of Tomorrow: Geeks, Gangsters, and the Birth of the*

Comic Book, Gerard Jones vividly describes *Superman* as "an *allegory* that echoed for immigrants and Jews: the strange visitor who hides his alien identity."

AMAZON

A legendary river in South America; a mythic race of female warriors from Scythia. Today whenever we hear the word we think of the forests of South America, Wonder Woman, Buffy the Vampire Killer, Billie Jean King. But the word was originally used by the ancient Greeks to describe a tribe of warring women who lived at the remote reaches of the then known world, the shores of the Black Sea and the Caucasus mountains, in Asia Minor. The first historian, Herodotus of Ephesus, described them as fierce warriors who fought against the Greeks, *a-masos*, without one breast, allegedly to more easily let fly their arrows. According to travelers' tales of the time, theirs was a society without men; any son born to an Amazon was either slain or exiled. Shakespeare's *A Midsummer Night's Dream* takes place the night before the wedding of Theseus and Hippolyta, the *Amazon* queen. In 1541, the Spanish conquistador Francisco de Orellana, who was the first European to navigate the length of the river, named it after the infamous warriors after being surprised in an attack by the Tapuya Indians, whose women, he reported, were as fierce as his own soldiers. Out of such unsettling events, a legend grew of a ferocious tribe of women warriors living in a world without men. Curious companion words include *Amazonian chin*, beardless, like a female warrior, as evoked in Shakespeare's *Coriolanus*: "When with his *Amazonian chin* he drove / the bristled lips before him."

AMUSE

To divert, entertain, occupy, please, or pleasantly ***bewilder***. Its 500-year-old origins are rather...*amusing*, a revelation, rooted as they are in the Middle French *amuser.* Captain Francis Grose, in his scintillating 1811 dictionary of ***slang***, deftly defines its earliest use: an attempt to deceive or cheat. But Grose adds a colorful use as a noun, and his definition is worth quoting in full. "*Amusers*," he writes, "are rogues who carried snuff or dust in their pockets, which they threw into the eyes of any person they intended to rob; and running away, their accomplices (pretending to assist and pity the half-blinded person) took that opportunity of plundering them." Some lexicographers insist on important degrees of *amusement*: *amusing* is a light and pleasant distraction, an activity that kills time; *entertaining* is an agreeable experience, as in a performance of some brio that heightens awareness; *diverting* suggests amusing ourselves to death, turning off the intellectual faculties, by a sporting contest or comedy. "Ha, ha! You *amuse* me, Mr. Bond," snarls the slitherly villain Max Zorin in *A View to a Kill*. Companion words include *amusia*, the inability to hear or appreciate music. And, dare we add, the *amusing* term from the English countryside *Ha-ha's*, which is humorlessly defined by the OED as "sunken fences bounding a park or garden." This is an ungainly description for a clever invention that prevents animals from escaping because the fences or walls are hidden from view—until the last possible second to unsuspecting country hikers, who are so surprised and delighted they've been known to shout, "Ha-ha!" Now, *that's* amusing!

ANIMATEUR

A teacher who infuses life into a subject. An obscure word from the French worthy of widespread use to vividly describe all those mentors, coaches, and therapists who teach with "a little bit o' soul," as they say in Motown, thereby *animating* their subjects and their students. The wordsmith Howard Rheingold suggests that *animateur* might even be able to bring to life the writing that deadens technical and scientific books. Similarly, the art of *animation* is the ability to create cartoons that appear to hum with life, such as the work of the Warner Brothers legend Chuck Jones, who brought Bugs Bunny, the Roadrunner, and Pepe Le Pew to life. Jones said in a 1999 interview, "Indeed, we wanted our characters to be alive. I take the term '*animation*' very seriously. … The expression is what gives life, the movement of the eye." Speaking of sketches that seem to move, the Swiss painter Paul Klee said that drawing to him was "taking a line out for a walk." Thomas Pynchon writes in *V.*, "All he believed at this point, on the bench behind the Library, was that anybody who worked for *inanimate* money so he could buy more *inanimate* objects was out of his head." Companion words include *animal*, a creature that breathes, and the miniscule *animalcule*, a tiny creature observed under a microscope, a discovery by Dutch lens-maker Antonie Philips van Leeuwenhoek that sparked a worldwide interest in microbiology, thereby *animating* science. Look again, you'll see *anima* and *animus*, the feminine and masculine aspects of the soul, respectively, according to Swiss psychologist Carl Jung. And, as Bill Bryson points out, in *The Mother Tongue*, it is wonderful to know that among the many early names for movie theaters are *phantascope*, *thaumatrope*, and *animatoscope*.

APHILOPHRENIA

The haunting feeling, however fleeting, that one is unloved. Not to be dismissed as just another "inkhorn term," but a case of an "invisible ink term," a word to be borrowed because nothing close to it exists in English. Entire phrases, proverbs, or song lyrics are required to express what these six brief syllables say. Its roots are Greek *a-philo*, not loved, and *phrenia*, mental disorder. To name it may take some of the sting out of it, knowing we aren't alone in this fear. If you listen hard to this word, you can hear an echo of B. B. King singing at the Cook County Jail, in Chicago, "Nobody loves me but my mama—and she could be jivin' too!" The most moving expression of this universal fear I've ever heard came one night in 1989, at the Village Voice Bookstore in Paris, when Raymond Carver read his poem "Late Fragment": "And did you get what / you wanted from this life even so? / I did. / And what did you want? / To call myself beloved, to feel myself / beloved on this earth." Mother Theresa concluded, near the end of her days, "I have come to realize more and more that the greatest disease and the greatest suffering is to be unwanted, unloved, uncared for, to be shunned by everybody, to be just nobody [to no one]." Companion words include the soft-sounding but hard-meaning *amourette*, French for an unloved lover. There is also the hard-to-translate Russian *razbliuto*, which refers to the amorous feelings you once had for somebody but just cannot conjure up again, which sounds far more like what it means than the clunky *anagapesis*, lost feelings for an old lover. And encompassing all of the above is *erotomania*, the ***melancholy*** that sweeps over lovers, as diagnosed in John Coxe's London medical dictionary in 1817.

ARACHIBUTYROPHOBIA

The fear of peanut butter sticking to the roof of your mouth. Curious, right? Every time I read or hear the word I think of spiders, from the Greek *arachne*. But it's really a very long and potent word for a very peculiar phobia, stemming from the Greek *arachi*, a glutinous oil present in peanut butter;

butryo, to stick or adhere; and *phobia*, fear. As someone who has been afflicted with esophageal and swallowing problems all his life, I can swear to what appears to be a universal fear of getting something stuck in the throat. So it's not difficult to imagine someone, especially with a peanut allergy, being terrified of its buttery version clogging up her mouth. The problem is mythic, a larger-than-life fear, or *phobia*—a word that can be traced back to *Phobos*, son of Ares, god of terror, but the symptoms are real, persistent, an unrealistic fear that seizes the whole person, resulting in symptoms of nausea, dizziness, and shame. That said, there is no shortage of curious phobias, such as: *erythrophobia*, the fear of blushing; *ablutophobia*, fear of washing or cleaning; *euphobia*, fear of good news; *chromophobia*, fear of color; *gnomophobia*, fear of ***gnomes***; *catoptrophia*, fear of mirrors; *Venustraphobia*, the fear of beautiful and alluring women; *kakorrhapphiophobia* is the fear of failure and *hippomonstrosesquipedaliophobia*, fear of long words, and perhaps longer definitions. Speaking of frightful words, a curious fear I've suffered from on occasion, especially on long airplane flights, is *abibliophobia*, the fear of not having enough to read. To be fair, let's conclude with an antidote of a word, *counterphobia*, which refers to "the desire or seeking out of experiences that are consciously or unconsciously feared." It's not unlike the advice your mom gave you after your first bad fall from a bicycle—climb back on.

ARGONAUT

A bold and daring sailor. A smooth-sailing word that combines the ancient Greek *argos*, swift; the beauty of a fine ship, *naus*; and the sailor courage of a *nautes*. They merge in *Argo*, the galley on which the *Argonauts* set sail, which in turn was named after *Argus*, its ingenious builder. Webster's succinctly defines an *Argonaut* as "any of a band of heroes who sailed with Jason in quest of the Golden Fleece." I vividly recall my father's Heritage Club edition of the book by Apollonius of Rhodes, *Argonautica*, which we read aloud as a family over one long Michigan winter. The legend recounts how Jason persuaded forty-nine sailors to accompany him on a perilous mission from Iolcos to remote Colchis, in what is now Georgia, at the far end of the Black Sea. Their mythic task was to capture the golden fleece, which hung on a sacred oak guarded by a fire-snorting dragon. Curiously, in 1849, many of those who left home and hearth for the California gold mines were called "*Argonauts*," in honor of Jason's adventure, as well as "'49ers," an uncanny echo of the forty-nine sailors who traveled with him in search of the resplendent wool. The *Argonauts* adventure lives on in *Argos*, a constellation in the northern sky; Captain Nemo's ship, the *Nautilus*, in *Twenty Thousand Leagues Under the Sea*; the spiral-shelled *nautilus*, which the ancients believed sailed underwater; and *nausea*, seasickness, from *naus,* ship. Another haunting echo of the word is found in one of the most touching scenes in all of literature, from the final book of the *Odyssey*, when the ***hero*** returns home to Ithaka after his twenty-year long adventure and is recognized by his faithful dog *Argos*—who wags his tail, then dies quietly.

ASSASSIN

A hired killer. The word comes hissing to us like an arrow across the battlements. It hails from the 13th-century Persian *hashshashin*, the *hashing* ones, those who smoke hashish. These were specially trained executioners, from the Shia sect, hired by Hassan ben Sabbah, the "Old Man of the Mountain," and trained at his fortress of Almamut to punish their Seljuk enemies, and later the Crusaders in northern Syria. For 200 years they stealthily murdered infidels, princes, soldiers, sultans, and other mercenaries. Their training was singular and stealthy. As a reward for their dangerous work, the Old Man created a kind of paradise on earth for these killers, plying them with stupendous amounts of hashish, the lubricious services of nubile young women, and the use of luxurious quarters in the palace. Eventually, the group became identified with the thing they smoked. Steadily, the reference to *hashshashin* wore down, like a plug of hash, to *assassin*, and now is commonly used to describe any trained executioner. The troubadour poet Bernard de Bondeilhs wrote, "Just as the Assassins serve their master unfailingly, so have I served Love with unswerving loyalty." Companion words include *cannibidulia*, the addiction to hashish, and the menacing *murthering*, as cited by John Bullokar in 1616: "A robbing, spoiling, or murthering in the highway." Nearby lurks *thug*, the infamous East Indian brand of *assassin* whose specialty was strangling his or her victims.

ASTONISH

To strike with thunderous surprise; in a word, to be thunderstruck. When the Norse god Thor was provoked he hurled thunderbolts made of gold that stunned all who had invoked his wrath. Likewise, to be *astonished* in English is to be *a-stunned*, a vivid word picture we've inherited from the Vikings, as well as the Old French *estoner,* to stun, and the Latin *extonare*, to thunder. Thus, to *astonish* someone is to stun them with the thunder of your ***wit*** or ingenuity. Two stunning remarks I caught over the years help clarify our meaning. First, I recall how my father roared with laughter when he read in Mark Twain's *Pudd'nhead Wilson*, "Do the right thing. It will gratify some people and *astonish* the rest," a line that he quoted for the rest of his life. Years later, living in France, I read in *Rilke's Letters on Cézanne* how the painter announced his entrée into the art world: "With an apple I will *astonish* Paris." Recently, Mexican novelist Mario Bellatin confessed, "I want to read my own production and *astonish* myself, as if I were a reader coming to my own text for the first time." It's amazing to note that Van Gogh found Gauguin's self-discipline "*astonishing.*" "Words, words, words," as Hamlet said.

"Explanation separates us from *astonishment*," said Eugène Ionesco, "which is the only gateway to the incomprehensible." To hear the real thunder underneath the word, let's remember Sergei Diaghilev's challenging words to Jean Cocteau, as a way to demand better direction for a new ballet he was designing for him: "*Astonish* me!"

Astonish (Paul Cézanne)

ASTRAL

Coming from, influenced by, or resembling, the stars. Star-like; starry; star-crossed. There's an Irish proverb that says, "The stars make no noise." Maybe so, but they sure do inspire wonder-seeking words. *Astral* regards an intangible substance said to exist next to or above the tangible world, the *astral* plane, which has long been regarded as the source of the *astral* spirits or *astral* bodies. Our English word dates back to 1605, when it emerged from the Old French and Late Latin *astralis*, revealed by the stars; *astrum*, star; the Greek *aster;* and the even earlier Proto-Indo-European *aster*, simply, a star. This gives rise to a constellation of astronomy terms, including *asteroid*, a small star; *astrolabe*, star-catcher; *asterisk*, star-shaped; *disaster*, literally two stars, but in collision; *sidereal*, referring to stars. *Asterism* is the terrific term for the naming of *constellations.* Consider the marvel of *consider*, thinking under the stars. *Astrobleme* means "star-scarred," craters from meteors; *astrolatry*, star worship; *estellation* was an ancient word for astrology, as uncovered by Herbert Coleridge. All these star-crossed words reflect the awe and wonder of our *starry*-eyed ancestors, who were undeterred by city lights and undistracted by the klieg lights of modern pop culture. *Astral Weeks* is the legendary album by Irish soul singer Van Morrison, which wanders celestially in the firmament of rock history. The medieval term *dignitie*s refers to the alleged *astral* advantages of a planet in a sign of the zodiac that strengthens "its influence, which is its Essential Dignity," and if in a House that strengthens its influence is its Accidental Dignity. And now you know why *astral* is a cosmic term.

ATHLETE

One who competes in sporting contests. An *athlete* is to a competition as an actor is to a play. Few words exercise the imagination as much as this one. Since the very beginning of competitive sports, in the Ancient Olympics (776 BCE), the athlete has been on stage. The Greeks believed that every *athlete* was an actor, every actor an *athlete*; every sporting event a drama, every drama a kind of *athletic* competition. This was acted out, in every sense of the word, since the Greeks used the same word for both, *athlein*, in the *stadium*, from *stadia*, the length of the ancient footrace; and in the *theater*, from *theatron*, a place for viewing, and the earlier *theasthai*, to behold. What is so compelling to me is what the root *thea*, to view, and its derivative *theates*, spectator, can tell us about why we love sports, theater, and the movies. They are all stages for *transport*. We compete or play, we dramatize our lives for others to see; we view the way that others play and compete. At the heart of these two dramas was the notion of the *athlos*, the competition, and *athlein*, contesting for the *athlon*, the prize. An *athlete* was someone who performed in a contest, in a ***gymnasium***, from *gymnos*, naked, reflecting the rule that Greek *athletes* performed in the nude, to ensure no cheating. So a true *athlete* hides nothing, plays fair. The word first appears in English in 1528, in one of the first health books, *The Salerno Guide to Regimen: This Booke Teachyng All People to Governe Them in Health*, by Thomas Paynell. *Athletics* followed in 1727, *athlete's* foot, in 1928. Thus, *athletes* play and compete for themselves and for the spectators as a way to stage the pursuit of excellence in mind, body, and spirit. When all three come together, everybody wins.

ATLAS

A volume of maps or a catalog of illustrations, named after the demigod who was said to support the world on his shoulders. The mythic association reaches back to 1585, when the first collection of modern maps was published by Gerhardus Mercator, the inventor of the Mercator projection. His son Rumold used an engraving of Atlas on the title page of his father's book. His inspired choice has inspired mapmakers ever since. Atlas had been one of the Titans, who were defeated by the new reign of gods, and he was condemned for all eternity to carry the world on his shoulders—an echo of *atlas*, being old Greek for "support, sustain, bear." *Brewer's Dictionary of Phrase & Fable* relates how Atlas came to call home the mountain range in Morocco that was later named after him. Figuratively, *Atlas* was resurrected as the poster boy for muscle men everywhere, such as circus strongmen and weight lifters. A young bodybuilder named Angelo Siciliano adopted the moniker Charles Atlas, after a buddy flattered him by comparing him to the statue of

Atlas that straddled a hotel on Coney Island. His fitness ads focused on "97-pound weaklings" having sand kicked in their faces by bullies at the beach, a threat that persuaded untold thousands of adolescent boys to send in a dollar for his popular workout program. "Step by step and the thing is done," he advised. "I'll prove in only seven days I can make you a new man." Which proves that men have long had a hankering to develop shoulders wide enough to support their world—and to avenge insults to their manhood.

AUGUR

One who reads the signature of all things. A Roman priest who interpreted the *auspices*, the signs observed in sheep's intestines, bird flight, the waves on the sea, and the stars in the sky. Since the *augurs* were believed to have the power to read the will of the gods, they were expected to declare whether the signs were favorable or unfavorable. Virtually every decision of public importance during the reign of the empire was taken "under the auspices." Consider the Roman historian Livy: "Who does not know that this city was founded only after taking the divinations, that everything in war and peace, at home and abroad, was done only after taking the divinations?" Plutarch distinguished between details that the augurs discovered on the left, or *sinister* side of the sacrificial animal, which foreboded evil because left was associated with the setting sun, (as were death and departure); and the details on the right, or *dexterous* side, which *augured* well because it symbolized the sacred East, the rising sun, the return of life. To "*augur* well" came to mean a favorable prediction, as did the later phrase to "bode well," a *bode* being a herald or messenger. Companion words include *inaugurate*, to begin; *auspicious*, favorable signs; and *euphemism*, to use words of good omen, as the great Skeat wrote; plus *portent* and *portentous*, to point out, stretch toward. While scrying crystal balls may be rare these days, there is no lack of sources for trying to predict the future, such as reading tea leaves, interpreting horoscopes, playing the stock market, and betting the odds on sporting matches. After reading the troubling *augurs* of history, novelist Rebecca West predicted that the modern world would be marked by "a desperate search for a pattern." Speaking of which, the desperate quest can also lead us astray, seeing patterns or connections where they ain't, which is the very definition of *apophenia*.

AWARE

The great sigh of things. To be aware of *aware* (pronounced ah-WAH-ray) is to be able to name the previously ineffable sigh of impermanence, the whisper of life flitting by, of time itself, the realization of evanescence. *Aware* is the shortened version of the crucial Japanese phrase *mono-no-aware*, which suggested sensitivity or sadness during the Heian period, but with a hint of actually relishing the

melancholy of it all. Originally, it was an interjection of surprise, as in the English "Oh!" The reference calls up bittersweet poetic feelings around sunset, long train journeys, looking out at the driving rain, birdsong, the falling of autumn leaves. A held-breath word, it points like a finger to the moon to suggest an unutterable moment, too deep for words to reach. If it can be captured at all, it is by haiku poetry, the brushstroke of calligraphy, the burbling water of the tea ceremony, the slow pull of the bow from the *oe*. The great 16th-century wandering poet Matsuo Basho caught the sense of *aware* in his haiku: "By the roadside grew / A rose of Sharon. / My horse / Has just eaten it." A recent Western equivalent would be the soughing lyric of English poet Henry Shukman, who writes, "This is a day that decides by itself to be beautiful."

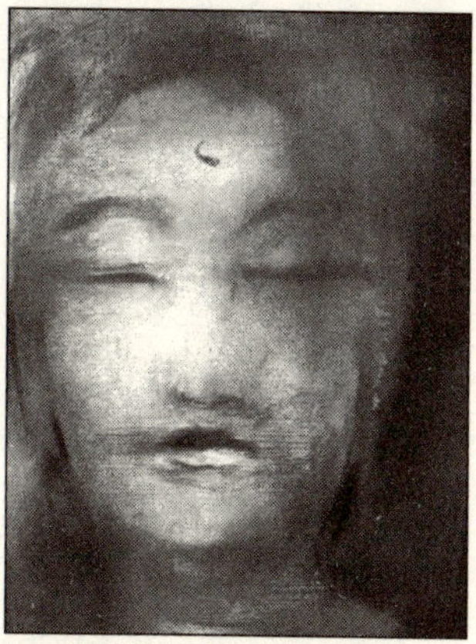

Aware (The Great Sigh of Things)

B

BAFFLE

To confuse, discombobulate, or foil. A word that could be cited to describe its own curious origins, which was the *baffling* punishment of a knight errant, or should we say, an erring knight? The word dates back to 1548, and paints a ***bewildering*** picture of public disgrace worthy of Brueghel. Richardson writes, "*baffull* is a great reproach among the Scottes, and is used when a man is openly perjured, and then they make of him an image paynted reuersed, with hys heles vpwarde, with his name, wondering, cryenge, and blowing out of [i.e. at] hym with hornes, in the moost despitefull manner they can." So a disgraced knight, or an effigy of him, was hung upside down by his heels for perjury or other dishonorable conduct. Richardson adds that the word may be a Scottish corruption of *bauchle*, to treat somebody contemptuously, or to act tastelessly, which possibly traveled across the North Sea from Icelandic *bágr*, uneasy, poor, also a struggle. Others speculate that *baffle* is linked to the French *bafouer*, to abuse, hoodwink, and *baf*, a natural sound of disgust, like *bah*, still heard in Parisian cafés, as *bof*. The legendary Associated Press reporter Mort Rosenblum describes the word as unspellable and the delivery as being "in the aspiration, like getting unwanted air out through fluttering lips, impelled by colossal ennui, with a rolling of the eyes, and a slight tossing of the head." Thus, to *baffle* is more than *confuse* but less than *vilify*; it is to turn somebody upside down with contempt, disgrace them ten ways from Sunday, with your reproach. Biologist Edward O. Wilson writes, "Sometimes a concept is *baffling* not because it is profound but because it's wrong." Companion words or senses include the *baffle* in a sound studio or mechanical device, whose first published use was in 1881.

BAKSHEESH

A tip; a favor, gratuity, charity; a reward. A benevolent bribe offered to smooth out service in the bazaar or market; a subtle gift to grease the wheels of a business deal; alms for the poor to fulfill a religious obligation. As an integral social custom in Islamic cultures, *baksheesh* is a familiar, almost incantatory word, heard on the streets from Cairo, Damascus, and Jerusalem to Baghdad, Beirut, and Calcutta. It is an echo of the American cry of "Brother, can you spare a dime?" but carries the spiritual overtones of the medieval practice of giving alms, whereby spiritual merit is earned. Its roots are in the Persian *bakhshish*, a gift, which stems from the verb *bakhshidan*, to give or forgive. The first written appearance in English dates back to 1625. A passage in the classic travelers' tale *The Great Railway Bazaar*, by Paul Theroux, illuminates the custom as practiced in Iran in the 1970s: "It is an old country; everywhere in the gleaming modernity are reminders of the orthodox past—the praying steward, the portraits, the encampments of nomads, and on what is otherwise one of the best run railways in the world, the ***yearning*** for the *baksheesh*."

BAMBOOZLE

To fool, guile, trick, or *hoodwink*. Those long *o*'s and that hard *z* lends the word a "grifterly" feeling, to coin a phrase, evocative of an Elmore Leonard detective novel riddled with deceitful women and swindling men. *Bamboozle* is first recorded in 1703, a ***slang*** or ***cant*** word, derided by Johnson as "not used in pure or grave writings." However, Brewer traces it back to the Chinese and Gypsy *bamboozle*, meaning to "dress a man in *bamboos* to teach him swimming," which gives rise to an image of a kind of human raft. Even though it's nearly impossible to rhyme in a poem—*bamboozle* and *ouzel?*—it is still a raffish word that lifts a smile on the face of anybody who uses it. The Scots can take credit, tracing it back to *bombaze*, to perplex, though it may also be connected to the French *bombast*.

If you can feel a wild animal ***writhing*** around in the word when you say it out loud, you're not far wrong. There was a popular epithet in Old French, "To make a baboon out of somebody," an uncanny reference to *embabuiner*, to make a fool out of. Not all have been charmed by the word. Jonathan Swift included it in his dubious *index expurgatorius*, his list of words to be expunged from the language. Nonetheless, it could not be repressed, and Benjamin Disraeli used it deftly in a letter: "It is well known what a middle man is: he is a man who *bamboozles* one party and plunders the other." Carl Sagan warned, "One of the saddest lessons of history is this: If we've been *bamboozled* long enough, we tend to reject any evidence of the bamboozle. The *bamboozle* has captured us. Once you give a charlatan power over you, you almost never get it back." Finally, if you just happen to be using *bamboozle* in a poem or song lyrics and you're stuck for a rhyme, you might try *gongoozle*, a rare but useful word meaning "to stare at, idly watch," as those whose leisure activity centers around watching boats drift by in the canals of England.

BANDERSNATCH

A monster so horrible, so terrifying, nobody has ever stayed around long enough to get a description of it. Beware, for it is outside your door, licking its chops. If you look up the hideous verb *transmogrify*, you'll find the bodacious *bandersnatch* nipping at its heels. Try to picture the horripilating ("hair-raising") incident in the *Voyages of Sinbad* in which the sailors are driven to mutiny by the strange cries of unseen monsters and the terror of the churning sea. If asked about the origins of the dreaded beast, a researcher into such things might say it is born of the scritching at the door of our imagination, and our ***eldritch*** fear of the unknown. However, the doughty Lewis Carroll dared name the dreaded beast in his diabolic poem "Jabberwocky." "Beware the Jabberwock, my son! / The jaws that bite, the claws that catch! / Beware the Jubjub bird, and shun / The frumious *Bandersnatch*!" Companion words include *catathleba*, "a noxious monster," which Pliny mentions in his *Histories*, and according to Coleridge, the *deutyraun*, which was "some monstrous animal." Finally, there is the odious beast in Al Capp's "Li'l Abner" cartoon strip, which he introduced "offstage" as the unseen but memorably named Lena the Hyena.

BARBARIAN

An uncivilized, uncouth, uneducated foreigner. The Greeks and Romans disagreed on many issues, but they held fast to this suspicion of the outsider. Those who couldn't speak their language were *barbaros*, stammerers or babblers. To both cultures, the speech of strangers was incomprehensible, reeking of roughhewn sounds like "bar bar bar to bar." No inconsequential prejudice, this. If you couldn't speak Greek you couldn't compete in the Olympics, own land, or vote. If you couldn't speak Latin, you were forever regarded as pagan. Dr. Johnson holds forth on the evolution—or devolution—of the word, tracking down its origins in the fear and loathing of strangers: "[*Barbarian*] seems to have signified at first only foreign, or a foreigner; but, in time, implied some degree of wildness or cruelty." Since then *barbarians* have arrived at the gate in virtually every land, as immigration and exile is now a constant in modern life, reviving the ancient disdain for strangers in the now universal phrase "It's all Greek to me." All is not lost. After being criticized by August Strindberg for the paintings he made in Tahiti, Paul Gauguin wrote, "You suffer from your civilization. My *barbarism* is to me a renewal of youth." Companion words include *gringo*, a regional Mexican-Spanish expression for the dreaded *Yanqui*, often used, with almost shocking similarity, to describe gibberish spoken by strangers. Word maven John Ciardi traces its derivation back to *griengar*, "to speak like a Greek," suggesting that American English was *barbaric* to Mexican ears, which brings us full circle, like Odysseus, back to Greece.

BATHOS

False depth, sentimentality, triteness, mawkishness. Bathos is the sinking feeling of being pulled down by sentimentality, dragged down by false emotion. *Bathos* is exaggerated pathos, which, as readers of James Joyce, Thomas Aquinas, or Greek tragedy know, is the "quality that arouses pity or sorrow." The original sense of *pathos* is "what befalls one," related to *paskhein,* to suffer, and *penthos*, grief, sorrow. So powerful were the old associations with *pathos* that when *bathos*, the old Greek word for "depth," was floated by Alexander Pope, in 1727, its echo was clear to most educated people. Current usage suggests that *bathos* sinks to the depths of what used to be called "low writing," in contrast to "high writing," which is reputedly loftier. *Bathos* is also a synonym for *anticlimax*, the sudden descent to the depths, in the pejorative sense, in speech or writing or at the end of a work of art. Otherwise known as third-act problems. Or as Napoleon famously remarked to De Pradt, the Polish ambassador to France, a drop "from the sublime to the ridiculous is but a step." Charlotte Brontë evoked its true profundity (*profundus*, depth) in *Jane Eyre*, when she wrote: "I like you more than I can say, but I'll not sink into a *bathos* of sentiment." Companion words include *bathykopian*, deep-bosomed, from *bathos*, deep, and *kolpos*, cleft; *bathyscape*, a small submarine designed to explore the depths of the ocean; and *bathetic*, which is a *pathetic* drop in the gravitas of the word *pathos*.

BEAUTY

The quality or perception that pleases. Some say *beauty* is the inner quality that brings ***calm*** to the observer. Others, like Stendhal, say it is "the promise of happiness." *Beauty* is a *beaut',* as we use to say of a ***gorgeous*** shot on the basketball courts of Detroit, where I grew up. She dates back to around 1275, from the Anglo-Saxon *beute*, and Vulgar Latin *bellitatem*, the state of being handsome, from Latin *bellus,* fine, beautiful, used mostly of women and children. Companion words include *beauty sleep,* the rejuvenating rest taken just before midnight, *beautician, beauty parlor, beauty shot, beauty shop,* and *bonify,* "to make good or beautiful. *Callipygian* means "gifted with shapely buttocks," such as those of prehistoric goddess sculptures. *Callisteia* was the name of a sought-after beauty prize won in beauty competitions in ancient Greece. *Callomania* is the delusion that one is beautiful, after the goddess *Callisto. Calligraphy* describes the ability to write *beautifully. Kalokagathia* is the harmonious Greek worldview that joins the beautiful (*kalo*) and the good (*agathia*). The subtle French *jolie laide* combines "pretty and "ugly" to describe an unconventionally attractive face you can't stop looking at. The sublime Navajo *hozh'q* refers to the ultimate aim in life being the beauty that can be created by human beings. Shakespeare's Romeo sighs of Juliet, "I never saw beauty until now." Art critic Elaine Scarry underscores all the above when she writes, "Beauty is sacred." "Beauty in art," Charles Hawthorne told his art students, "is the delicious notes of color one against the other." And in an old leather-bound book of travel poems at Ansel Adams's cabin in Yosemite, I catch the tender dedication that Everett Dawson wrote to Ansel and his wife, Virginia: "*Beauty* has its roots in the fitness of things. May 27, 1930."

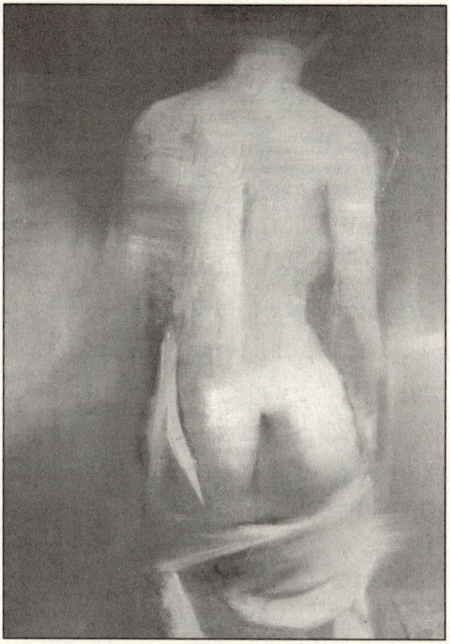

Beauty

BEDSWERVER

A wandering, lusting lover. A lubricious Shakespearean term, from *A Winter's Tale*, for a woman who swerves from the marriage bed. In 1753, Dr. Johnson defined a *bedswerver* with avidity, as one who "is false to the bed; one that ranges or swerves from one bed to another." A playful euphemism for an adulterer from a time rife with bed references. Consider the lubriciously descriptive *bedganging*, a beguiling *bedventure* in which a lover seeks a *bedworthy* partner, an *ibedde*, or *bedsister*, whom Herbert Coleridge calls a "concubine," or a *bedfellow*, in "a bed of sin." The male equivalent to a *bedswerver* was a *bedpresser*, a john-among-the-maids, knave-of-hearts, or belly-bumper. Companionable *bed* words include *curtain-lecture*, which Dr. Johnson defined as "a reproof given by a wife to her husband in bed." Memorably romantic terms from Old English include *hugsome*, huggable, and *kissworthy*, worthy of a kiss; and in hipster ***slang***, *bedwarmer*, bed partner, and *bedroom furniture*, a woman, doll, or dame. Figuratively, essayist E. B. White described his *bedfellows* as Fred, his pet dachshund, as well as Harry Truman (in the *New York Times*), Adlai Stevenson (in *Harper's*), and Dean Acheson (in *A Democrat Looks at His Party*). Recently, I caught up with *shrimping*, a clever coinage from Sarajevo writer Aleksandar Hemon, which he describes as "curling up in a fetal position" with a lover, which is a remarkably clever alternative to the Victorian *spooning*.

BEKOS

Bread. Not only the most famous Phrygian word, but some say the very first word, period. According to Herodotus, *bekos* meant bread, and he then said why. In his *Histories* he tells the yeasty story of Pharaoh Psammetichus, who believed there was one proto-language, the source of all languages, like the mythic source of the Nile. To attempt to prove his point, he exiled two babies to a hut in the mountains and left them there to live in silence, visited occasionally by a shepherd who brought them food. Eventually, the story goes, the children spoke. What they said was *bekos*, which the Pharaoh interpreted as meaning that Phrygian was the mother of all languages. Never ones to leave a colorful folk etymology alone, modern linguists connect *bekos* with the Albanian *buke*, also meaning "bread," and to the eventual English *bake*. Companion "first" words include one that many of us devour with the *New York Times* Sunday crossword puzzle. A historian of dictionaries, Jonathan Green, recounts a study in *Chasing the Sun* about the search for traces of the earliest words common to all Indo-European languages. After the elimination of thousands of words, the true and noble survivor was the noble friend of bagels everywhere, *lox*. *Hmmmmm*, you say, and I say we're on to something. Roy Blount Jr. cites Stephen Mithen's work in *The Singing Neanderthals*, "that the first stirrings of language were *hmmmmm*." All origin stories have the strange contours of poetry. The physician and etymologist Lewis Thomas speculates: "'*Kwei*,' said a Proto-Indo-European [PIE] child, meaning 'make something,' and the word became, centuries later, our word 'poem.'" Incidentally, the oldest *phrase* in continuous use in English is the still popular "Woe is me," which first appeared as "Woe unto me," in the Old Testament, Job 10:15.

BERSERK

Ferociously out of control; displaying superhuman strength in battle. In 1822, Sir Walter Scott raided the Old Norse language for the right word to convey the sense of utterly bloodthirsty warriors for his novel *The Pirate*: "The *berserkars* were so called from fighting without armour." After the book was ***published***, *berserk* became all the rage. Within fifty years the word shape-shifted into its figurative sense of deranged behavior, so that "to go berserk" became the English version of the Malaysian "running amok." North Beach photographer Mikkel Aaland, whose family hails from Norway, told me what his uncle told him, "The *Berserkrs* were a Viking tribe so called because they wore bear, *ber*, skirts or garments, *serk*. They were known as ferocious fighters who went to battle after eating psychedelic mushrooms. They were known to tear the flesh off their opponents with their teeth, and so, *berserk*, uncontrollable rage, is derived from this behavior." Howling like animals, foaming at the mouth, and biting the edges of their iron shields, the *berserkrs* spread terror from Ireland to Russia, and were frenzied champions when they returned home to plow their fields and tell their tales in front of the home fires. Why the bear skin? Some say donning the bearskin was sympathetic magic. If you kill the bear, wear its skin, you absorb its ***fury***, display its courage and strength. In 1908, Kipling wrote in *Diversity of Creatures*, "You went *Berserk*. I've read all about it in Hypatia. … You'll probably be liable to fits of it all your life." Companion words include *anger*, from the Viking *angr*, their red-face response to injustices of the world; and Herb Caen's "*Berserkely*," or "*Berserkelier-than-thou.*"

BEWILDER

To confuse, bespudder, or discombobulate. A 16th-century folk memory from the days when most people in Europe lived either in the forest or in towns surrounded by woodland. *Bewilder* derives from the Old English *be*, thoroughly, and *wilder,* to lead one astray. Figuratively, it means to be lost in the pathless woods, and by extension to lure an innocent into the wild. Scholars suggest that it's a "back-formation" from *wilderness*, whose roots are in *wilde'or*, the wild deer that once roamed the untamed land. Companion words include *bedevil*, *bewitch*, and the wonderfully clangorous *bewhape*, an archaic English word from the 14th century meaning "confused." According to the charming Charles MacKay's culling of *Lost Beauties*, *mask* surprisingly meant "*bewilder*" back in the 13th century, and the verb *maze* meant "to *bewilder* and confuse." As for the old saw that men can't ever admit they are lost, let's consider the ingenious response of Daniel Boone when asked if he'd ever been lost: "No, but I was once *bewildered* for three days." His kindred spirit of a more recent time is Isadora Duncan, who urged other women artists, "You were once wild here. Don't let them tame you!"

BIBLIOTHÈQUE (FRENCH)

A library, a paradise for book lovers. The earliest written record dates back 4,500 years to ancient Sumeria's *eduba*, translated by its Akkadian conquerors as the "tablet house," for its thousands of cuneiform books. Originally, *bibliothèque* meant "a box or warehouse of papyrus scrolls." The word *derives*, drifts downriver to us like a reed along the Nile, from the Greek colony of Alexandria, whose famous library consisted of 700,000 *biblion*, papyrus scrolls, from *biblios*, the heart of the papyrus stalk, and *byblos*, rolled scroll or rolled book, the word used to describe what came from the Phoenician port that shipped papyrus rolls to Egypt. [Green] *bibliophile* Alberto Manquel describes the Library of Alexandria as "a very long high hall lined with *bibliothekai,* niches for the scrolls." This was the Museion, The House of the Muses, The Place for the Cure of the Soul. Companion words: *bibliography*, a book list; *bibliomancy*, divination through books; *biblioclast*, destroyer of books; and *biblioburro*, "a rural book mobile system," via donkeys, in Colombia. *Bibliocaveat*: beyond the uplifting aspects of libraries, a gentle warning about the addiction to books. H. L. Mencken tells us there are *bibliobibuli*, those who are *book-drunk* because they have read too much. "I know some who are constantly drunk on books, as other men are drunk on whiskey or religion. They wander through this most diverting and stimulating of worlds in a haze, seeing nothing, and hearing nothing." *Bibliophobia* is the fear of running out of things to read, a familiar dread for those on long plane flights or train rides. Eudora Welty visited her local Carnegie library every day as a young girl for her "sweet devouring" of the two books a day doled out by the librarian.

BONA FIDE

In good faith, authentic, honest; without bad intentions, fraud, deceit, or deception. Today, we say, "He's got the *bona fides*, he's a five-tool ballplayer." Or: "She's got *bona fide* talent as a singer; she's the real deal." Figuratively, it points out authentic credentials. One of my favorites is the following example, from a pub custom in late-19th-century Dublin, Ireland. In those days the pubs closed at the traditional hour of 11:00 P.M., but it was also an hour when the back roads of Ireland still saw plenty of wanderers afoot, such as the gypsies, the traveling people. Often, they would knock on the doors of pubs they knew stayed open late for travelers, those who wanted a late meal or drink. But there was a law in Dublin that pubs could only sell alcohol to those who were true, authentic out-of-towners, so as to keep the locals from drinking after hours. Since those were days when many people still knew Latin, the phrase *bona fide* was used as a kind of password at the threshold of the pubs: "Aye, lad, are ye *bona fide*?" Meaning, "Are you telling me in *good faith* that you are truly from outside Dublin?" If so, the lad could enjoy a late-night whiskey. In the Coen brothers' rumpus of a movie *O Brother, Where*

Art Thou? Ulysses Everett McGill (George Clooney) asks his ex-wife, Penny Wharvey McGill (Holly Hunter) why she's told everyone that he was hit by a train. Exasperated, she says, "Lots of respectable people have been hit by trains... What was I gonna tell them, that you got sent to the penal farm and I divorced you from shame?" Ulysses responds, "Uh, I take your point. But it does put me in a damn awkward position, vis-a-vis my progeny." Rolling her eyes, Penny says: "Vernon here's got a job. Vernon's got prospects. He's *bona fide.* What are you?" Companion words include the anguished antonym *malafide*, bad faith, a word well worth reviving.

BONDMAID

A woman bound to the land or the lord, as a bondman was bound. One of the notorious "lost words" from the first edition of the OED. It's editor, the venerable James Murray, who was the very personification of "philosophical calm," was mortified to learn that shortly after the "B" volume had been mailed to the publisher the white slip with the inscription of *bondmaid* was found under an unturned pile of fellow words. In 1901, fourteen years after the famed first edition appeared, Murray wrote to a caviling correspondent: "I am afraid it is quite true that the word *bondmaid* has been omitted from the Dictionary, a most regrettable fact." Upon review of that project the omission becomes understandable, if you consider that Murray had to comb through 5–6 million slips or citations, from which he and his assistants in the "Scriptorium" chose 1.25 million headwords. Later lexicographers have rued the seemingly random process by which some words were included and others went missing, for lack of time or lack of space, such as the incandescent *lamprocarpous*, defined as "having shining fruit," and the clangorous *collide*, to crash into.

BOONDOCKS

A distant place, the remote mountains, the farthest reaches of civilization. A favorite word of mine, popularized in books and movies, as well as by baseball announcers such as the legendary Tigers announcer Ernie Harwell, who used the word to describe long home runs: *"Kaline swings—and it's a long belt to left field—it's long gone—way back into the boondocks!"* Its origins are as surprising as they are fascinating: not the docks of longshoremen like Terry Malloy in *On the Waterfront*, but the rice terraces and head-hunting villages of the far, faraway Philippines. The root word is *bundok*, a Kapampangan word for "mountains" learned the hard way by American GIs who were captured by the Japanese army during World War II while fighting in central Luzon. The few who escaped the Bataan Death March disappeared into the remote villages of northern Luzon, where Filipino rebels and the last of the headhunters still controlled the rice-terraced *bundoks*. Those who survived described where they'd waited out the war as "in the *bundoks*," which later became our *boondocks.* Companion words include the short version, the *boonies*, and its distant cousin *boondoggle*, a *sonicky* word, as Roy Blount, Jr. calls the ones that sound as great as they appear on the page, for a useless task, a futile project that wastes time and money, coined in 1929 by American Scoutmaster Robert Link.

BORBORYGMUS

Stomach growls; the rumble in the jungle of your tummy. Our word descends from the Greek *borborugmos*, from *borborygzein*, to rumble (no kidding) which meant the same then as it does now, the burbling sounds issuing forth from your intestinal passing of gas. This is a great word to pull out around the Thanksgiving table when the snarls and growls coming from within the bowels of your guests threatens to drown out the cheers and jeers coming from the football game on television. Kids tend to be especially delighted with this word because it sounds as goofy as the Looney Tunes sounds coming from their own stomachs. For those who are uncertain how the word can possibly be used, see Vladimir Nabokov's novel *Ada*: "All the toilets and water pipes in the house had been suddenly seized with *borborygmic* convulsions." Companion words include *eructation*, commonly called *burping*, the expulsion of air from the stomach, and *flatus*, the explosion from the other end, an exercise school kids and "bromance" screenwriters call *farting.* And a severe case of *borborygmi* results in what my elegantly Victorian English Grandpa Sydney used to call *collywobbles*, severe cramping and diarrhea. Incidentally, the art of listening to the symphony of stomach sounds and discerning what they mean is called *auscultation*.

BOUDOIR

A private room where a woman goes to be alone to brood to her heart's content. When dinner parties would break up during the glory days of France, the custom was for the men to withdraw to the smoking room for cigars, brandy, and manly talk. Women, in contrast, were expected to retreat to the *boudoir*, to brood, after the French *bouder*, to pout, sulk. If the reader is brooding over the origins of the selfsame word *brood*, it derives from the Anglo-Saxon *brod*, for "heat." Centuries of careful farmyard observation taught farmers that when hens sit on or *brood* their eggs, their heat will help hatch the baby chicks. Eventually, that long, slow process stood for the prolonged meditations of those *brooding* over problems and "hatching" plots. "As she sallied forth from her *boudoir*," wrote William Manchester, "you would never have guessed how quickly she could strip for action." Novelist Kathleen Winsor writes, "It was a woman's bedroom, actually a boudoir, and no man belonged in it except by invitation." A curious companion word is *parlor*, which was the room reserved in an otherwise silent monastery for speaking, from the French *parlez*. Companion words include *gueuloir*, a "shouting room," which is what

Gustave Flaubert called his study. More often than he liked, he spent hours searching for *le mot juste*, just the one right word to use in his stories or novels. So he tended to alternate the usual writer's brooding with yelling at himself.

BRICOLEUR (FRENCH)

One who assembles, creates, puts together. Coined by French anthropologist Claude Levi-Strauss to explain how the "primitive mind" works. He writes that a *bricoleur* is "someone who works with his hands and uses devious means compared to those of a craftsman. … Mythical thought is therefore a kind of intellectual 'bricolage.' … Like 'bricolage' on the technical plane, mythical reflection can reach brilliant unforeseen results on the intellectual plane. … The *'bricoleur'* is adept at performing a large number of diverse tasks. … The rules of his game are always to make do with 'whatever is at hand.'" Levi-Strauss's work was enormously important in Paris during the 1940s and '50s, and he inspired artists such as Picasso and Braque. Psychologists such as James Hillman use the word to illuminate how the soul works: "Let us imagine the dream-work to be an activity, less of a censor than of a *bricoleur.* … The dream *bricoleur* is a handyman, who takes the bits of junk left over from the day and potters around with them." Companion words include *bricolage*, the result of the *bricoleur's* handiwork, "an assembly, montage, or reconstruction that is intended to reflect the complex and rich form of its subject"—a word soon discovered by French artists, who saw in the word an apt ***metaphor*** for the assembly process of many avant-garde artists. In 1965, *American Anthropologist* described man as a "creator of Culture, like a *bricoleur* … who makes constructions for the fun of the thing out of anything that is lying around." From the French *bricole,* trifle, and Italian *briccola.*

BROADCAST

To spread the good word. Originally, it meant "to scatter seed," which was recorded in 1767, and in many paintings, such as Van Gogh's *The Sower,* which depicts a shadowy farmer throwing seeds across his fields. In *The Yellow House,* an account of the years in which Van Gogh and Gauguin lived together in Arles, Martin Gayford writes, "In addition to the familiar terrain, the sower *broadcasting* his seed was an image that had been with him almost since he had become an artist." In 1921, only thirty years after Van Gogh's death, at 37, the verb was applied to spreading the word over radio waves, casting word seeds so ideas might grow. During the war in Southeast Asia, the notorious Hanoi Hannah said, "Because the GIs were sent massively to South Vietnam, maybe it's a good idea to have a *broadcast* for them." Hall of Fame baseball announcer Ernie Harwell says, with his trademark modesty, "I've been lucky to *broadcast* some great events and to *broadcast* the exploits of some great players."

BROWNSTUDY

Melancholic reflections in the soul's own studio. As the lifelong melancholic Dr. Johnson defined it, "Gloomy meditations; study in which we direct our thoughts to no certain point." Earliest mention comes in a 1532 book, *Dice-Play*, which ***augured*** the coming meaning: "Lack of company will soon lead a man into a brown study." Here we have a 16th-century word for deep, or to some, gloomy, meditation, from the color brown, which used to refer to a gloomy mental condition, and study, which meant during the late medieval period any form of intense meditation. This monochromatic word was used by the Scottish novelist Robert Louis Stevenson to describe his ***melancholy*** in several letters. It derives from the French *sombre-reverie,* and later *brow-study*, as in "fevered brow," from Old German *braun* or *aug-braun*, eyebrow. Today, in creative circles, it refers to abstraction, absentmindedness, deep thought. Brewer cites a verse from William Congreve's "An Impossible Thing": "Invention flags, his brain grows muddy, / And black despair succeeds *brown study*." Judy Garland's version of "Melancholy Baby," in the 1954 movie "A Star is Born," captures the heartrending emotion of one overcome in the *brownstudy* of life. There are many modern equivalents, the most colorful being "in a blue funk," which the OED defines as "extreme nervousness, tremulous dread."

BUCCANEER

A pirate, swashbuckler, adventurer. The first *buccaneers* looked very little like the debonair Errol Flynn in *The Pirate*, or even the demented Johnny Depp in *Pirates of the Caribbean*. Instead, they were ordinary islanders, *boucans*, who smoked meat on a wooden rack placed over an open fire. *Boucan* was what 17th-century French settlers heard of the original Tupi Caribbean word *mukem*, which makes you wonder how closely they were listening. Later, *boucanier* became a sobriquet for the privateers and outlaws who hid in the remote woods of the West Indies and later grew fond of barbecuing their meats over a fire. Speaking of which, if you look up *buccaneer*, you'll soon come across the Dominican *barbacoa,* from which we get one of our favorite backyard activities, the *barbecue*. Companion word: *pirate*, as in the five-time World Champion Pittsburgh *Pirates*, so called in 1890 because of the reputed "piratical" practices of the new owners, who switched from the old American Association to the National League. Today, their nickname just happens to be "the Bucs" or "the Buccos," short for *buccaneer.* Considering how many Pittsburgh *Pirates* star players have come from the Caribbean, such as Puerto Rico's charismatic Roberto Clemente and the Dominican Republic's versatile Felipe Alou, *buccaneer* is another wonderful example of how words can often go home again.

BUDGET

An idealistic plan to spend only what is earned. Originally, a *budget* was a small sack full of money, which shouldn't surprise anyone who has tried to keep to a budget ever since, but it evolved into the act of sorting money into several little bags. This is a useful visualization for sorting out expenses. Our English word derives from the Latin *bulga*, a bag, from French *bouge*, and its diminutive *bougette*, a pouch. Traynor writes that it was "a tinker's traveling bag for holding implements of his trade; hence a tramp's bag." Companion words would have to include *bankrupt*, the condition of those who haven't kept to a *budget*. This unfortunate word that dates back to 1533, from the Italian, *banca rotta*, a broken bench, from *banca*, a moneylender's shop or bench, and *rotta*, broken, defeated, interrupted. The 18th-century lexicographer Brewer lends a colorful backstory in his indispensable *Fables and Phrases*: "In Italy, when a moneylender was unable to continue business his bench or counter was broken up, and he was spoken of as a *banca rotta*—i.e., a *bankrupt*." Updating this observation, novelist John Updike writes: "*Bankruptcy* is a sacred site, a condition beyond conditions, as theologians might say, and attempts to investigate it are necessarily obscene, like spiritualism. One knows only that he has passed into it and lives beyond us, in a condition not ours." Companion words include *banquet*, from *banchetto*, and *rupture*, from *rotta*. The modern sense of "morally or intellectually *bankrupt*" means ethically or mentally bereft. Consider also *mountebank*, a charlatan, from *montare*, to mount, *banca*, bench, figuratively, someone who lends money at usurious rates to *bankrupt* people.

BULL

A large animal, a papal decree, a ludicrous statement. Three wide-ranging definitions for one of the most mythic words. The *bull* is there at the beginning of time, a robust beast with which our ancestors deeply identified, longing as they did for the virility of the animal, and its horned association with the phases of the moon. Going back to the source, we find the PIE root *bhel-*, to blow, to swell, like a snorting *bull*, pawing at the ground in a *bullring*. It enters Old English as *bula* and the diminutive *bullock*. This is evident by the rituals of *bull-riding, bull-dancing, bull sacrifices, and bull coins*, all of which were rife in the ancient world. During the 13th century edicts issued by the Vatican were sealed with *bullets* of wax, from the Latin *bulla*, seal; hence, a papal *bull*, and later, *bulletin*, little edict. The third meaning enters like the proverbial *bull* in the china shop, probably from the Middle English noun *bul* for "falsehood," and the 15th-century verb *bull*, to mock or cheat, and Old French *bouller*, to deceive. Companion words include *bullshit*, the smelly epithet; *bulldoze, bulldozer, bull's-eye.* Roy Blount Jr. cites the *American Heritage Dictionary's* tracing of *bull* back to" the PIE root *bhel*, to blow, swell with derivates—referring to various round objects and to the notion of tumescent masculinity: boulevard, balloon, ballot, and fool." Speaking of the devil, Will Rogers once quipped: "After eating an entire *bull*, a mountain lion felt so good he started roaring. He kept it up until a hunter came along and shot him. The moral: When you're full of *bull*, keep your mouth shut." And I still recall my father's advice when I went into the offices of the *Wayne Dispatch* to interview for my first newspaper job: "If you can't dazzle them with brilliance, buddy, baffle them with *bull*."

BUMMER

In recent slang, a lousy deal; originally an idle, worthless fellow, a rascal. Older than you think, the root word *bum* was first recorded in 1387, possibly imitative, as the OED says, of a "protuberance, swelling." Five centuries later, we find *bum*, as in hobo, tramp, in 1864, from *bummer*, loafer, idle person, 1855, possibly deriving from British *slang* for "butt, backside, bum," and also German slang *bummler*, loafer, from *bummeln*, go slowly, waste time. Thus, a picture emerges of the hordes of German immigrants in the Northern army during the Civil War, using the word to describe how the war was going slowly, wasting their lives away. *Bummer*, for a terrible experience, like the fraternity running out of beer in *Animal House,* arises in the 1960s. But even so there is startling evidence of 19th-century usage that might have been muttered by John Belushi: "Thus San Francisco has been called the Elysian of *bummers*." In California, men who profess to be journalists, and so obtain free dinners and drinks, are called "literary *bummers*." Companion words or phrases include *bum's rush*, for forcible eviction, like being tossed out of a bar or ballgame. To wit, the great crepehanger of a comic George Carlin said, "If God dropped acid, would he see people? *Bummer*." The Hindu shopkeeper Apu says to Ned Flanders on *The Simpsons*: "That's the problem with your religion: it's a *bummer*—but the sing-alongs are okay." And the Dude in *The Big Lebowski* sighs "Bummer" no fewer than a dozen times, which is far less than the 283 "f-bombs" that are dropped during the movie.

BUNDLING

A pioneer custom of sleeping fully clothed in the same bed with members of the opposite sex. A tradition formerly in vogue in Wales and New England during a time when beds were scarce, men and women slept together in the same bed without removing their clothes. *Halliwell's Dictionary* cites the Duke de la Rochefoucauld's *Travels in America*: a practice wherein "a man and woman slept in the same bed, he with his small clothes, and she with her petticoats on; an expedient practiced in America on a scarcity of beds, where, on such an occasion, husbands and parents frequently permitted travelers to bundle with their wives and daughters. This custom is now abolished." Could it be that the coo of lovers, "little *bundle* of love" came from *bundling*? Since you asked, *bundling* comes from the Middle Dutch *bondel*, from *bond,* and *binden*, to bind, binding, and German *bundilin*. The modern sense of *bundling* a baby or a package, "to wrap up in warm heavy clothes," was recorded in 1893.

C

CAHOOTS

To collude with, to be in league with, to deal with secretly. So furtive is this word, no one really knows its origins. It hides in etymology dictionaries like a crow in a dark cave. Some scholars suspect it derives from the old Roman word *cohorts*, a troop of soldiers, and others say it comes from Old French *cahute*, hut, which provides a shadowy word picture of clandestine deals made in remote cabins in the woods. More recently, Daniel Cassidy suggests, in *How the Irish Invented Slang*, that its roots are in the Irish *comh-udar*, co-author, co-instigator. Thus, to be in *cahoots* with your collaborator on your next spy novel would be as redundant as sending a keg of Guinness to Ireland. Writing in the *New York Times* in 2000, columnist Molly Ivins asked, "Where's the outrage? I've got plenty for ya!" When she interviewed the director of the Intermountain Tissue Center in Salt Lake City about the highly profitable trade in body parts, he told her, "If donors were told at the time about profits, they wouldn't donate." Ivins adds, "Duh. The nonprofit foundations involved in this grisly trade are in *cahoots* with the for-profit corporations."

CALCULATE

To count; a method of reckoning. If you visualize the Roman fresco of a definition that the venerable Skeat provides, "to reckon by help of small pebbles," you'll never look at *calculation* the same way. For it comes from the Latin *calculus*, pebble, and *calx*, stone, specifically stones for the Roman (or Chinese) abacus to be used for accounting purposes. These stones also contributed to a clever Roman invention that only Mel Brooks could've staged. Mounted onto a chariot that carried passengers was a box full of pebbles with a small hole in the bottom. This box was attached to another box into which the pebbles dropped as the chariot rumbled along. When the chariot reached its destination, let's say the Colosseum in Rome, the dropped pebbles were counted or *calculated* and the "fare" determined. Imagine the stones dropping like those numbers that click over on the old taxicab meters, and you'll appreciate this Fred Flintstone-like device as the first taximeter. Who knew that math could be so much fun? Companion words include *calculus*, Newton's invention of the branch of mathematics, and *calculation*, the act of figuring out stock prices, baseball averages, or the odds at a roulette table. "I can *calculate* the motion of heavenly bodies," Newton said, "but not the madness of people." Calculus is also a medical term for a stone in the bladder. Curious companions include *cancel*, Old Latin for "fenced in," represented by the # symbol, which is what we have to do with some of our *calculations*. And yet, not everything is *calculable*. Bertolt Brecht reminded us: "I want to go with the one I love. / I do not want to *calculate* the cost. / I do not want to think about whether it's good. / I do not want to know whether he loves me. / I want to go with the one I love."

CALM

Sheer tranquility amid the storms of life. This diminutive beauty comes down to us from the Provençal French *chaume*, to describe the time when flocks of sheep rested. Now that you've *calmed* down, think of how *chaume* evolved from the Latin *caume*, for the heat of the Mediterranean noonday sun, an utterly sensible time to rest, and the earlier Greek *kauma*, heat, and *kaiein*, to burn. Thus, we find compacted into a crisp, cool syllable the old folk ***wisdom*** that is wise to *calm* down when life heats up. If we don't learn how to *calm* down, we will end up "burning down the days," as novelist James Salter titled his memoirs. Companion words include the ironically stressful-sounding *ataraxy*, the psychiatric term for *calm*, according to the American Psychiatric Association. Stranger still, the APA resorts to defining *calm* not by what is, but what it isn't: the "absence of anxiety or confusion," adding that tranquilizers are called *ataractic* drugs, which makes me nervous just typing it. Fortunately, companion images abound: *halcyon*, as in the "halcyon days," so named after the kingfisher bird that nested on seas, *calming* them at the period of the winter solstice. Later, *halcyon* coolly evolved into a popular synonym for idyllic, youthful, soothing, evergreen *calm*. One of the most *becalming* lines of poetry I've ever encountered was by the 11th-century Arabic poet Abu al-Alaa' al-Ma'arrii: "The world's best moment is a *calm* hour passed in listening to a friend who can talk well."

CAMERA

A curve in classical Greece, an arch in ancient Rome, a shadow-catcher instrument invented in 19th-century Paris, a dream-maker in Hollywood. Our sense of *camera* originates with *chamber*, in Old Latin; later it becomes a scientific term for any wooden box with a lens. As the box grew larger, with ever-stronger lenses, it came to be called *camera obscura*, a dark room, an innovation that aided such early painters as Vermeer and Caravaggio and later ones like Andy Warhol and David Hockney. By the early 19th century the box and the term shrank to become simply *camera*, the basic tool of a photographer, who can proudly and literally call herself a "light-writer." Thus, a *camera* is a little room you hold in your hand by which you write with light. To keep going with the metaphor, here is an intriguing sidelight.

When the first colonial *cameras* arrived in 19th-century South Africa they were advertised side by side with the first affordable rifles. The verb to shoot developed for both simultaneously. Little wonder that indigenous people around the world were suspicious of all those newfangled *cameras* aimed at them. "Shooting" was in the air, and the *cameras* caught it. In his autobiography, Ansel Adams gratefully remembered the summer of 1916: "One morning shortly after our arrival in Yosemite, my parents presented me with my first *camera*, a Kodak Box Brownie." His sense of awe lasted a lifetime. In *The Camera*, he wrote, "Sometimes I do get to places just when God's ready to have somebody click the shutter." In the late 1980s, I enjoyed

Camera (Ansel Adams at Point Lobos)

a few Proustian privileged moments watching Henri Cartier-Bresson wandering with his Leica around the Luxembourg Gardens in Paris, looking, looking, looking through his *camera* before he ever snapped the shutter. Years later, when I read his humble admission, "Your first 10,000 photographs are your worst," it made sense how he waited and watched, and watching, finally *saw* what he wanted to shoot. *Bon courage* to all those who follow the light. Lest we think artists are humorless, let us recall Larry the Cameraman's words in *Groundhog Day*, "People think that all cameramen do is point the *camera* at things, but it's a heck of a lot more complicated than that!"

CANADA

A country in North America; the land of my ancestors. According to Alberto Manguel, the name of his adopted homeland was granted when the first Spanish explorers landed in British Columbia and exclaimed: "*¡Acá nada!*" (Here's nothing!"). In "A Case of You," Saskatoon, Saskatchewan's' own Joni Mitchell described one of the most unusual tributes to a lover on record, so to speak, when she wrote about how she took a cardboard coaster and in the light of a blue television screen, "I drew a map of Canada / Oh Canada / With your face sketched on it twice." From down under, in Australia, comes a story that's almost too good to be true; it goes like this. In 1770, the intrepid Captain Cook was exploring the northeast coast, near a river he named the Endeavour, when a peculiar animal carrying her young in a pouch on her stomach came bounding by. Cook asked an Aborigine from the Guugu Yimidhirr tribe what it was. "*Gangurru*," he was told, which the English sailors heard as *kangaroo*, and later entered folklore as "I don't know." Cook duly recorded it in the ship's journal as "kangaroo." And it's said that when Spanish explorers arrived in southeastern Mexico they asked a leader from the Yucatec Maya people where in blazes they were, and were told: "Yucatán!" which actually meant "What do you want?" or "I don't understand your words!" Whether or not these folk etymologies are literally true, they reveal the rare cracks of light and humor from the official reports of these colonial powers, as if to say, yes, there were misunderstandings.

CANOODLE

To caress, pet, fondle; lovemaking. A titillating verb, an amorous euphemism. Cuddling, with the promise of a little action; a humorous way to describe fooling around without sounding like one—a fool, that is. A word that snuggles up to you and asks to be embraced. *The American Heritage Dictionary* suggests that it could be related to the English dialectal *canoodle*, donkey, fool, and it's not hard to imagine Eddie Murphy's donkey in *Shrek* asking a girly donkey to *canoodle* in the back of the barn. But it is the suggestion of being a *Fool for* ***Love***, as Sam Shepard wrote about in his tumultuous stage play, that gives the word the mule-kick of meaning. The AHD also hints at a connection with the colloquial German *knudeln*, to press or mold with your fingers, as with dough, which conjures up the possible origin of how a little *canoodling* could lead to sighing to your lover, "my little dumpling." Here is a case of being so delighted with a new word that I went racing home—in Berkeley, circa 1981, on my 850 Yamaha—to check my dictionary. I had just seen *The Lady Eve* at the now sadly defunct University Theater and heard Ann Sheridan purr these lines about what she planned to do with her beau: "[I'm going to] finish what I started. I'm going to dine with him, dance with him, swim with him, laugh at his jokes, *canoodle* with him, and then one day about six weeks from now…" She didn't have to say more. Companion words to use with your *inamorata*, your lover, include *croodle*, which Robert Hunter tenderly defines in his collection of words from Chester as "to snuggle, as a young animal snuggles against its mother." And who can forget the amorous alliteration of Ian Dury and the Blockheads, in the mellifluously named "Honeysuckle Highway," when they sing, "Cruising down carnality canal in my canoe can I *canoodle*?"

CANT

Any jargon used for secret purposes. The language or "slanted talk" of street gangs, criminals, mendicants, villains, beggars, prisoners, artistes, or rogues (also called "rogers")—all those who feel the need for angled, ***skewed***, coded language. According to Dr. Johnson, *cant* is probably from Latin *cantus*, implying the odd tone of voice used by vagrants; but some imagine it to be a corruption of *quaint*. "Clear your mind of *cant*," he scolded Boswell, for he thought it "barbarous jargon," and one of his ideals with the language was to purify it. *The Oxford Dictionary of Word History* defines *cant* as an allusion to "singing," from *cantare*, the singing of choirs in the streets or beggars "singing" for alms. Skeats writes that it was "at first a beggar's whine; hence, hypocrisy." Cassidy makes a persuasive case that Irish was the "first literate vernacular in Europe," providing English with thousands of words, among them *cant*, which he suggests hails from the Irish *caint*, "speech, talk, and conversation." Thus, *cant* is evidence that there are always at least two levels of any given language, the official and the unofficial, the surface and the subterranean. Some *cant* survives, like the talk of gypsies; some is lost forever, such as the secret language of women in classical Greece. Companion words include *cantankerous*, a blend word of *cant* and *rancorous*, bitter talk. *Recant* then means something like "to take back your whining words." *Gibberish* is another form of the secret language of rogues, imitative of chattering sounds, possibly a corruption of *jabber*, which in turn derives from French *gaber*, to cheat. Coming full circle, we find that *cant* is considered *gibberish* by the threshold guardians of language who often feel cheated—or left out—by the secret language of the street that is often far more alive and vibrant than their own.

CAPPUCCINO

Espresso coffee mixed or topped with steamed milk or cream. For me, the perfect cup of *cappuccino* resembles one of Morandi's still-life paintings, trembling with earthen browns and whites. However, the word arose from the beverage's inspired resemblance to the *cappuccio,* or long, pointed brown hoods worn by the Capuchin order of Italian friars. From the monk's habit to the coffee habit didn't take long; the word appeared in English in 1785. The first use of *cappuccino* in American English is recorded in 1948, after the rapid rise of cappuccino machines in America's postwar fascination with European culture. Thus, a true *cappuccino* is a divine breakfast drink in Italy that begins with a strong shot of espresso followed by a dollop of velvety steamed milk, which insulates the drink, and often, like a monk's hood, which helps him focus by keeping away the outside world, it leads to ***contemplative*** thought. Either way, *cappuccino* is a habit that's hard to break. In the comedy *So I Married an Axe Murderer* the mock beat poet Mike Myers holds up a manhole-cover-sized *cappuccino* at a North Beach, San Francisco café and snarls to the waitress, "Excuse me, but I think I ordered a LARGE *cappuccino!*" Companion words include the *capuchin* monkey, so called for the tuft of black cowl-like hair, and *feather,* the slight verb favored by certain *baristas* to describe "the rising of cream on the surface of a cup of tea or coffee."

CATAWAMPUS

Awry, askew, askance. A bumptious-sounding Appalachian word, first recorded in 1840, for "mixed up; out of balance." As the lexicographers say, it's O.O.O., of obscure origin, but we can rest assured in this case that it is probably of "humorous formation." If you're on the mountain overlooking Knoxville and an old hunter says, "You're all *catawampus*," he means you're lost, or you've lurched off track, or maybe you need a chiropractor, or maybe he thinks you're as crooked as the road you just meandered down in your '32 Ford truck. For some recondite reason that should keep the word mavens busy for a thousand years, there is a wide raft of companion words for this *helter-skelter* condition. They include *farrago*, another country word, meaning a mix of available grains to feed animals; *mishmash,* and *mumblejumble. Hodgepodge* is a French-Dutch corruption of *hotchpot*, a confused medley, according to Skeat. In "The Place of Humbug" Lewis Carroll wrote, "I dreamt I dwelt in marble halls, / And each damp thing that creeps and crawls / Went *wobble-wobble* on the walls." Companion words include *catawamptious*, crooked, like a politician on the take, and Old Western slang for "chawed up, demolished, utterly defeated."

CATCH

An 800-year-old word used to describe a game that's been played for at least thousands of years. Recent excavations along the Nile reveal Egyptian tomb paintings forty-five centuries old of a pharaoh playing catch with his priests and swinging a black stick at a palm-leaf-wrapped ball. Compared with that veteran status, our English word *catch* is a rookie, first brought up from the minor leagues of language in 1205 AD. The sequence is familiar to all hunters and ballplayers. *Catch* ricochets to us from Old French *cachier*, to hunt, chase, from the Latin *captare*, to seize, and *capere*, to take hold. Thus, to *catch* is to take hold of what has been chased down, whether a long belt to left field or a long-tailed rabbit. The expression "a good *catch*" took on romantic connotations at the end of the 16th century as a way to describe a nubile young woman or a winsome lad as someone "worth *catching*." Jane Austen adapted the phrase for one of her characters who was vying "to *catch* the eye" of someone who had caught hers. Companion words include *capable*, meaning "with ability," and *catchy*, memorable. *Catchword* is a dictionary term for a word printed in the lower right-hand corner of each page of a book that signals what the first word will be on the following page. *Catchy* phrases include *catch as catch can,* recorded in 1393, and the foot-tapping song "Catch Me If You Can," recorded by the Dave Clark Five in 1965. *Catch-22*, Joseph Heller's famous novel title, refers to a notorious "*catch*" (or gotcha) in military law that relates to a bomber pilot's decision to fly or not to fly combat missions. If the pilot never asks to be relieved, he can be officially regarded as insane—and thus eligible to be grounded. But if he does ask, it is interpreted as him having the wherewithal to recognize the danger involved, a sign that he isn't ***crazy***. So he has to keep flying more missions. And there is the lesser-known, but to some of us just as stirring, "Catch 25." Legend has it that during a break on the set of *Citizen Kane* the 25-year-old Orson Wells shouted: "Who's got a baseball? Let's play *catch*!" Finally, there is *wordcatcher*, an alert reader who is always ready for the coruscating *catch* of a particularly beautiful, unusual, precise, or eye-opening word in a book or ***conversation***—and then equally ready to throw it over to the next reader, a playful act that keeps the game of *wordcatching* going on, infinitely.

Catch *(Catch 22)*

CHANTEPLEURE (FRENCH)

To sing and cry at the same time. A word to fill a void in our language, one that we've all felt and rarely been able to describe. Recall the time you attended your child's school Christmas concert and when the sing-along time came at the end, with *O Holy Night,* you could barely lift your voice for all the emotion swelling in your heart. No English word fills the need to describe that beveled-edge moment on the verge of both elation and sorrow. But there is the lovely *chantepleure* in French, which defies precise derivation, other than from *chanter*, to sing, and *pleurer*, to weep. Perhaps it is the result of centuries of concerts in the bejeweled Saint-Chapelle, in Paris, or in that stone poem, Chartres Cathedral, or the triumphant tears inspired by the singing of "La Marseillaise" in the French classic *Les Enfants du Paradise.* Whatever its source, *chantepleure* is to language what sweet-and-sour sauce is to Chinese food. Companion words include *chanticleer*, clear-singing, as well as *Chauntecleer*, the proud rooster in the French fable *Reynard the Fox.* During the French invasion of Russia in 1812, those Russian prisoners who did not sing for their French captors were insulted as *chanterapa.* Then there's *merry-go-sorry*, a merry-go-round of emotion, spinning you around from laughter to weeping. Synchronicity lives: as I type this word story, my son Jack brushes by me, casually chanting "Singin' in the Rain," the American equivalent of singing through your tears.

CHARACTER

An impressive life; the life that is incised on the soul. A sharp word with an incisive story. I'm reminded of the description of the face of a lovely old woman in Ballyconneelly, Connemara, where I lived in the 1980s. My neighbor, Mr. Keaney, called it a "lived-in face." Originally, a *kharacter* was an engraving or stamping tool in ancient Greece, deriving from the verb *kharassein*, to sharpen, cut, incise, furrow, scratch, engrave. In Skeat's dictionary of 13th-century ***slang***, *character* has the meaning of "an engraved or stamped mark." Not used in its modern sense of "distinctive qualities" until the 17th century, by the historian Clarendon (*History of Great Rebellions*), and later in the 18th century, when Noah Webster defines *character* as qualities that are "impressed by nature or habit" onto someone, distinguishing them from someone else. Thus, the early sense of *kharacter*, "to impress or stamp in a way that marked one thing differently from another," has been likewise stamped deep into the language. *Character* is the etching of life's trials and tribulations into our faces and souls, which distinguishes us from everyone else. Eventually, this sense led to *character drawings* and *character portraits* in literature and memoirs, and to *character acting*. The French essayist Michel de Montaigne wrote, "To compose our *character* is our duty, not to compose books, and to win, not battles and provinces, but order and tranquility in our conduct. Our great and glorious masterpiece is to live appropriately." UCLA basketball coach John Wooden said, "Sports don't build *character*; they reveal it." Annie Lamott, in *Bird by Bird*, writes, "Find out what your *character* cares about the most in the world, because then you will have discovered what's at stake." An obscure but compelling meaning for *character*, in Skeats, is as a synonym for "handwriting," a belief that lives on in the work of handwriting experts. Companion words include *characteristics* and *character flaw.*

CHICANERY

Tricky talk, clever deceptions, unfair artifice. The deliberate practice of obscuring the truth that this tough-sounding word evokes is similar to the speculation about the word itself. The root word here is the unfortunately lost verb *chicane*, from French *chicaner*, to deceive, to wrangle. But the stratagem within chicanery reaches back to *chicane*, a dispute in the French bridge game described as "a whist hand without trumps." The modern French verb retains the smoky atmosphere of an argument in a tense card game, "to quibble." Skeat tracks it back even further to the Persian *chuan*, a crooked mallet, from *mall*, a club or bat. Still others insist it is an echo of a precursor to golf played long ago in Languedoc. In his day John Adams captured the pettifoggery of politics: "Abuse of words has been the great instrument of sophistry and chicanery, of party, faction, and division of society." The 19th-century Romantic novelist Ouida (a favorite of Oscar Wilde's) wrote, "To vice, innocence must always seem only a superior kind of chicanery."

CHIRM, CHYRME

Melancholic birdsong. A word you never thought possible for a moment you thought could never be expressed with mere language. Have you ever been outdoors in those air-crackling moments just before a rainstorm when a branch full of birds in a nearby tree begins to chirp or sing? Well, this is the word, in the lovely phrasing of the 18th-century Scottish wordhunter Joseph Jamieson, "the mournful sound emitted by them, especially when collected together." The OED's definition is dolefully prosaic, chiming in with "noise, din, chatter, vocal noise, especially birds, with a secondary meaning of the noise of children on a playground, especially the mingled noise of many birds." Murray's anonymous contributor for this word must not have been fond of birdsong. Curious companion words include *jargon*, from Old French *jargoun*, twittering of birds. The Scottish *chavish* is second cousin to *chyrme*, defined by Rev. W. D. Parish as "a chattering or prattling noise of many persons speaking together. A noise made by a flock of birds." We may collect these marvelous bird words in a "birdcage," which in French is *cajole*, which gave us *cajoler*, to persuade by flattery or promises or to chatter like a blue jay. These words are birds-of-a-feather, what I like to think of as "observation words" that emerged from a lifetime of closely watching nature's own theater, including bird behavior. It's sweet to think that our own mating calls may have been inspired by untold generations listening to the cajoling, the flattery, the sweet-nothings of our fair-feathered friends, the birds, which adds a grace note to the romantically alluring power of Frank Sinatra's crooning or Ella Fitzgerald's scatting.

CLICHÉ

An overused, meaningless expression. Originally a printer's term, from the French *clicher*, to stereotype, inspired by the sound *cliquer*, to click. The imitative sound is heard, *The American Heritage Dictionary* says, "when the matrix is dropped into molten metal to make a stereotype plate." The stereotype block that reproduced the same word or image over and over led to the expression "stereotyped speech," a word or phrase repeated time and time again, as if from a single engraving plate. Piranesi's enormously popular engravings of the ruins of Rome come to mind because they were struck so often they darkened until their details were smudged and imperceptible, not unlike a word that can't be seen or understood anymore because it's been repeated *ad nauseam*. In 1946, George Orwell described his bottom line for *cliché*-busting: "Never use a ***metaphor***, simile, or other figure of speech which you are used to seeing in print." On the other hand, Jack Kerouac playfully reminds us, in his novel *Big Sur*, "*Clichés* are truisms and all truisms are true." Thus, at the end of the day it boggles the mind that we're still between a rock and a hard place when it comes to using incredibly unique words that are dead as a doornail.

CLOUDERPUFFS

Scarcely visible summer clouds. Coined by Conrad Aiken, exercising his poetic license, which should inspire the rest of us to use our own while cricking our head to ***contemplate*** the marvels of the clouds once in a while. *Clouderpuff* is as subtly *sonicky* as it is dulcetly descriptive. Can we call them "sound-alikes"? It's a little less showy than *onomatopoeia.* Ironically, this is one etymology that isn't cloudy; it's origins call for clear skies. *Cloud* derives from the Middle English *clud*, a mass of vapors, which happens to be the same word as the Anglo-Saxon *clud*, a round mass, mass of rock, hill, from the Teutonic root *kleu*, to stick together. *The American Heritage Dictionary* points out that until the 12th century *cloud* and *sky* were essentially the same word in English, presumably because the skies were so often cloudy even seven centuries ago. These two seemingly unrelated words eventually gave us *clew,* and *clod.* If you look up *cloud*, so to speak, you'll see the poetic classifications that weren't officially decided upon until Luke Howard, an 18th-century amateur meteorologist in London, named the three basic families: cirrus, cumulus, and stratus. The mirror image for the melodic *clouderpuff* could be *blunderhead*, coined by essayist Verlyn Klinkenborg. In autumn 1870 the English poet-priest Gerard Manley Hopkins saw a flotilla of clouds and described them in his inimitable way: "One great stack in particular over Pendle was knoppled all over in fine snowy tufts and penciled with bloom-shadow."

COMPANION

A close friend. In the Old World wayward travelers were so respected that if one knocked on your door and asked for food and shelter, you were bound by tradition to help. The Old Testament and Greek myths exhorted everyone to treat a stranger well because he or she could be an angel or a god in disguise. The custom evolved that once you invited a stranger inside your home and broke bread with them you were expected to treat them well; to harm them was considered an act of treachery, a breaking of millennia-old rules of hospitality. The custom of breaking bread in the spirit of friendship is present to this day in the intimacy of the word *companion*, which derives from the Latin *com*, together, plus *panis*, bread, and by extension, "someone to share bread with." Thus, a *companion* is a friend with whom you break bread, a bread-brother or sister. Likewise, the marvelous phrase *boon companion*, which adds the yeasty *boon*, meaning "benefit, good ***fortune***, or timely blessing," and is related to the Scottish *bonnie*, by way of the Latin *bonus*, good. *Boon* reappears in *bon vivant*, one fond of good living. Taken together, *boon companions* are jolly friends such as Robin Hood and his Merry Men, or Gertrude Stein and Alice B. Toklas and theirs. As the English proverb has it, "Be kind to your friends; if it weren't for them, you would be a total stranger."

CONTEMPLATE

The act of thinking deeply, observing attentively. The ancients described it as the urge to consider "the signature of all things." The word comes down to us from the 13th-century Latin *contemplationem*, the act of looking at, and *contemplari*, to observe. From *con*, with, and *templum*, an open space, originally an open space reserved for observation of ***augurs***. Figuratively speaking, whenever we are thoughtful, deeply considering life's perennial questions, we have stepped inside a temple, where we consider the signs within the sacred precinct. Traditionally, this was marked off with a line drawn in the ground by the augur, and was later demarcated with stones, gates, and doors. The earliest temples were where augurs read the signs; *temple* later entered English as the site for religious activities or musings of priests, ministers, and rabbis. In this *holy* place, from Old English *haelan*, to heal, and PIE *kailo*, whole, uninjured, the pilgrim believes he or she is closer to the gods. The Latin *profanum*—*pro*, before, *fanum*, the temple—provides an image of the *profane* person hovering outside the threshold or even being banished from the House of Holies. Closely related is *fanatic*, Latin *fanaticus*, one who is inspired by the gods to the point of frenzy, transported with "temple madness." Of course, this has devolved to *fan*, one who has an obsessive, near-religious relationship with a celebrity or a team. Taken too far, the affection can be *sacrilegious*, Latin for "picking up and carrying off sacred things." Of such matters, we can say of ecologist Rachel Carson that she believed it was *sacrilegious* not to ponder the sacred wonders of nature. “It is a wholesome and necessary thing,” she wrote, “for us to turn again to the earth and in *contemplation* of her beauties to know of wonder and humility.”

Contemplate

CONVERSATION

An exchange of words, thoughts, and friendship. Conversation is communication by way of dialogue. Its origins are a walk through history, reaching back to 1352 with the Latin *conversatio*, literally "to turn around with," from *com*, with, and *vertare*, which also gave us *versus*. Slowly, this was adapted by the French to *converser*, to live or deal with—figuratively, a way in which people conduct themselves. By 1580, we can see a classic painted word beginning to appear: two or more people walking and *talking* together, which is the very heart of *conversing*. By the 16th century, *conversation* was a euphemism for "sexual intercourse," presaging the expression *criminal conversation*, which became a legal term for adultery by the late 18th century. Companion words include *conversant,* familiar with, *reversation,* switching directions in talk, and *tergiversation,* the evasion of the truth in *conversation*. The euphonious *eutrapely* was Aristotle's word for someone "pleasant in *conversation*." His teacher's teacher, Socrates, often invited to dinner a man named Deipnoso, "a wise and witty *conversationalist*," which gave us the word *deipnosophist*. Conversely, *deipnophobia* is the *fear* of dinner parties. The cross-dressing Scottish poet and traveler William Sharpe's middle name was "Conversation." According to Boswell, Dr. Johnson loved "the sport of *conversation*." Companion words include *persefleur*, a banterer, *persiflage*, light conversation, *subtilist*, a subtle conversationalist, *causeur*, a talkative person. And from the great Canadian essayist Alberto Manquel, a reminder that in Turkish *muhabbet* means both "*conversation*" and "***love***."

COOL

In the know, ***hip*** *to the connotations.* According to the *Hipster Dictionary*, *cool* is "A-OK, hep, unworried, **calm**, relaxed," as in "real gone daddy, dig dong daddy, hepcat." A very *cool* definition. Still, it's a living paradox of a word. The moment anything is labeled *cool* it's immediately something else, which is the sleeves-rolled-up job of street ***slang***, jargon, argot, and ***cant***. It's ***cant*** that can do, a quality that an ordinary dictionary can't *cant*. A *cool* caveat has been registered by jazz historian Ted Gioia in *The Birth (and Death) of the Cool*, where he writes that the term has become "a verbal tic expressing approval of any sort … applicable to anything that is current or popular or even just acceptable." *Cool* is possibly from the Yoruba, where it was once defined thus: "*Coolness* is correct way to present yourselves to human beings." Calvin confides to Hobbes in the Sunday funnies, "What fun is it being *cool* if you can't wear a sombrero?" Biographer Frank Buchmann-Miller writes, "Lester Young remains one of the great ***jazz*** icons—the first *paragon of cool* and an inspiration to countless musicians, from Charlie Parker to Stan Getz." Thus, asking what *cool* is is like asking Louis Armstrong what jazz is: "If you have to ask, there just ain't no telling ya." You know it when you see it; you're it without even trying. To dig the essence of *cool*, you have to know the depths of *dig*, which means "to get it, be in on it, comprehend, approve," and which Cassidy claims for Irish *tuig*, to understand. The paragon of *cool*, jazz man Sidney Bechet, called his music "the remembering song. There is so much to remember." Now that's *cool* without ever uttering the word, a hip revelation of ***character***.

CORNUCOPIA

An inexhaustible source. We say that a great bookstore is a *cornucopia* of reading pleasure, a farmer's market is a *cornucopia* of food, or, as my son reminds me, an Apple store is a *cornucopia* of computers. When we use the word we are echoing an old story that comes down to us in the Latin *capricornus*, from *cornu copiæ*, literally a "horn of plenty." There is myth aplenty stored up in the word. According to the old taletellers, Zeus placed his wet nurse, Amaltheia, the "horned goat," in the sky in thanks for acting as his nursemaid when he was an infant. So grateful was he that he took one of her horns and transformed it into the "horn of plenty," one that would replenish itself forever with food at the mere whim of the owner. In literature, the word is often used metaphorically, as when William Styron answered George Plimpton's question, in *The Paris Review*, about competition in the world of writers. "I'm enormously pleased when one of my contemporaries comes out with a good book because it means, among other things, that the written word is gaining force. It's good for us to be throwing these fine novels into the cultural *cornucopia*." In art and architecture a *cornucopia* is usually depicted as a curved goat's horn overflowing with flowers, fruit, and grain, signifying abundance. So a dictionary is a *cornucopia* of words; a *cornucopia* is a dictionary of myth. Companion words include *capricornified*, defined by the inimitable Captain Grosse, in his *Dictionary of the Vulgar Tongue*, as "cuckolded, hornified."

CRAIC (IRISH)

A good time, where the action is, the real thing. Old Irish, used in the most common expression from Galway to Dublin: "Where's the *craic*?" [pronounced "crack"]. It is asked in pubs, streets, schools, after mass, and before leave-taking, meaning, "Where's the fun, the good time, the best people, the night life, the *craic*?" To go in search of the *craic* could refer to the best pint of Guinness, the best *seisun* (a spontaneous music session), the prettiest colleens, or the hunkiest lads. In Ireland, *craic* is to social life as Joyce's *Ulysses* is to literature, U2 to music, and Tullymore Dew to whiskey. Its discovery is the result of an all-day, all-night search, not unlike Leopold Bloom's twenty-four-hour odyssey in search of love around Dublin. James A. C. Stevenson explains, in his *Dictionary of Scots Words & Phrases*, that the Scottish word *crack* as a sharp noise, as chat or ***conversation***, and offers up the old Scottish expression, "Gie's your crack" ("Tell me your news.") In "Yesterday's Men," the Irish rock band Celtic Thunder sings: "Farewell to the paydays, the pints and the *craic* / Oh, We gave them our best years now they've paid us back."

CRAZY

Cracked, off-kilter, cockamamie, insane. Originally a verb, *craze*, which meant to "break, crush, or shatter," from Old French *acraser* and the Old Norse *krasa*, "to crackle." The Swedish phrase "Sla I kras" renders a dynamic picture of its original meaning, to be "dashed or broken to pieces." Figuratively, it came to refer to how the mind and spirit can be dashed or broken, and eventually led to the current sense of a psychological "crack-up," worthy of F. Scott Fitzgerald. In street slang, *crazy* means "good, superlative, wild, the best, real gone." Companion words include *craze*, a mania or fad; *crazy quilt*, an eccentric pattern, and *crazy*, the Roaring Twenties slang for "***cool, hip***, with it." Colloquial phrases include "*Crazy* as two left shoes," "*crazy* like a fox," and Willie Nelson's "Crazy," his first hit song: "I'm crazy for crying, crazy for trying, and I'm crazy for loving you." A vibrant companion word is *derange*, from French *déranger*, and Old French *desrengier*, disarrange, from the Indo-European prefix *des-*, to do the opposite of. Thus, Baudelaire was right when he suggested that a poet had to be a little crazy and intentionally *derange the senses*, as in rearrange them to reflect the shattered reality of life.

Crazy as it sounds, the Swedish actor Peter Stormare tries to explain the secret meaning behind the cult movie *The Big Lebowski*, where he appears as one of the demented enforcers, like this: "The *craziness* of being a human being, and ending up in such a mess."

CRUISE

To sail, cross, ease by, search for love trouble. The word didn't begin with luxurious associations of bourgeois people cruising the Seven Seas. *Cruise* began as a term for pirate attacks. Around 1651 it arrived in the port of English usage from the Dutch *kruisen*, to sail to and fro, and *kruis*, cross, from Latin *crux*. Thus, to *cruise* is to cross a body of water, preferably exotic; figuratively, a *cruise* was closer to a *crisscross*, a medieval sailing pattern, up and down, back and forth, used by ships to avoid being captured by those dreaded pirates. Companion words include the *naval cruiser* from 1679, and 250 years later, in 1929, the *police cruiser.* Later, the rapscallion association was co-opted, like so much bohemian behavior, by the well-to-do who went sailing on their own leisurely ***schedules*** rather than officially ordained schedules, thereby operating outside protocol, outside usual time. To say they were *cruising* to be amusing wouldn't be sailing off course.

CUSHLAMOCREE (IRISH)

A rarified expression for "darling" or "sweetheart." A ***lullaby*** of a word, a sweet nothing with a brogue. The crusty Clint Eastwood played a boxing trainer who reads an Irish–English dictionary between training sessions in the movie *Million Dollar Baby.* While riffling those pages he discovered this honey of a word, which literally means "vein in my heart," deriving from *Cushla*, from O cuisle, meaning "the vein or pulse of my heart." Companion words include *sweetening, sweetie,* and *sweeting*, Old English for "sweetheart, lover," used by Shakespeare in *Othello*: "All's well *sweeting*, / Come away to bed." A sweetheart in Yorkshire, in less-than-sweet contrast, is the rough-and-tumble *wonder-wench*. A ladylove in Italy is the more dulcet-sounding *inamorata*.

D

DAMN

A cuss world; a mild expletive-deleted; no small escape valve. Origin stories differ radically (from *radix*, root). The traditional but conservative derivation, issuing from the hallowed halls of *The Oxford Book of Word Histories*, traces *damn* back to the Old French *dam(p)ner*, from Latin *dampnare*, to inflict a loss on, from *damnun*, loss or damage. *Damn*, if there isn't an alternative reading. Captain Grosse offers a far more picturesque source: *dam*, a small Indian coin, mentioned in the Genoa code of laws. Accordingly, the common English expression "I do not care a *dam*" arose, for "I do not care a farthing for it." Not to worry. Recent research reported in *The Week* suggests that a little swearing after hitting your thumb with a hammer may be good for your blood pressure. It could just as well be called the "Professor Higgins syndrome," after the speech teacher in *My Fair Lady* who falls hopelessly in love with the fetching Eliza Doolittle, singing, "*Damn, damn, damn,* I've grown accustomed to her face…" Companion words include *damnation* and *damage*, plus innumerable euphemistic variations such as *darn, dagnabbit*, and the Appalachian euphemism *dad-burned*.

DASTARDLY

A varmint of an adjective, a villainous word dressed up in a black hat and handlebar mustache, signaling cowardly, ignoble behavior. Although *dastardly* may sound as if it hails from a 1940s Western shot in Monument Valley, it actually derives from *adastriga*, an old Anglo-Saxon word meaning "dwarf; a ***poltroon***; a man infamous for fear." Ansel Adam writes in his memoirs about his seventh-grade teacher who scolded him for reading Mary Shelley's *Frankenstein*: "Shelley was a *dastardly* atheist!" If you're wondering, as I did, whether there is a noun at the heart of the word, consider these lines by John Dryden (not John Ford), who wrote, "*Dastard* and drunkard, mean and ***insolent***; / Tongue-valiant hero, vaunter of thy might, / In threats the foremost, but the last in the fight." Similarly, a certain George McDuffle alliterated this amazing apothegm: "He who dallies is a dastard, he who doubts is damned."

DAYMARE

An anxiety attack, personal pandemonium. Obscure but useful, and dating back to 1713, *daymare* refers to sudden claustrophobic or crushing mood swings while wide awake. Today, we call them "panic attacks," from *pan,* god of terror. *Daymare* is to nightmare as daydream is to nightdream. It is a circus mirror image, twisting, turning, elongating, foreshortening our worst fears. The Anglo-Saxon *daymare* derives from the old Sanskrit *dah,* to burn, and *mare,* horse, with possible influence from the ancient demon horse-god Mare. During medieval times the reigning belief about the cause of nightmares was that the spirit of a horse lay on the stomach of an anxiety-ridden sleeper. Dr. Johnson provides us with another of his inimitable definitions: "a morbid oppression in the night, resembling the pressure of weight upon the breast." Thus, a *nightmare* is the mythic image that embodies the terror of being unable to breathe in the dead of night, and the torment of feeling crushed by psychological pressure, tormented by bad dreams; and a *daymare* is the mythic image of morbid fears that come like an incubus between dawn and dusk. In *Dracula: Dead and Loving It,* the silliest prince of darkness of them all, Leslie Nielsen, moans, "It is nighttime, so it wasn't real. I was having a *daymare.*"

DELPHIC

An oracular word, a divine proclamation, a piece of ambiguous advice. During classical times *Delphic* meant divinely inspired ***wisdom*** and then reversed direction in modern times. Its origins are echoic, from the sacred site of *Delphi*, after the oracle who sat on her tripod in the Temple of Apollo. Her proclamations were famously ambiguous, even riddlic: "Thou Shalt Go Thou Shalt Return Never By War Shall You Perish," For centuries afterward, the debate raged: Where does the comma go? The anonymous and ignominious Greek warrior who asked her the question chose to believe the comma went before the word *never*, rather than after it—and died in the battle he had been subtly warned about. Considering the curious fact that only seventy-three or so recorded utterances of the oracle have been identified, its hold on Western memory has been tenacious. To doubt its wisdom was inadvisable, as Aesop learned the hard way. When he mocked the oracle in one of his stories he was thrown off the cliff that overlooks Delphi. Thus, advice from Delphi was considered wisely ambivalent, revealing the ***character*** as well as the destiny of the one who asked the question. Companion words include *oracular*, from the Latin *orare*, to pray; *Apolloniac*, Apollo-like; and *Sibylline*, the Roman equivalent of *Delphic*, like the Sibyl of Montparnasse, Gertrude Stein.

DESULTORY

Unplanned, unconnected, unsatisfying. To be *desultory* means to jump around, meander from topic to topic without any rhyme or reason, a practice that makes it hard to finish anything. The backstory tells us why. The Romans called the circus performer who made the mob gasp by jumping from one horse to another a *desultory*, from the Latin *desilio*, to jump down, from *desalire*, to leap. Picture a cross between *Ben-Hur, Mr. Hulot's Holiday,* and *Indiana Jones*. The Roman orator Seneca wrote, "*Desultory* reading is delightful, but to be beneficial, our reading must be carefully directed." Since 1581 we have used the word in English to describe someone who leaps around in a conversation or speech. But the word has an upside, if you can stay with me for a moment. Consider the marvel of a fiercely focused horse-leaper, actually called a *desultory*, whose job it was to stay focused on the job at hand, an ability which also lent us the word *consultant*, as well as the word *result*, which is the consequence of an experience that "leaps back" at you. Companion words for the versatile *desalire*, from the Latin *salire*, include *sally*, to leap ahead (as in "to sally forth") and the lascivious *salacious*, which originally referred to a male animal that lustily "leaps upon" a female. If you're feeling slightly *jaded* about all these old words, remember that *jaded* is Middle English for a horse whose spirit has been broken, and has been crippled by old age.

DICTIONARY

A collection of words organized alphabetically, a collision of meanings, a river of origins, a garden of citations. "The universe in alphabetical order," in the marvelous description by Anatole France. Historian Jonathan Green credits Aristophanes of Byzantium with the compiling of the first *dictionary*, which he simply called *Leixis*, or *Words*, in 200 BC. So now we know that folks have been consulting them for at least 2,200 years, but they offer more meaning than meanings alone. Théophile Gautier read them to improve his poetry, Walter Pater regularly consulted them to keep his prose warm and marmoreal. Of all people, Mae West may have the most memorable line about one. After learning that she had inspired the name for a life jacket, she said, "I've been in *Who's Who* and in "What's What" but this is the first time I've ever been in a *dictionary*." What would she have said if she knew her ample bosom had also inspired the name for what happens to a parachute when one of the lines comes across the top and it forms a giant bra? Finally, I find it boundlessly charming to discover that one of the very first *dictionaries* for young people was called the *Promptorium Parvuloru*—in English, "The Prompt for the Young" or "Treasure House of Words for the Young." Thus, a *dictionary* doesn't merely give us a little information about a word or two we are looking up, but it *prompts* us to think longer and harder about them. Writing in a letter to Fransesco Sastres (August 21, 1784), Dr. Johnson said, "*Dictionaries* are like watches: the worst is better than none, and the best cannot be expected to go quite true." For some reason, in Spain and Mexico *dictionaries* are called "donkey-killers," perhaps because of the mulish demands on them to carry great loads of meaning across treacherous lands of meaninglessness.

DINOSAUR

A humungous, mostly carnivorous, occasionally herbivorous, now extinct reptile of the Mesozoic Era. Coined, in 1841, by Richard Owen, from the Greek *deinos*, terrible, and *sauros*, lizard. No ordinary neologism, but a dramatic coining that was minted shortly after Darwin's radical publication of the *Descent of Man*. Together, the discoveries of fossils and human origins were arguments marshaled against the contemporary belief that the world was only 6,000 years old. Bishop Ussher, of Dublin, pinned the time down to the precise day and hour: January 1, 4004 BCE at 9 A.M. In its own way that historical fact underscores Emerson's definition of language as "fossil poetry." In defense of science, paleontologist Stephen Jay Gould wrote, "*Dinosaur* should be a term of praise, not opprobrium. *Dinosaurs* reigned for more than 100 million years and died through no fault of their own. *Homo sapiens* is nowhere near a million years old, and has limited prospects, entirely self-imposed, for extended geological longevity." Figuratively, a *dinosaur* suggests something or someone terribly outdated. Companion words include *saurian*, lizardlike, and the ever-popular *lounge-lizard*, a ladies' man or a bar slut who slinks around bars chatting up rich women or men with come-on lines a million years out of date.

DRACHENFUTTER

An olive branch to your lover or spouse. This raspy but funny-sounding word is Old German for "dragon fodder," or "food for the dragon." According to *The Concise Oxford Dictionary, dragon* derives from the Latin *draconem*, and the earlier Greek *drakon*, serpent, and *derkomai*, to see, which Skeat says reflects its "supposedly sharp sight." If the reader dares to edge up close enough to feel the breath of this beastly word, you'll learn that it refers to a timorous peace offering, a guilt gift, to an angry spouse or doubting lover. Think of a box of chocolates, red roses, a diamond ring. The word suggests that we starve the beast of lust, feed the dragon of ***love***. For the temptations are never-ending, as suggested in that "sparkler of a word," as Novobatsky and Shea call the old gems, *gandermooner*, a man who takes more than a *gander* at other women during the *moon* or month after his wife gives birth. Companion words include *draconian*, strict in discipline, and *dragoon*, a mounted soldier who bore a standard festooned with a *dragon*.

DUDE

A city slicker who vacations on a Western ranch; a flamboyant dresser; an informal greeting, as in "Hey, dude." For centuries a *dude* was a dandy, a swell, a fastidious aesthete, according to *Thorndike-Barnhart.* For such a ***hip*** expression, its origins and definition have tended to be so hopelessly opaque in traditional dictionaries that some have simply surrendered, as the OED does in its attribution of O.O.O., "of obscure origin." By far the most compelling definition comes from Daniel Cassidy, who devotes an entire chapter in *How the Irish Invented Slang* to the Irish root *dúd*, a foolish looking fellow, a dolt, a numbskull, an eavesdropper, and later, Irish-American street slang for young swells on a spree in the bohemian circles of the concert halls, saloons, and theaters in late-19th-century New York. He cites a clipping from the *Brooklyn Eagle* in 1883: "A new word has been coined, *d-u-d-e.* … Nobody knows where it came from, but it sprung into popularity in the last two weeks and now everybody's using it." Thus, what began as a *dud* in Ireland, a dolt, a clown, a rubbernecker, came to America with the immigrants, evolving into the Irish-American *dude.* How cool is that—117 years ago everybody was saying "*dude.*" By the 1950s, *dudes* are "suave cats" hitting the bongos, which evokes an episode of *Dobie Gillis* on the old Philco. But as Bill Cosby says, I told you those stories to tell you this one. In 2004, I came home one night to several messages from a guy who claimed to be "the Dude." I felt a Cheshire Cat grin crawl across my face when I looked up his website. His real name was Jeff Dowd, the inspiration for "the Dude" in the Coen Brothers' *The Big Lebowski.* As played by Jeff Bridges, "the Dude" is the love child of a hundred years of *dude* lore, a hippie slacker trapped in a Chandleresque detective story. The plot is baroque, the banter raunchy, and the humor as subtle as a machine gun. What holds it together is a word—*abide*, as in "the Dude abides." To *abide* is to endure, outlast, continue, hold out, wait, prepare for; from *a*, to, and *bide*, dwell. Thus, a *dude* lives according to his or her own *dudeness*, which is a philosophy, a credo, a way to conduct yourself, a way to keep it together, stay cool, outlast everyone else who gives in, a way to stand by your friends, man, while the whole world changes around you.

DUENDE (SPANISH)

The blood surge, the vital force, the source of all impassioned art. When passion pales as an expression, *duende* is a fierce alternative to sentimental notions of inspiration. The Gypsies gave us this word for "little folk," or "the blood of the earth," from the Spanish *duen de casa*, master of the house. *Duende* eludes ordinary definitions, such as the pallid "power to attract via personal charm," according to one usually reliable dictionary. Instead, *duende* is a lapidary word, with more levels than Troy. Traditionally, *duende* was simply a "playful hobgoblin," a prankster spirit. To comprehend it, you need to turn to a poet like Federico García Lorca, who knew of an older, deeper aspect of the word in his native Andalusia: a power that could be found in the "deep songs" of certain poets, on the dance floors of flamenco dancers, the cries from truly gifted guitar players, and the flourishes of toreros; from artists who possessed—or were possessed by—*duende*. More than virtuosity, different from inspiration, *duende*, Lorca believed, couldn't be developed; it needed to be wrestled to the ground, subdued, then absorbed. For Lorca, art, poetry, music, playwriting were

Duende (Lorca in Havana)

a quest for the truth of life, not entertainment; it was irrational, earthbound, and profoundly aware of death, down in the "bitter root." "The *duende*," he wrote in *Deep Song*, "is a momentary burst of inspiration, the blush of all that is truly alive, all that the performer is creating at a certain moment." Later, plumbing the depths of *duende*, he wrote that it is "the mystery, the roots that probe through the mire that we all know, and do not understand, but which furnishes us with whatever is sustaining in art."

DUNCE

A fool, a backward thinker. "Introduced by Aquinas' disciples in ridicule of disciples of John Duns Scotus, from Dunce, Berwickshire, supporter of old theology vs new theology, opponents of progress." A contemptuous word, named after the controversial Scottish philosopher John Duns Scotus, who was widely read in the Middle Ages, then widely reviled in the Renaissance. His influence led to a veritable war of words between the old learning of the *Dunsmen, Dunses,* or *Dunces,* and the new scholasticism. As usual, Dr. Johnson had a thing or two to say about them: "It was worthwhile being a *dunce* then [in the days of Swift and Pope]. Ah, sir, hadst thou lived in those days! It is not worth while being a dunce now, when there are no wits." Companion words include *dunce's cap*, as worn by Alfalfa in *The Little Rascals*, whose punishment for his antics was to sit in the corner of the one-room schoolhouse with the traditionally conical hat of shame plopped on his pointy little head. A *dunce's corner* is the place where bad kids, like Dennis the Menace, are banished. The clever website that is also named *Dunce's Corner* includes this witticism: "Oh, you play chess, huh? That's sort of like checkers, right?"

DUPE

One who is easily fooled, a chump, patsy, sap, sucker, or *pushover.* An old hunting term from the French *duppe* (first recorded in 1426), and *le huppe*, the *hoopoe*, an extravagantly feathered but easily caught bird. The hunters knew a ***metaphor*** when they saw one, and the name naturally evolved into *dupe*, the personification of one who is equally easy to catch, or, in the argot of thieves, "a deceived person." Thus a *dupe* is one who is easily *gulled*, an imitative word for an unfledged bird, and *gullible*, easily fooled, possibly from *gullet*, the esophagus, which tightens up whenever we try to swallow a lie, while its verb form, to *dupe*, is "to fool, to deceive, to take advantage of." *Mrs. Byrne's Dictionary* offers *gobemouche*, French for "swallowing flies," a person who swallows anything, as in *gullible*. An illuminating antonym is *morosoph*, a wise fool. Speaking of which, *the On the Road* journalist Charles Kuralt once defined a *dupe* as someone "trying to learn how to fool a trout with a little bit of floating fur and feather."

E

ECLIPSE

To leave out, fail, overwhelm, pass by, suffer. In Skeat's phrasing, "a failure, especially of the light of the sun." The word's origins are overshadowed only by its euphony. Our current word dates back to Middle English *eclips*, and the Greek *ekleipsis,* a leaving out, and *ekleipein*, to omit, forsake a usual place, fail to appear, from *ek*, out, and *leipein*, to leave. Eventually, *eclipse* came to refer to the complete or partial obscuring of one celestial body by another, as well as the passing into the shadow of a celestial body; figuratively, it came to mean "falling into obscurity, decline, the shadows," as to one's reputation. Companion words include the celestial *ecliptic* (c. 1391), "the circular path in the sky followed by the Sun, whose light is *eclipsed* when the moon approaches the line." In a letter to Galileo, in 1611, Kepler wrote: "The Ptolemaic Astronomy was barely able to prognosticate a lunar *eclipse*." Almost four centuries later, Stephenie Meyer presents the dilemma of the vampire hero of her novel *Eclipse*: "The clouds I can handle, but I can't fight an *eclipse*."

ELDRITCH

Eerie, uncanny, terrifying. A 14th-century word that stretches over the moors of language like a supernatural mist. *The Concise Oxford Dictionary* has only "***weird***, hideous," as if it's the scary uncle in the attic. We do know that by the late 18th century it had come to mean "frightful, repulsive, inexplicable." and that *eldritch* is possibly a compound of *elf* and *rich,* kingdom. Thus, James A. C. Stevenson tracks down *eldritch* to the scratching sounds at the door, at midnight, in a cabin deep in the woods, which is a nastifying echo of the shenanigans of elves. Not the Keebler Cookie kind, but the ferocious spirits of the forest who guard a loathsome treasure that we may or may not wish to dig up. The Scottish national poet Robert Burns wrote, in "Address to the Deil": "I've heard my reverend grannie say, / In lonely glens ye like to stray / Or where old ruined castles gray / Nod to the moon, / You fright the nightly wandering way / With *eldritch* croon." Writer and essayist Cecil Day-Lewis wrote, in *From Feathers to Iron*, "Do not expect again a phoenix hour, / The triple-towered sky, the dove complaining, / Sudden the rain of gold and heart's first ease / Traced under trees by the *eldritch* light of sundown."

ENCYCLOPEDIA

A comprehensive book or collection of books. In every sense of the word, an *encyclopedia* attempts to provide a well-rounded education. If you look it up, you'll find it derives from the Greek *enkulclios,* which originally meant "cyclical, periodic, ordinary," plus *paideia*, learning. This led to the Latin *cyclo*, circle, and *pedia*, learning. As Skeat defines it, "circular or complete instruction," from *encyclo*, to circle, and *paeda*, instruction. Such was the influence of Johnson's prodigious English dictionary that when the French

Encyclopedia (Diderot)

attempted to translate it they appointed the essayist Denis Diderot, who promptly gave up and forged ahead with a completely original work, the *Encyclopédie,* which became a hallmark of the French Enlightenment. Diderot's goal was, he wrote, "to assemble the knowledge gathered over the face of the globe and to expose its general system to the men who come after us, so that the labors of centuries past do not prove useless to the centuries to come." The most surprising interpretation of the word I know of comes from baseball star Yogi Berra, whose young boys once asked him to buy them an *encyclopedia.* His response deserves an old Bob Seger once-over-twice: "I had to walk to school, and so do you."

ENIGMA

A secret, a riddle, a shadowy saying, a puzzling person. An arcane mystery, obscure or hidden meaning, or even more precisely, "a dark secret." If you peer behind the curtain, you find the Greek *enigmae*, to speak darkly; *enigmarein*, dark sayings ("I speak in riddles"); *aivos*, tale, story; and finally *enigmatic*, meaning "from the stem." Altogether, we find "a dark riddle told as a story from the stem." Jane Austen wrote often about dark, mysterious strangers: "One cannot love a reserved person. ... He's my *enigma*." One of the century's most memorable lines was delivered by Winston Churchill in a description of Russia in a 1939 radio ***broadcast***, "It is a riddle, wrapped in a mystery, inside an *enigma*." Later, he evoked the "dark saying" for the name of his "*Enigma*" project, which helped keep secret the Allies' battle plans during World War II. Italian essayist Umberto Eco updates Churchill when he writes, "I have come to believe that the whole world is an *enigma*, a harmless enigma that is made terrible by our own mad attempt to interpret it as though it had an underlying truth." And the Riddler's name in the *Batman* comics was Edward Nigma—*E. Nigma*.

ENTHUSIASM

Commonly reckoned as the luster of inspiration. More precisely, to the ancient Greeks *enthusiasm* signified the glow of "the god within," or "to be full of the gods," from the Greek *enthousiasmos*, possessed by a god. To my lights, *enthusiasm* is a form of inspiration but with the addition of passion and joy. By the early 17th century, the French evolution of the word, *enthousiasme,* took on the connotation of "religious fervor," such as the ability to speak in tongues, but possibly also referring to persons who were mentally unbalanced, full of violent passions, suspicious because they claimed God spoke to them. Dr. Johnson wrote that an *enthusiast* was "one who vainly imagines a private revelation; one who has a vain confidence of his intercourse with God." Personifying this posture for Johnson was poet John Milton, whom he denigrated as being "no better than a wild enthusiast." But the shift to the modern sense was already under way, as evidenced by Boswell's prescription for the well-lived life: "He who wishes to be successful, or ***happy***, ought to be *enthusiastical*, that is to say very keen in all the occupations or diversions of life." The eminent microbiologist René Dubos writes, "The phrase 'a god within' symbolizes for me the forces that create private worlds out of the universal stuff of the cosmos and thus enable life to express itself in countless individualities." For Marlene Dietrich, "Latins are tenderly *enthusiastic*. In Brazil they throw flowers at you. In Argentina they throw themselves." Companion words include the verb *enthusing*, as in "the critics were *enthusing* among themselves about Pavarotti's performance," and *giddy*, from the German *gudiga*, also possessed by a god. Thus, the modern figurative sense of *enthusiasm* evokes the God or gods or the divine in all of us.

EPIPHANY

A sudden shining forth, a blazing insight. This luminous word comes to us like light from a distant star. The Greeks saw the light first, as *epiphaneia*, a manifestation, striking appearance, from *epiphanies,* manifestation, and the earlier *epiphainein*, to display, from *epi-* on, to, and *phainein,* to show. This was the Greek word the New Testament used to express the advent or manifestation of Christ, and later used as the name of the Festival of the Manifestation of Christ to the Gentiles, *Epiphany*, celebrated on January 6. By the 17th century it was used to describe the appearances of other divine beings. Its current literary sense was established by Thomas De Quincey in 1822, and James Joyce in his famous short story "The Dead." Joyce uses it doubly, setting the action in Dublin on January 6, the *Epiphany*, but also figuratively to suggest the sudden blaze of painful light and truth about the marriage of his two main characters. A modern, mythic example of an epiphany took place thousands of miles above the earth, as described by the astronaut Edgar Mitchell: "On the return trip home, gazing though 240,000 miles of space toward the stars and the planet from which I had come, I suddenly experienced the universe as intelligent, loving, and harmonious. My view of the planet was a glimpse of divinity." Companion words include *phantom*, a vision, specter, or apparition; *pharos*, lighthouse; and *fantastic*, a display of the incredible. And then, whoops, there is the near *epiphany* sometimes called *presque vu*, French for "nearly seen," a kind of epiphany-manqué, or frustrated light.

ESPÉRANCE (FRENCH)

Hope. But not just any pie-in-the-sky wish fulfillment. As the beloved French Provençal writer Jean Giono used it, there is a quality of hope that keeps the heart kindled and the soul intact, despite the degradations of life. Giono's translator, Norma Goodrich, wrote that *hope* pervaded his novels and short stories, reflecting his own boundless but sober confidence in the future. Furthermore, she adds, his use is more closely aligned with the feminine noun *espérance*, "designating the permanent state or condition of living one's life in hopeful tranquility," than the masculine noun for hope, *espoir.* Giono's brand of hope sprang, she wrote, from literature and poetry. Compare the Portuguese *esperança*, and Spanish *esperanza*, and the related *aspiration*. Thus Giono's careful, life-affirming use of *espérance*, stands in dramatic contrast to the often effete use of "hope," what the 16th-century writer Robert of Gloucester called "*over-hope*," a much-needed word to combat the fatuous faith that the future will turn itself around without our own avid participation. The legendary Knoxville songwriter, playwright, and poet R. B. Morris cites a memorable use of the word from the mountains overlooking his hometown. "Up on the mountain, the word *hope* is used as the past tense of 'help.' It's a fairly common phrase usage in the mountains, like 'He *hope* me good' as in 'he helped me out.' I've always liked the way it seemed to imply that to help someone was to give them *hope*."

ESPRIT DE L'ESCALIER (FRENCH)

A brilliant comeback, witty response, quick rejoinder—that comes to mind too late. Coined by the French philosopher Denis Diderot as he walked downstairs after a party at the home of Joseph Necker, wishing he had been wittier during dinner. Hence, "the spirit of the staircase." A figurative expression, it refers to that universal feeling of wishing we'd had the *esprit*, the spirit, the inspiration, the ***wit*** to say just the right thing, *un bon mot*, a few moments before, at the party or in the business meeting. But words that lodged in your throat don't come up until you're on the way home, or as you're on the staircase, leaving the room. The redoubtable *Oxford Book of Quotations* renders it as "An untranslatable phrase, the meaning of which is that one only thinks on one's way downstairs of the smart retort one might have made in the drawing room." Companion words include the German *Treppenwitz* and Yiddish *Treppverter*, from *treppe*, steps, and *verter*, words, those you finally think of on the way down the steps and out of each other's lives, and their distant cousin, the Spanish *ocurrencia*, a sudden, bright idea or witty remark, whether on the staircase or in the subway. Then there is *O'Hara's Disease*, the great S. J. Perelman's term for "the ability to remember all the cunning things I did last night." Unfortunately, no one knows which O'Hara he is referring to. Once in a while someone tries to conjure up an English equivalent for these foreign expressions; sometimes they're embraced, sometimes not. The American humorist Gelett Burgess, best known for coining the word *blurb*, also thought up *tintiddle*, defined as "a witty retort, thought of too late." Not too late, though, if a few kind-hearted readers begin to use it.

F

FADO (PORTUGUESE)

A Portuguese song of sadness and longing. One of two must-translate ***untranslatable*** Portuguese words (see also: ***saudade***), the better to understand the complexities of human longing. When I lived in a 200-year-old stone house in Penedo, on the west coast of Portugal, in the early 1990s, a local Portuguese friend, Fernando, told me that the only way to understand the national soul was to know the almost excruciatingly nostalgic feeling of ***yearning*** for something once loved but now irretrievably lost. He described it as "the ***melancholy*** that lurks behind every happiness." As may be expected, *fado* issues forth from Latin *fatum*, fate, on the collective as well as individual level. All extraordinary words fill a void, and *fado* is one such word, expressing the deep sorrow of Portugal's lost national destiny after the Age of Discovery. This is reflected in mournful songs about sailors lost at sea, somber dances about lovers wrenched apart, and lugubrious poetry about brave explorers, all performed by *fadistas* who infused their work with ***saudade***. In Stephen Olsson's documentary *Sound of the Soul*, a *fado* singer, Katia, explains, "*Fado* is the most pure expression of the Portuguese soul. And our soul, our ***saudade***, stays in our soul, in our way of living all the time. And the faith is very strong. The faith that everything will be okay just believing in something bigger." And she sings mournfully: "Forget the time and the pain, / and think only of our love / Come now, give me your hand, / Climb the mountain with me / Because when we love someone / No one can silence the heart / Climb the mountain with me / Because when we love someone / No one can silence the heart."

FALSE FRIEND

A word in one language that looks similar to a word in your own—but isn't. False friends (*faux amis*) are pairs of words in two different languages that seem to be genuinely similar ("to agree or be friendly") but are actually "strangers" because they are so different. The French *préservatif* sounds and looks like the English *preservative*, a chemical added to cereal to give it longer shelf life. In fact, it is their word for "condom." The English *ale* in Finnish means "sale." A *magazine* in English is a publication; but *magazin* in Russian is a shop. ***Gorgon*** is not the root word for *gorgonzola*, the legendary blue-veined cheese from the ancient town of

Gorgonzola, near Milan, Italy, but a stone-souled, snake-haired Greek goddess. The graphic *cocksure* isn't a bawdy term for an overly confidant Lothario, but an allusion to, as Brewer describes it, "the cock of a firelock, much more sure to fire than a match." Similarly, the old English word *undergrope* isn't as naughty or improper as it first appears. Its proper meaning is "to conceive or understand." A *urinator* is not a "urinal," but "a diver, one who searches under water, according to Dr. Johnson. *Fakir* and *faker* are homonyms but not synonyms; the first is a member of a religious order of mendicants, and the second is a person who ***dupes*** others. And *teetotaler* doesn't mean "totally tea" for those who've "given up the drink," but has a stranger derivation in the stammer of a Lancashire temperance activist in 1830 who demanded "*t-t-t-total* abstinence."

FIREDOG

An andiron, often featuring a sculpted dog. The name may seem arbitrary, but therein lies a tale or two. Technically, it is the name for the thin metal supports for firewood mounted on short "legs," which are anchored in the stone floor of the hearth. Of unknown origin, but first appearing in 1309, possibly inspired by the Old French *andier*, from the Gaulish prefix *andero*, a young ***bull***, an echo of the practice of throwing bull's heads into the fireplace. The animal associations live on. During the Middle Ages meat was prepared over an open fire, often by rotating a spit by hand, which was hard, sweaty work. Eventually, a contraption was invented that allowed a dog to run on a leash, which turned a flywheel, which turned the spit. That is, until animal rights groups abolished the device as cruel. Thus, centuries of animal presence around the hearth, from the meat grilled there, to the resemblance to legs, and dogs that turned the spit, are compressed into the image that lives on in the iron shapes of dogs on the andirons. A curious footnote: The town of Abergavenny, Wales, has a museum that displays an old engraving of a *turnspit*, which happens to be the name for a small dog that was bred to run inside a wheel cage placed inside a fireplace. Eventually, the caption says, the canine mechanism was replaced by a clockwork mechanism that' rotated the spit (I'm paraphrasing here), but the memory of the live dogs was honored in the name for the old andirons.

FLÂNEUR (FRENCH)

A soulful urban wanderer. Not someone who makes *flans*, as I once overheard from a misguided American tourist in a Paris café, but also not one who is merely "a loafer or idler," as dismissed by the prim Mrs. Byrne in her otherwise delectable dictionary. Her suspicion has deep roots in the ancient enmity between townsfolk and those who are constantly on the move, such as Gypsies and bohemians, as in *The Grand Panjandrum's* pointy-headed definition: one who is "usually not a vagrant, but an unsettled idler with little concern for others." Hardly so. The *flâneur* comes from a noble tradition, strolling to savor the city, in contrast to the flashier *boulevardier*, who strolls in hopes of being savored *by* the city. The roots of *flâneur* would appear to be French or Flemish, but the word actually comes from Old Norse *flana*, a wanderer. Their patron saint, poet Charles Baudelaire, writes: "For the perfect *flâneur*, for the passionate observer, it's an immense pleasure ... in whatever is seething, moving, evanescent and infinite; you're

Flâneur

not at home, but you feel at home everywhere." Or as the great humorist James Thurber wrote, "It is better to have loafed and lost than never to have loafed at all." Companion words include *flânerie*, the actual practice and activity of the *flâneur*; *boulevardier*, one who walks city streets in hopes of being recognized as an artiste or philosopher; and *promenadier*, ***saunterer***, and *ambulist*. Those great hikers the Scots also gave us *stravaig*, to wander from place to place, from the Scots *extravage*, to wander about, to stray in ***conversation***, from Latin *extravagare*, related to *extravagant*. Thus, a *flâneur* is an extravagant wanderer.

FLIRT

To signal romantic or sexual interest, but more theatrically than seriously. So much romance compacted into such a short word. Curiously, in its 16th-century adolescence the Early Modern English word *flurt* was loaded with meaning, "to turn up one's nose, to sneer," "to flick something away with the fingers," and even "a stroke of ***wit***." This evolved into the fluttering French *fleuterer*, to use flowery language or talk sweet nonsense, which creates a word picture of bees flitting from flower to flower. Similarly, *flit* is an old Scottish word for "moving house," as the Anglo-Saxon *flurt* means "to move constantly from object to object, in short, quick flights." *Flirt* is the love child of all this illicit commingling, a tricky word that signals many conflicting messages, from the witty to the cheeky attentions of a "flighty girl." Dr. Johnson considered a *flirt* to be a "pert young hussey." Shakespeare's *flirt-gill* (Jill) was "a woman of light or loose behavior." Altogether, the common meaning for *flirt* has changed little since its 1777 definition, "to play at courtship." Ronda Rich writes in *What Southern Women Know about Flirting* that it is like making a mint julep: "making the drink even stronger is a recipe for a good time to be had by all." Gregg Mortenson writes in *Three Cups of Tea* that the Pakistani word for *flirt* is *Eve-tease.* Companion words include the whirligigging *flirtigig* from Yorkshire, a giddy, *flirtatious* girl. Thus, to *flirt* is to *flit* from one sweet thing to the next, while *flicking* back the attentions of anybody who picks up on your signals. Ultimately, *flirting* is alternately frustrating, frenetic, and fun.

FLIZZEN

To laugh with every muscle in the face. To say it is to see it. *Flizzen* is another *sonicky* word, as well as an "eloquent tighten-up word," like *flinch, clinch, winch,* and shrink—words that make you pucker up and contort your face. There's just something about those double *z*'s. If you happen to look it up and keep riffling pages, you'll find *flodder,* to disfigure [the face] in consequence of weeping. It contains an allusion to the marks left on the banks of a river by an inundation, from Swedish *flod-a,* to overflow. Wherever the cup of emotions runneth over, at roisteringly funny parties or dirge-sad funerals, we can feel a kind of sympathetic magic with the natural world. The antonym here is also illuminating: to *ridicule* is the polar opposite of hearty, full-faced laughter, for it really means "to laugh *at*," and it wouldn't be too much to add "with every muscle in the face." To dig deeper into *ridicule* is to discover how words can turn in on themselves. Eventually, *ridicule* referred to words or actions that evoked sarcastic laughter, contemptuous language, derisive humor. Its roots are 17th-century Latin *ridiculum*, to make a joke out of, and *ridere*, to laugh at. And why do we need to laugh? One of the most heartbreakingly funny writers of our time, the late Frank McCourt, wrote in *'Tis: A Memoir*, "We tell jokes because every joke is a short story with a fuse and an explosion." And when we do, we *flizzen* with laughter, even if we've never heard of the word.

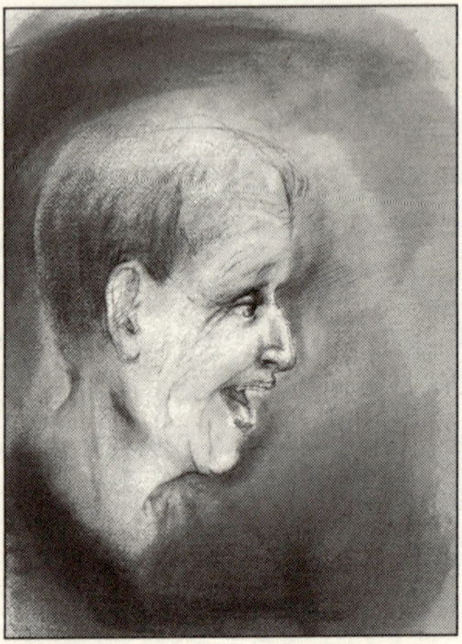

Flizzen

FLOCCINAUCINIHILIPILIFICATION

The act of regarding something as absolutely worthless or useless, such as this very word. If you didn't have a soft spot in your heart for long words that are fun to say and thrilling to hear, this one, from the halls of Eton, might convert you. A rhythmic example of a *sesquipedalian* word, one that's six and a half feet long, *floccinaucinihilipilification* is often regarded as the longest word in *The Oxford English Dictionary*, notwithstanding James Joyce's jawbreaker word for "thunder," *bababadalgharaghtakamminarronnkonnbronntonnerronntuonnthunntrovarrhounawnskawntoohoohoordenenthurnuk*, which he created from untold numbers of obscure languages. (To deride his neologism as a literary parlor trick would be a florid example of *floccinaucinihilipilification*.) The origins of our word are obscure, but possibly date back to a college parody of one of Eton's lexicons, in which four Latin words were linked together: *flocci-nauci-nihili-pilification*. Sir Walter Scott gave the word its ***bona fides*** when he used it to describe money. If pushed to use it today, one might describe someone, let's say an antique dealer, who is notorious for his habit of *floccinaucinihilipilification*, the belittling of his clients when they asked him to evaluate their artifacts. Companion words include *floccify*, to consider something worthless, which is a fancy way to say ***trivialize***.

FLOUNDER

To fall, stumble, thrash about. A nature-based word, from folk observation of generations of fishermen watching the way in which the *flounder* dives awkwardly, clumsily, as if trying not to drown. Metaphorically, it is used in common parlance for failure. But the critic Jacques Barzun plays off a famous observation: "As Henry James said, 'art is our *flounderings* shown.' And in the light of contemporary art one must even say: our *flounderings* shown *up*." Etymologically, it dates back to 1592, perhaps a corruption of *founder*, from the Dutch *flodderen*, to flop around, move clumsily. Alternately, it could be a blend word, bringing together *blunder* and *founder.* Figuratively, it now means to struggle awkwardly, in deep water, mud, or snow, or in action, such as getting lost in a speech or task. Margaret Atwood wrote, "We *flounder,* the air ungainly in our new lungs with sunlight streaming merciless on the shores of morning."

FOCUS

Sharp concentration. Sit down by the fireplace and I'll tell you where this good old Roman word comes from. Actually, I just did. *Focus* is Latin for "fireplace," the hearth, the center of activity in the home for millennia. Over time other languages *focused* on their own related fire words, such as French *feu*, Italian *fuoco*, Spanish *fuego*, and English *fuel* and *fusillade.* When the astronomer Johannes Kepler, in 1604, needed a term for the "burning point" of a mirror, the point where light rays converge, chances are he stared into his hearth and said, "Aha!" and co-opted *focus* for science. The figurative use of *focus* for the "center of activity" dates to the early 19th century. Actor Lawrence Olivier used to *focus* on the farthest seat at the back of the theater; baseball slugger Mark McGwire would spend a half hour before a game staring deep into the recesses of his locker, *focusing* on imaginary at-bats so he wouldn't be surprised by any pitches during the game. Tennis star Jennifer Capriati said, "You have to block everything out and be extremely *focused*

Focus (Looking for Degas)

and be relaxed and mellow, too." And Mark Twain: "You can't depend on your eyes when your imagination is out of *focus*." Companion words include *focal, focus group,* and *foyer,* a public lobby used by audiences during intermission of a performance, or by guests at a hotel who may want to *focus* on their ***travel*** plans.

FORNICATE

To do the deed, to make the beast with two backs, to make love but not be too delicate when you describe it. The street-tough version of "making love" betrays its bawdy (from *bawd*, prostitute) roots, which is the Latin *fornix*, a vaulted brick oven or furnace often found in the arched subterranean rooms of ancient Rome. The *fornix* was furtive enough to be commonly used as a brothel by prostitutes; the noun evolved into a verb for visiting the place, then transformed into a word for the act itself in the brothel. Thus, to *fornicate* really means—nod, nod, wink, wink—to pay a visit to a small, dark, warm, vaulted place. If you think about it this way, it's a far sexier word than that old reliable but crude Anglo-Saxon *fuck*, from Old English *fokken*, to beat against. According to folk wisdom, however, there may be an uncanny connection between the two potent verbs. The legend goes that when the Black Death was the scourge of Europe, during the Middle Ages, the ruling powers tried desperately to limit the populations of the peasants, even requiring couples wishing to have children to obtain permission from local lords, or from the royalty. Favored homes hung signs that read "Fornicating Under Consent of King," which was shortened over time to *FUCK*. Companion words include the obsolete English *swyve,* to have sex, which was the ***slang*** term that was upended by *fornicate* by the 14th century.

FORTUNE

A large sum of money; luck, chance. As ambiguous as casting one's fate to the winds. By extension, a *fortunate* person is one on whom the Fates are smiling, and an unfortunate person is one being ignored or cursed. Burrowed deep within the word is an important association. *Fortune* comes from the Roman *Fortuna*, the goddess of chance or luck, the Latin equivalent of the Greek goddess Tyche. The ancients believed that Fate ruled all, was even more powerful than the gods, but they also believed in the power of chance, personified by Tyche, the daughter of Oceanus, god of rivers, the flow of life. Mythically, one's *fortune* was a turn of the "lottery wheel," the dispensing of one's "lot in life," spun by the cosmic spinners, the Fates. In turn, *Fortuna* was depicted in medieval engravings in the center of a spinning circus wheel, which suggests that our fortune is in the flow of our future—but we have to do our part by actually moving the wheel, which requires taking destiny into our own hands. Companion words include *fortunate, fortune-teller,* and *fortuitous,* all variations on chance, luck, one's allotment in life. From the Roman catacombs, circa 2nd century AD, comes a timeless piece of graffiti from a grieving mother who has just lost her young child: "Oh, relentless *Fortune*, who delights in cruel death. Why is Maximus so early snatched from me?"

FREELANCE

An independent worker, originally a soldier who was free to lend his lance to anyone. Since I first walked into a newspaper office at sixteen and sold my first sports story and photographs, I have relished the idea that I was a *freelance* writer, a word warrior, a pen-for-hire. The word has never lost its magic for me. Originally, *free-lancers* were medieval mercenaries who sold their services to kings, lords, and captains alike. Free-lancers, earlier called free-companions, were free to pledge their loyalties and their lancers to whomever they pleased—free of their own will, not free as in without cost. This freedom retains its allure to this day. Though the practice is centuries old, the word didn't enter English until the prolific Sir Walter Scott introduced it in his novel of 1819, *Ivanhoe*, a book I recall reading aloud in a beautiful Heritage Club edition with my parents in the late 1950s. Scott wrote, "I offered Richard the service of my *Free Lances*, and he refused them—I will lead them to Hull, seize on shipping, and embark for Flanders; thanks to the bustling times, a man of action will always find employment." The modern sense of a freelance writer as independent, working outside the system, arose in the late 19th century, and is illustrated in the *New York Times*'s obituary for the poet Amy Clampitt: "She worked … as reference librarian at the National Audubon Society from 1952 to 1959. Through the 1960's and most of the 70's, she was a *freelance* writer, editor and researcher. From 1977 to 1982 she was an editor at E. P. Dutton. Initially self-published."

FRIBBLE

To trifle, waste, dodder, potter, stammer, falter, totter, kill time. What we do when we're procrastinating. Though people have been *fribbling* for as long as there were important things to avoid, the word didn't enter the English lexicon until 1633. The 1913 edition of Webster's isolates a *fribbler* as a frivolous kind of fellow. An idler. Companion words include *fiddle, fritter,* and *doodle*, truncated from "do little," and the *wunderbar* German *Dudeltopf*, a fool, a simpleton, best remembered in the Revolutionary War ditty "Yankee Doodle Dandy." Despite the legions of famous doodlers from John Keats to Virginia Woolf, the implication is that those who are sketching in the margins of life are wasting their time. Thus, to *fribble* in all these cases is to kill time, which violates a central thesis in Western life, that people must use their time wisely (though the verb "use" betrays its own Calvinistic bias). You say "fritter," and I say *fribble*. Fritter, *fribble*—let's call the whole thing off.

FUNGO

A practice fly ball in baseball. One of the great unknowns and so one of the most fun words to speculate about. It dates back to at least 1867, possibly to a similar practice in the game of cricket. For words like this we entertain all possibilities. A colorful one is that *fungo* refers to an early cricket exercise of tossing the ball up in the air, whacking it, then running after it. Hence, it's "fun" to "go" hitting a ball and running after it. Fellow words do not include *fungology*, dating back to 1860, which is the study of mushrooms rather than balls thunked into the outfield. But they do include *fungo hitter*, a coach who specializes in hitting 300-foot-long fly balls to precise spots in the outfield, sometimes no larger than a silver dollar. It's said that poet Robert Frost once told George Plimpton his dream was to hit a poem so high it would resemble a *fungo* that never came down. *Fungo* stories are as rare as good *fungo* hitters, but presumably what they have in common is a sense of awe and wonder for anything that reaches so high. Incidentally, *fun* is a word that seems to have been around forever but only dates to the 17th-century verb *fun*, to cheat or ***hoax***, probably a variant of the early-15th-century *fon*, to befool, to trick, ***hoax***, or turn practical jokes. Thus, *fun* came to mean "merriment, diversion, sport, make a fool of." Cassidy makes a strong parallel case for the Irish *fonn*, delight, pleasure, song. Collecting its ***false friends*** is fun, too: *funambulist*, a ropedancer or tightrope walker, from *fun*, rope, *ambulare*, to walk.

FURY

A ferocious passion. If you are in a *fury*, you are enraged because you've been touched by the Furies. If you are *furious* you are more than angry, which derives from *angr*, an old Viking word meaning the emotions that arise from realizing the injustices of the world, but less than *berserk*. *Fury* derives from the Latin *furia*, a violent passion, rage, madness; *furiosos*, furious; and *furere*, mad, enraged. The Romans translated the Greek name *Erinyes*, the three personifications of vengeance sent by Hades to punish evildoers, as *Furiae*. Later, *fury* takes on the metaphorical, embodying a woman's rage. Companion words include *furtive, secretive,* and the frightening verb *furify*, to infuriate. A companion quote to consider, by Francis Bacon: "A man who contemplates revenge keeps his wounds green." John Dryden wrote, "Beware the *fury* of a patient man." Shakespeare's *Macbeth* declaims: "Life's but a walking shadow, a poor player, / That struts and frets his hour upon the stage, / And then is heard no more. It is a tale / Told by an ***idiot***, full of sound and fury, / Signifying nothing."

G

GALAXY

A vast group of stars; an assemblage of brilliant persons or things. Named after ancient Greek sky gazers who named the twinkling bands of light in the night sky *galaxes*, from their word *gala*, milk. Later, astronomers in medieval Europe described the "light-studded path" across the sky as a *galaxy*, from the Greek word for "a circle of milk" and its Latinized form, *lacteus*, lactate, milky. For centuries, the Western world has been able to enjoy the origin story of the myth of Hera nursing the infant Hercules. Never one to know his own strength, the infant bit her nipple; when Hera pulled away from him her milk went spurting across the night sky, leaving the bright white lights we've since called the "Milky Way." Companion words or usages include the Ford *Galaxy*, one of the most stylish sedans produced by Ford Motor Company, in the 1960s, and the famous text crawl at the beginning of the first *Star*

Wars movie, in 1977: "In a *galaxy*, far, far away..." When naturalist and mountaineer John Muir needed an exultant phrase to describe his tumultuous ride in an avalanche of snow down the side of a mountain in Yosemite he reached for a *galactic* metaphor: "This flight in what might be called *a milky way* of snow-stars was the most spiritual and exhilarating of all the modes of motion I have ever experienced."

GLAMOUR

Enchantment, a spell, a fascination; the illusion of beauty. A mysterious attraction that evokes the exotic. This Scottish beauty has cast a spell for centuries, as if it were created through sheer sorcery, which in a sense it was. Originally, *glamour* was a magic spell, and *glamorous* meant "magic, supernatural." It is a cognate of the Icelandic *glamr*, a legendary ghost spirit, as well as "a kind of haze covering objects, and causing them to appear differently from what they really are." The Danish *glimmeri* means "glitter, false luster, glamorous, supernatural." Charles Mackay wrote, "Once supposed to be from the Gaelic *glac*, to seize, to lay hold of, to fascinate, and *mor*, great; whence 'great fascination,' or magic, not to be resisted." In 1851 Black wrote, "When devils, wizards, or jugglers deceive the sight, they are said to 'cast *glamour*' over the eyes of the spectator." During medieval times the word *glamour* described a certain power that modern people might call *charisma*. Eventually, these magical associations adhered to language itself. Mackay recounts how a certain Lord Neaves thought that *glamour* was a corruption of ***grammar***, "in which magic was once supposed to reside." According to the Shakespeare scholar Stephen Greenblatt, *glamour* was feared enough by the Inquisitors to be called an actual spell. *Glamour* is one of the more than 700 contributions of Sir Walter Scott, who introduced it in *The Lay of the Last Minstrel* (1805): "And one short spell therein he read: / It had much of

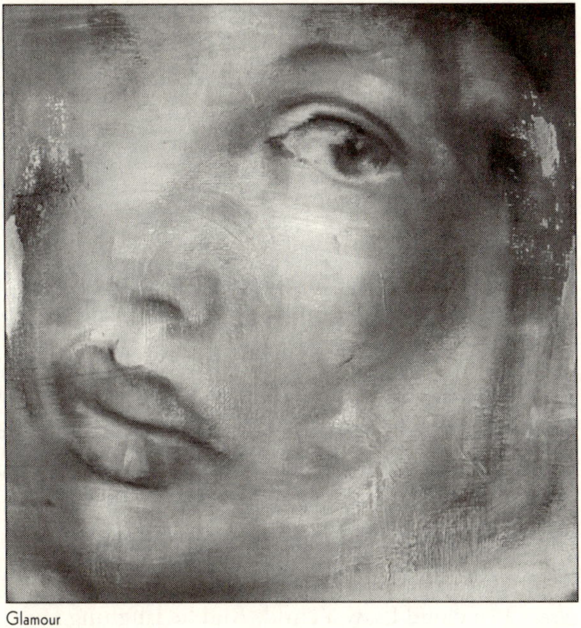

Glamour

glamour might / Could make a ladye seem a knight." Scott explained: "in the legends of Scots superstition, means the magic power of imposing on the eyesight of the spectators, so that the appearance of an object shall be totally different from the reality. ... a special attribute of the Gypsies." And who would know better than Marilyn Monroe about the silken cage of *glamour*: "I don't mind being burdened with being *glamorous* and sexual. Beauty and femininity are ageless and can't be contrived, and *glamour*, although the manufacturers won't like this, cannot be manufactured. Not real *glamour*; it's based on femininity. We are all born sexual creatures, thank God, but it's a pity so many people despise and crush this natural gift. Art, real art, comes from it, everything."

GLEE

Sheer beatific happiness. Originally, simply, music. The magic lies in those two gloriously long *e*'s, the joyful vowels of a child with her toys and the music fan *shrieking* in the front row at a concert. A ***happy*** word, by chance, borrowed directly from the Scandinavian *glee*. Mackay writes at first haltingly, then cheerfully, "by which by the progress of change and corruption, has come to signify that state of mind which music is so calculated to produce, joyfulness and pleasure." In *Songs of Innocence* William Blake writes: "Piping down the valleys wild, Piping songs of pleasant *glee*, On a cloud I saw a child, And he laughing said to me,

'Pipe a song about a lamb!' So I piped with merry cheer. 'Piper, pipe that song again!' So I piped. He wept to hear." The Rolling Stones sang, in "Sympathy for the Devil": "I watched with glee / While your kings and queens / Fought for ten decades / For the Gods they made." From the ***melancholic*** genius behind "Peanuts," Charles Schultz: "All the loves in the strip are unrequited. All the baseball games are lost, all the test scores are D-minuses, the Great Pumpkin never comes, and the football is always pulled away. … For me the operative response is *glee.* And its *glee* that I never get tired of." Companion words include a *glee*, a part-song scored for three or more usually male and unaccompanied voices that was popular in the 18th century; *gleeman*, a singer, teller of tales; *gleeful*, ***happy***; and *glee-music*, which Hunter defines as "merriment caused by minstrels."

GLOM

To *grab, grasp, grope, snatch, steal.* This is a stealth word. It snuck in under the radar, quietly evolving from the Scottish *glaum*, the tool used to geld horses. The careful groping around under the horse and then the quick emasculating cut made a stark impression, coming to mean over the centuries any quick, dangerous, thieving move. A later influence was *glam*, Irish-American gangland slang, to handle awkwardly, grab voraciously, devour, thieve, snitch, nobble, nab. Over time, the two words merged into the popular street word *glom*, to understand, to get it. Curiously, Dashiell Hammett used the former spelling but took the latter meaning in *The Dain Curse*: "Looks like him and another guy *glaumed* the ice." Cassidy offers an alternate reading, the Irish *glam*, to grab, snatch, and cites O'Leary's *Dictionary of the American Underworld*: from *glom,* to grab, as in stealing. Either way, to *glom on* to something is to suddenly snatch it away. At the risk of being indelicate, it takes some balls to suggest the following companion words: *glomerate*, from Latin *glamus*, to collect into a ball of yarn, and *conglomerate*, to wind into a ball, heap together, as in having the balls to gather together a group of businesses. Our word *globe* rolls to us from *globus*, as if the gods rolled all of creation into a ball when they created the round world we live on. Uncannily, the original sense of *glom* lives on faintly, a faint echo—or is it odor—of the furtive behavior in Scotland's horse stables, whenever we try to grasp the meaning of anything difficult to reach.

GNOME

An ageless sprite. Old reliable Skeat attributes the word to the alchemist Paracelsus, who suggested "the notion that gnomes could reveal secret treasures." Now there's a new light on the old *gnome* in the neighbor's garden, rooted as he is in two old Greek words, *gnosis*, intelligence, and *noetics*, to know, especially hidden knowledge. *Gnosis* in turn gave rise to *gnostic*, a sect devoted to the teaching of immediate knowledge, from *gnositiko*, wise, good at knowing. To call somebody *gnomic* isn't to say they're annoying little garden spirits, but that they're prone to "wise sayings or aphorisms," like Oscar Wilde and Gertrude Stein—or John Belushi, who both looked and sounded *gnomic.* The astrophysicist Sir Arthur Eddington's mysterious observation "Something out there is doing we don't know what" is numinously *gnomic.* Marvelously related words include *gnomon*, the index of a sundial; and also from the Greek, *gnosis*, interpreter, one who knows. While researching my book *Riddle Me This* in the early 1990s, I caught sight of a book of gnomic verse in the San Francisco Library special collection of humor, *Early English Poems,* by Pancrost and Spaeth, published in 1911. Here is "The Book-Worm": "A moth ate a word! To me that seemed / A Strange thing to happen, when I / heard that wonder,—A worm that / would swallow the speech of a man, / Sayings of strength steal in the dark, / Thoughts of the mighty; yet the / thieving sprite / Was none the wiser for / the words he had eaten!" Thus, it's safe to say that a *gnome* is an elemental reminder that there are those who *know* the secret knowledge, maybe of time itself, one that eats and spits it out again.

GODSEND

A blessing, a gift from back of beyond. Originally, a term in Orkney and the Shetland Islands for the flotsam washed ashore from shipwrecks in the outrageously rough North Seas. The god behind the word riddles much of the language. *Godhopping* is the act of pretending religious interest to get help from missionaries. Not as unusual a construction as one might believe. A *goditorium* is ***slang*** for a church, the place where one listens to a *godbox*, a rare but colorful term for a church organ. Our English word *god* has the oldest of roots, the Proto-Indo-European *ghut*, that which is invoked, which grew into the Icelandic *guth*, which sired such European words as the German *Gott*, Dutch *god*, and Danish *gud*. There are many euphemisms for the divine, such as *Zounds!* from "God's wounds," *good-bye* from "God be with you." *Gadzooks* comes from "God's looks." *Gee whiz* is a contraction of "Holy Gee ("G")," possibly from old Irish *dia*, God, a god. *Gossip* was overheard from an old expression for "a sponsor in baptism." Skeats derives it from *godsibb*, a reference to relatives, which gave us godfather and godmother, a person related in God, someone regarded as spiritual enough "to have God's ear." All that intimate talk invariably involved some betrayal of secrets, which evolved into the "idle talk" known as gossip. "Oh, Deuce!" comes from "Deus!" A comic expression for God in the South is *Old Wind-maker*: "Old Wind-maker's blowin' liars right out of North Car'lina." And ordinary stones are called "God's biscuits" in the old saloons of Knoxville, Tennessee.

GORGEOUS

Showily, splendidly beautiful. The hidden meaning lurks in its French origins, *gorgias*, elegant, from *gorge*; and *gorget*, throat, throat-covering. A fully embodied word. In 1611, Randle Cotgrave pointed out in his French–English ***dictionary*** a tantalizing connection with the earlier French *reggorger*, which he cleverly traced to the habit of proud people to "hold down the head, or thrust the chin into the neck, as some do in pride, to make their faces look fuller." Figuratively, this action evolved into *gorgias* and *gorget*, to reflect the proud behavior, "from the swelling of the throat in pride." Thus, a painted word comes into ***focus***: an attractive woman who coquettishly tucks her head down, exposing more of her beautiful neck, and thus appearing simultaneously more modest and more alluring. In a word, *gorgeous*, which when uttered is usually stressed—*italicized,* if you will—far more than the soft-spoken *beautiful*, as in "She's *gorgeous*!" When I was teaching screenwriting at the American Film Institute, I searched through their library for a perfect quote for a talk I was to give on the history of humor in the movies. Finally, in *Hollywood Quotes*, I caught this sumptuous use of the word from flame-haired Lucille Ball: "Once in his life, every man is entitled to fall madly in love with a *gorgeous* redhead." Companion words include *gorge*, to overeat, an act which tends to enlarge the throat; *gorge*, as in the throatlike passage in a canyon; and *gorget*, throat-armor.

GORGONIZE

To turn to stone, demonize. The verb form of the infamous noun, as vivid as you'll ever hope to encounter, deriving, of course, from the three daughters of Phorcys and Ceto, called the Gorgons, from *gorgos*, the very embodiment of "fear, fierce." Originally, the three sisters, Medusa, Sthenno, and Euryale, were considered ***gorgeous***, famous for their beautiful hair. But after Poseidon "obtained their favors" in Athena's temple, the sisters were cursed, their fate repellent, their hair transformed into slithering snakes, their hypnotic eyes petrifying all who stared at them to stone. Together, the sisters personified different aspects of fear and trembling experienced by those entering into deadly realms. Medusa's epithet was "lightning," Sthenno's was "thunder," and Euryale's "wanderer." If a ***hero*** or hunter was foolhardy enough to gaze upon one of them, he or she was turned to stone. So lethal was their power that even after death their heads were placed on shields, as when Perseus slew Medusa and presented her still swithering head to Athena, as a talisman. For some mythically murky reason, Medusa was beloved by Poseidon, and when she died, their offspring, the flying horse Pegasus (later a symbol of the Mobil Oil Company), sprang up from the pool of her still burbling blood. Curious companion words include *gorgonia*, a sea-fan-shaped polyp that appears to turn to stone the second it is exposed to the air. Today, *gorgonize* is an obscure but still stone-cold word meaning, as it ever did, to "paralyze, petrify, or hypnotize."

Gorgonize

GOSSAMER

Gauzy, silky, flimsy. A mellifluous word; a diaphanous derivation. Seven centuries ago in 14th-century England, "goose" was *gos*, and "summer" was *sumer*, and together they referred to "goose-summer," the time when "summer goose" appear, what we now call Indian summer. As hunters and hikers know, it's the time of year when the "summer goose" are most seen, and since seen, hunted, and eaten; it's also the time of year for those silken filaments of goose down that float through the air like flying cobwebs. To picture the phenomenon, imagine the gauzy veils worn by the Three Graces in Botticelli's *Primavera*. Also, remember the uplifting photographs and video of Paul MacCready's invention, "Gossamer Wings," the first completely man-powered flight. Edgar Allan Poe wrote, "There is something in the unselfish and self-sacrificing love of a brute which goes directly to the heart of him who has had frequent occasion to test the paltry friendship and *gossamer* fidelity of mere man."

Gossamer

GRAMMAR

Originally, ***glamour*** was a version of *grammar,* alluding to knowledge, especially of the occult, and skill in words and syntax; originally, "knowing one's letters." The great Jamieson tried to comb out the knot of meanings between the two. He suggested that *glamour* was a subtle form of magic because of the folk belief that those who knew their *grammar* well were considered to be *magicians* by those who didn't. This is borne out by the Old French *grammaire,* a grammarian, a magician, and the earlier Greek *grammatike* and *techne,* the art or technique of making letters, as well as *gramma,* a written letter. The term *grammar school* dates back to 1387, and described a place where "the learned languages are *grammatically* taught." By the 17th century, *grammar* referred to any language taught *grammatically* or technically, but soon afterward Johnson saw the inherent pedagogical dangers when he coined the term *grammaticaster,* a mean and verbal pedant. The power to cast a spell for good or ill lives on in our word *glamour,* born of this sense of enchantment with words and education. Thus, *glamour* is the language of magical attraction, as *grammar* is *glamorized* language. To this day, if those 800-page issues of *Vogue* magazine are any indication, *glamour* is "magical beauty" conjured up to cast a spell, a fashionable enchantment, as *The Devil Wears Prada* revealed sulfurously well, designed to impress through a kind of hypnosis. Likewise, in literary circles *grammar* is language endowed with magical, mythical significance. Companion words include *glamour puss,* a person with an attractive face, and *grammaticaster,* a verbal pedant, low grammarian.

GREGARIOUS

Affable, sociable, agreeable. Words that flock together apparently stay together. Thus, *gregarious* literally means belonging to a flock of sheep, from the Latin *grex*, flock, but figuratively it suggests the quality of being amiable in a crowd, enthusiastic in the company of others. Companion words include *aggregate*, collect the flock, *congregate*, assemble the flock, and *separate*, keep apart the flock, plus *egregious*, standing out from the flock—figuratively, "excellent," and only later corrupted to mean "outrageous." The suave actor Peter O'Toole says of his own infamous social behavior, "I'm the most *gregarious* of men and love good company, but never less alone than when alone." Together, this flock of words illustrates the powerful influence of our ancient herding instincts on our language. In this sense, collective nouns are a *gregarious* use of imagination: a skulk of foxes, a crash of rhinoceroses, a parliament of owls.

GROGGY

Tipsy from overdrinking; unsteady; hazy, as after a nap. Aptly named after the coarse-grained *grogham* breeches/pants worn by the English Admiral Vernon, nicknamed "*Old Grog*" (c. 1740), who began the practice of diluting with water the rum or spirits allotted by law to his sailors to prevent them from "intoxicating themselves." Presumably, if they were only a little drunk—*groggy*—they would still be able to perform their naval duties for God and country. Incidentally, there are hundreds of words in the OED for being *zozzled*, or *spifflicated,* in Robert Cawdrey's 1604 dictionary. According to the BBC, in 2008 there were no fewer than 141 euphemisms for the besotted condition. However, wordsmith Paul Dickson has collected over 3,000 English synonyms for *drunk*, far surpassing Benjamin Franklin's legendary list of 228 "round-about phrases" to describe the *befuggered* state, which appeared on January 13, 1737, in the *Pennsylvania Gazette.* Woozy companion words include *besotted, befuggered, befuddled, blotto, crapulous, dipso, hooched, plotzed, shnockered, schnicked, soused, sizzled, stinko, zombied,* and *zonked.* Not to mention the all too visual *pavement pizza* to describe the painted results of being such.

GYASCUTUS

An imaginary creature with four telescopic legs. Miraculously, these legs lift up and down, depending on which side of a mountain it is grazing on, shorter legs on one side of its body enabling it to walk easily on steep hillsides, and a long, tough tail that can wrap around rocks to keep it from falling down the hill. These are frequent creatures that freckle the hills of Sonoma on our way to visit Grandma, as I used to tease my son. Look at *gyascutus* and you'll find a hillside full of fellow mythical creatures, such as the "sidewinder" and the "rickaboo racker." Stranger than fiction, however, is the axolotl, the Mexican salamander with a face like Charlie Brown and a body like the Marvel comic book hero Madcap, who owns the mutagenic power to regenerate his damaged body parts at will. Companion word-animals include *badger,* defined by Sir Thomas Browne as having legs longer on one side of its body than the other.

GYMNASIUM

A site for exercise, a school for ***athletes***. Literally from the Greek *gymnos*, and *gymnazein*, to exercise naked, a practice banned in 393 AD by blue-nosed Roman rulers who were offended at the sight of naked bodies cavorting in the gyms. Around fifteen centuries later the Germans, following their digs at Olympia, revived the word and applied it to their own upper school, whence it ran across to England and ultimately to the US. Fellow words include the 19th-century back-formations *gym, gymnast, gymnastic,* and *gymnosophist,* the last a peculiarly ambiguous description of a certain sect of Hindu gurus who taught buck naked. Curious citations include Vladimir Lenin's "Chess is the *gymnasium* of the mind." Companion words include the popular *gym rat*, originally used to describe basketball players who seem to spend every waking hour shooting hoops, but now taken to mean anyone who spends a lot of time working out.

GYNOTIKOLOBOMASSOPHILE

One who loves to nibble on a woman's earlobes. A voluptuous name for a tremulous habit. And you thought there wasn't a word to describe this kind of torrid lover. This mouthful comes from the Greek *gyne*, woman, plus *otikos*, of the ear, *lobos*, lobe, *masso*, chew, and *philos*, loving. Strung together, it makes for a rictus of risible pleasure, if whispered at just the right moment. Companion words include *gynopiper*, one who looks lewdly upon unsuspecting women; *melcryptovestimentphilia*, the love of black underwear, and *nympholepsy*, the throbbing trance produced by erotic fantasies of earlobes, black underwear, and other seductive triggers.

H

HAPPY, HAPPINESS

Content, without a care, and since the 14th century, fortunate. "Oh, Happy Day," sing the Edwin Hawkins Singers. Etymologically, it emerges from *hap*, a concise 14th-century word meaning "a chance occurrence, fate, ***fortune***, befall." Nothing *haphazard* there, nothing risky. A *happy* soul is a "lucky" one, a connection in many languages, with the poetically curious exception of Welsh where it meant "wise," one who is "very glad." Companion words include *hapless*, without luck; *perhaps*, by chance; and *happenstance*, what lies in store for us, originally meaning "very glad," but the kind of *happiness* that comes to us by chance, by accident. There is also *haply*, by good luck. Curiously, *perhaps* is connected, through Old Norse, "by chance," by the nod of the gods. *Flakhappy* means "frazzled from stress," *happy hour*, "twilight drink discounts," *happy-go-lucky*, "plucky," and "*happy as a clam*," which is a contraction of *happy* as a clam at high tide—*happy* to be left alone when the tides of time run over us, or, can't be dug up this time! The lilting Italian *cuor contento* means a "*happy* heart," suggestive of the way a *happy*, even-tempered person feels. Consider the felicitous words of young Mary Wollstonecraft Godwin, a few hours before eloping with her lover poet, "I hope, indeed, oh my loved [Percy] Shelley, we shall indeed be *happy*." Consider, too, the heart-stopping words of poet Jack Gilbert, in "Between Aging and Old": "Lying in the dark, / singing about the intractable / kinds of *happiness*." And we can't forget the traditional Greek farewell *Khaire!* "Be *happy*!" There, fair reader, are you *happy* now? And, sadly, there is *anhedonia*, incapable of feeling *happiness*.

HECKLE

To harass, make fun of, criticize, disconcert, challenge, gibe, badger, or 'question severely in a bid to find weaknesses.' A harsher version of the Scots *heckle*, an 18th-century word from *haeckle*, a way to comb flax or hem, from the Middle Dutch *hekelen*, to prickle, irritate. The Scots borrowed the word to describe those who got in trouble with the clergy for doing this simple manual labor on the Sabbath, and the word steadily evolved to include any kind of public ridicule, including that of government figures. Ironically, *heckle* came to mean the opposite of what it originally meant; from the trouble you caused by doing innocent work to the trouble you *made* for others whose work or ideas you don't appreciate. Years ago, at the Holy City Zoo in San Francisco, I caught an up-and-coming comic who dealt with a rash of *heckling* from the audience. "Did you hear the one about the blind heckler who shouted: "Get off!" at a really lousy comedian? Well, he waited for a long, lonely moment, then he said, "Are you still here?" In 1996, the whiplash-quick comedian Phyllis Diller told Janeane Garofalo, "You'd have to make an appointment to *heckle* me. My timing is so precise that either the audience is laughing or I am talking. *Hecklers* wait for a pause. They wait for dead air, and there's no dead air in my act." Curiously, many strong verbs for criticism come from humble labor, such as *excoriate*, to severely criticize, denounce, from the Latin *excoriare*, to flay or strip off the hide, from *ex*, off, and *corium*, hide, skin. Thus, to "tear the hide off." Companion words include *excruciate*, to torture, especially on a cross.

HERO

A demigod, a warrior, one to be emulated. A universal character, embodying the idea in ancient and modern cultures of someone who seemingly possesses superhuman abilities, but also lives for others as a defender of home and hearth, a protector. The earliest English usage dates to 1387, and defines a hero as "a man of superhuman strength or courage," from the ancient Greek *heros*. The Middle

English use focused on the mythological stories of persons with superhuman ability who were watched over by the gods. Later, the word came to mean more generally a model person, someone worth emulating, or as Emerson memorably defined a *hero*, one "who is immovably centered." The late 17th century saw the word taken to signify the main character in a novel, play, or story. The first use of *heroine* was recorded in 1659, and *hero worship* in 1774. Companion words include the New York *hero sandwich*, an American version of the Mediterranean *gyro* (from *gyrate*, "to spin"); and *heroin*, which made early users feel *heroic*. Since the two World Wars the idea of what an individual *hero* can do in the face of real evil has taken a beating, giving rise to the *antihero* in literature and film, someone not ideal, perfect, or divine, but imperfect, often selfish, and usually irredeemably alone. The gallery is crowded: Humphrey Bogart in *Casablanca*, James Dean in *Rebel without a Cause*, Sigourney Weaver in *Gorillas in the Mist*, Keanu Reeves in *The Matrix* movies.

HIP, HEP, HIPSTER

In the know, streetwise, keenly aware, socially clever, enlightened, sophisticated, inside the outside, in the pocket, someone who gets it. To be *hip* embodies the dance between the insider and the outsider, it is to see the truth that others don't; the hipster is able to put it to words, music, paint, stone, or film. Imagine a combination of Mark Twain, Miles

Davis, Billie Holliday, and Warner Brothers' Chuck Jones. The author of *Hip*, John Leland, writes, "*Hip* is a term for enlightenment," presumably in endarkened times. It was brought over on slave ships from Africa as the Wolof verb *hepi*, to open one's eyes and see, to be aware. Cassidy offers an alternate derivation, tracing *hip* back to the old Irish *aibi*, pronounced "hipi," for "mature, clever, quick, wise." With common use in the ***jazz*** and blues clubs and the brothels of Storyville, New Orleans, the word was burnished and shortened into *hip*, street patois for those who see through the lies of society. *Hipsters* were the "holy fools" in the Beat circles of the Fifties. Perennially hard to define, like jazz itself, you know *hipness* when you see it. Jazz drummer Tony Williams recognized it when he saw Miles Davis play, saying later, "That's the life I want to live." Companion words include *hep*, *hip*, ***cool***, righteous, in the know; *hepcat*, one who is *hep*, totally uncubistic (not square); and of course *hippie*, from the Sixties, as in the description of Jack Kerouac on the back cover of *On the Road* as the "*Hippie* Homer of the turned-on generation..." The *hipoisie* performers in the *funky* (from "heavy") blues music world learned how *to funkify*, or frighten the straight world with darkly menacing bass lines and sensuous lyrics. No coincidence, then, that the name of the legendary backup band in Motown was The Funk Brothers.

HOAX

A ruse, trick, deceit. Etymologically, a curiosity cabinet. Short for *hocus-pocus*, a nonsense phrase uttered by medieval jugglers and tricksters to distract their audience, and sometimes poke fun at them. Another influence on *hoax* was tall tales about the incantations of alchemists. There are many charming claims for the true origin of the word. Skeat simply says, "Short for *hocus*, i.e. to juggle, cheat." Others insist that *hoax* is a twist on the Latin words intoned at the moment of transubstantiation during communion: *Hoc est corpus*, "Here is his body." Still others claim that it derives from the faux Latin *Hax pax max Deus adimaxus*, employed by conjurers as a magic formula. By the 18th century it had simply become a shorthand verb for tricking or misleading and a noun for a fake. Famous *hoaxes* include the Piltdown Man controversy, and the fake memoirs of Howard Hughes, conjured up by a down-and-out Utah garage mechanic, Melvin Dummar. Companion words include *Hocus Focus*, a cartoon game of visual acuity enjoyed by children around the world (and that's no *hoax*), and several *hoaxy* words, including *hokey-pokey, hokum,* and that good old Tommy James & the Shondells song, "Hanky Panky."

HONEYMOON

The time between the wedding and everyday marriage, thought to be as sweet as honey, but only lasting the length of one moon. The earliest reference clocks in with the 1546 recording of *hony moone,* and yet the notion of a new marriage being as sweet as *honey* but as fickle as the waxing and waning *moon* must be as old as ***love*** itself. Hunter wrote, in 1894, that the term derived from old Teutonic practice of drinking a honeylike liquid, metheglin, for thirty days after marriage. During this charmed month the bridegroom intended to hide his bride from family and friends, thought to be an echo of an the ancient practice of capturing women for marriage. The French version is *lune de miel,* a moon of honey, and the German is *flitterwochen*, from *flitter*, tinsel, and *wochen*, week, which works out to a tinsel-like romance that lasts but a week. When asked why she was late with a writing assignment while on her *honeymoon*, Dorothy Parker wired her editor: "Too busy fucking, and vice versa." On the wall of a gas station outside Tucson I caught this graffito scribbled in red ink: "After our *honeymoon* I felt like a new man. She said she did too." Not to be confused with *gandermooner*, a man who chases other women in the month after his wife has given birth, probably from *gander*, to take a look, and *moon*, as in the month after the wedding.

HOPSCOTCH

A jumping game for kids. A 17th-century word for a 2,000-year-old game. Originally known as *scotch-hoppers*, and rooted in another old English game called hop-score, in *hopscotch* children hop over *scotches*; lines marking the squares to be hopped are scored or *scotched* in the ground. Companion words include *butterscotch*, from "scotched" or "burnt" butter. I recall catching a cartoon some years ago that imagined a young Neil Armstrong watching two kids playing *hopscotch* on a city sidewalk, and hearing one of them chant, "One small step for Jan, and one small step for Malcolm." In the early 1960s, jazz artist Calvin Hayes accompanied his record producer father, Mickie Most, to the Abbey Road studios to record the Beatles, and wandered onto the paving stones of Studio One. He recalls, "I spent a couple of hours being taught to play *hopscotch* by none other than John Lennon."

HYPERBOLE

Wild exaggeration. Word conoisseur Wilfred Funk cleverly defines *hyperbole* as "a wild pitch." If this seems a stretch, a tautology, consider that the word comes flying to us across the field of dreamtime from the Greek *hyper*, over, and *ballein*, to throw or to throw over. It classical times that would've referred to a javelin or the occasional gymnastic use of exercise balls, but today it means to pitch a ball over the head of a terrified batter, or in baseball parlance, to throw some "chin music." Incidentally, "wild pitch" is an actual category in baseball, referring to any pitch too high, too wide, too wild for the catcher to catch. The ignominious career record in the major leagues is 277, held by the fireballer Nolan Ryan, and the single-season record is 30, by Red Ames, in 1905. These stats are—and aren't—exaggerated examples of *hyperbole*! Companion "throw words" are no *problem*, from *pro-ballein*, to throw forward; *symbolic*, to throw together; and *diabolic*, to throw apart. And it wouldn't be *hyperbole* to say that the German philosopher Heidegger wrote that human beings must not take anything in life as predetermined, but instead must practice "throwing-oneself-free."

HYPOCRITE

*A pretender, a **phony**, a poseur.* The word twists and turns through the centuries, dating back to the Old French *hypocrisie*, in 1225, and reaching all the way back to the Greek *hypokrisis*, acting on the stage, and *hypokrinesthai*, to play a part, pretend, from *hypo*, under, and *krinein*, to sift, decide. As the playwright said, "All the world's a stage, and all the men and women merely players." However, some are acting authentic roles, and some are inauthentic. Thus, *hypocrite* describes someone who is adept at acting a part but is a persuasive pretender, one who exploits others with a phony sense of *crisis*. Companion words include *hypocrisy*, literally the acting of a part, according to the OED, and figuratively the "simulation of a virtue or goodness." The mordant Ambrose Bierce describes it as "prejudice with a halo." My father's old book of proverbs offers this one from Russia: "*Hypocrites* kick with their feet and lick with their tongues."

I

ICONOCLAST

One who shatters graven images. The original *iconoclasts* were Eastern Orthodox Christians during the 8th and 9th centuries who violently disagreed with the use of *icons*, religious images, and some took to smashing those they found in churches, monasteries, convents. These medieval Greek *eikonoklastes* gave us *iconoclasm*, icon-breaking, from *eikon*, likeness, image, portrait, and *klon*, to break. Used theologically to describe the refusal of the Protestants after Luther to bow down before any man, and also by social historians since the 19th century to describe someone who shatters sacred cows or barriers. Thus, both Martin Luther and Martin Luther King Jr. were *iconoclasts* in their own worlds, as certain artists such as Georgia O'Keefe, Jackson Pollack, and Gloria Steinem have been in theirs. "Rough work, *iconoclasm*," said Oliver Wendell Holmes, "but the only way to get at truth." Companion words include *iconic*, *iconography*, and that rare but great verb *iconify*. *Icons* as computer symbols seem to have been around forever, but only entered the language in 1982.

IDIOT

An ignorant person; someone with limited intelligence. Dr. Johnson succinctly defines one as "a fool; a natural; a changeling; one without powers of reason." If this seems overly harsh, consider its true origins. To the early Greeks, *idios* literally meant "one's own," but figuratively meant "a private person," one who was either unqualified for public affairs or far too much "his own man," a loner, an inexperienced man. Eventually, *idios* came to mean a person incapable of holding public office; later it took on the meaning of a person with the (believed to be enormous) privilege of voting who didn't participate in civic affairs or shirked his civic responsibility. One of the worst of epithets then and now, an *idiot* was someone who didn't vote or attend the Senate. By the early 1300s, *idiot* referred to a mentally incapable person, from the Old French *idiote*, for "uneducated person," Thus, an *idiot* has long been someone whose individuality far outweighs his or her commitment or connection to the community, as evidenced by its flowing into fellow words like *idiosyncrasy*, an individual's peculiar behavior traits, and *idiom*, an individualistic expression; *idiot box*, a description of a television set, from 1959; *idiot light*, the red flasher on the dashboard, from 1968. The sarcasm and disapproval that imbues the word is captured by Mark Twain's aside, "Reader, suppose you were an *idiot.* And suppose you were a member of Congress. But I repeat myself." Novelist Rebecca West, in an unguarded moment, suggested a subtle distinction: "The main difference between men and women is that men are lunatics and women are *idiots.*"

IGNORASPHERE

A layer of the sky sandwiched between the atmosphere and outer space. It is situated exactly where the word suggests, a place not-known, from *ignore*, not to know. This playful term refers to the most poorly investigated and misunderstood region of space, which is beyond the reach of ordinary aircraft and below orbiting spacecraft. A so-called derivative word, invented by meteorologists who wished to draw attention to a "sphere of air" surrounding the earth that other scientists had "ignored": hence, the jocular *ignorasphere.* But not only ignored—unrecognized. Not until recently has it been understood as the source of natural phenomena such as lightning storms, and as the region millions of meteors enter at their peril—and then disintegrate. Actually, it is a playful synonym for the mesosphere, from Greek *mesos*, middle, and *sphaira*, ball, the layer of the earth's atmosphere above the stratosphere and below the thermosphere, located between fifty and ninety kilometers above the surface of the earth. Thus, we ignore the *ignorasphere* at our peril, as it generates "atmospheric tides" and "gravity tides," and even the eerily beautiful *noctilucent*, night-shining clouds. Companion words include *atmosphere*, steam sphere; *troposphere*, revolving sphere; *stratosphere*, spreading sphere; *ionosphere*, violet sphere.

INSOLENT

Rebellious, arrogant, with a tincture of realizing a higher justice. Richard Chenevix Trench's definition, trenchant as it is, deserves to be quoted: "The *insolent* is, properly, no more than the unusual. This, as the violation of the fixed law and order of a society, is commonly offensive, even as it indicates a mind willing to offend, and thus *insolent* has acquired its present meaning. But for the poet, the fact that he is forsaking the beaten track … in this way to be *insolent*, or original, as we should now say, may be his highest praise." First recorded in 1386, "proud, disdainful, haughty, arrogant," from Latin *insolentem*, which may be related to *sodalis*, close companion. The modern sense of being contemptuous of authority dates from 1678. Aristotle is credited with the pithy saying "***Wit*** is educated *insolence*." Sharing a piquant observation about her friends Lauren Bacall and Humphrey Bogart, Bette Davis said, "She matched his *insolence*."

J

JAZZ

In a word, Louis; in two, Ella Fitzgerald; in three, Charlie "Bird" Parker; in four, Irish heat or passion. Its origins are as ***hip*** as its syncopated rhythm. *Jazz* jumped out of Black America's ***juke*** joints, those cheap bars in the South that flailed with bump-and-grind dancing and bad-ass music, as intertwined as two lovers on the dance floor swaying to an Eartha Kitt song. So *jazzin'* was slang for getting it on, *jazzy* became an adjective to describe the slick moves of a Pete Maravich on the basketball court. Cassidy's Irish–American ***dictionary*** offers the Irish *teas*, pronounced *j'as ch'as*, and meaning "passion, ardor, excitement, sexual heat and excitement." His persuasive research tracks the word to as early as 1917, in the Bay Area, where it was a "hot new word" heard in music halls and whorehouses and on baseball fields. He writes, *"Jazz* was so full of *jasm* and *gism* (*iteas ioma*, an abundance of heat) … It was a word you learned by ear—like *jazz* music." Often used together by the immigrant Irish, *jasm* and *gism* had a kind of bluesy "call and response" relationship, which resulted in *tch'as* pronounced, drum roll, please—*jazz*. Originally a kind of "spark." it appears in Northern California sports pages, in the 1890s, to describe ballplayers who performed with *gis*, sass, zest, pizzazz. In hipster slang, *jazz* means having sex, as in "I Want a Jazzy Kiss," by Mamie Smith, 1921. Companion words include *jazzbo*, boyfriend; *jazz water*, bootleg alcohol; *jazzed*, excited. *Jive*, as indispensable in *jazz* as syncopation, is defined in *Hip Slang* as "to kid, to talk insincerely, to use elaborate or trick language"—immortalized in Cab Calloway's crepuscular dictionary of *Jive Talk* in the 1920s.

JINX

To curse; an evil spell; a person or article that brings bad luck. Traditionally cited as O.O.O. "of obscure origin." But that doesn't mean we can't *speculate*, hold up a mirror, to the popular word, no matter how ***baffling*** it is to scholars. Long associated with witchcraft and witches, who used a certain *wryneck* bird for divination. Pindar and Aeschylus cite *iunx* as a peculiar contraption called a witch's wheel that turned with a "hapless bird," the *Jynx torquilla*, that is able to rotate its neck 360 degrees. Reportedly, onlookers were charmed. Biologist Lyall Watson traces it back to *jynges*, for "unspeakable counsels" in ancient Chaldaic philosophy.

Lexicographer and poet John Ciardi roots it in "*Iunx*, the wryneck, squawking European bird that can twist its neck in an extra way." Not until the 1910 does the word resurface—in the sports pages again—in a reference to a couple of hapless ballplayers who hadn't escaped "the *jinx* that has been following the champions." The New York Giants' Christy Mathewson, in his 1912 book *Pitching at a Pinch,* described a *jinx* as "something which brings bad luck to a ball player." Actress Gina Gershon says, "I've seen it too many times in Hollywood. Talking about a relationship in public can *jinx* it. And if you have your picture taken together, you might as well start packing your bags."

JUGGERNAUT (HINDI)

A huge wagon; an unstoppable force; an act of sacrificial devotion. A word with the strength of its image. What is now considered anything with runaway force, a team of horses, a locomotive, a political campaign, comes from an ancient Hindu ritual where a few thousand ardent worshippers pull a colossal statue or icon of a god in a religious procession, predominantly the Puri Festival in Orissa, India. The Sanskrit *Jacganatha*, from *jagat*, world, and *nathas*, lord, lends the immediacy of the image of an idol of the "Lord of the World," Krishna or Vishnu, parading through the streets and causing a rapturous havoc. Unsubstantiated to this day are those dispatches from early Western reporters who claimed to see worshippers throwing themselves under the wheels of the *juggernaut*, inspired by their religious fervor. Nonetheless, the stories inspired the ***metaphor*** of an inexorable, wild, crushing force, such as an invading army. At Caffè Trieste, in San Francisco, in the early 1970s, a young screenwriter named Francis Ford Coppola wrote in his script for *Patton*: "Meanwhile, the main body of Patton's army … resupplied now and rolling like a *juggernaut*, slashes toward the Saar."

JUKE

A roadhouse; music box; to fake in basketball. Street ***slang*** for sex, dancing, music, great basketball moves, funky roadside shack for food, music, and sometimes, good lovin'. Evidently, *juke* derives from *juke joint*, a kind of off-road brothel. Sociologists would describe a *juke* as a transgressive or liminal space. Etymologists trace the word to two languages in West Africa: the Gullah word *juk*, infamous, wicked, and the Wolof *jug*, disorderly, and *zug*, to live wickedly. Closely related is the Bambara *jugu*, a naughty person. Of course, other theories flail about, like those roadhouse dancers, tracing the word back to the French *jouer*, play, and Scottish *jouk*, hide, evade, dodge, and *jookerie*, a secret place where "marks" are swindled. So, like a good gumbo, the word was seasoned by many influences from the sensual subculture of New Orleans, which thrived in the *juke joints*, where "barrelhouse music" was played and "barrelhouse liquor" was served by the cup on a makeshift bar with a plank set across two barrels. Eventually, *juke* became shorthand for the music machines. Essayist Michael Ventura suggests that *juke* came from Storyville, in New Orleans. Originally, he writes, it meant "to fuck," while *jelly roll* was a risqué reference to the sex organs of both men and women. Buddy Bolden, it was said, "had the old moan in his cornet." Bolden was famous for his trance-inducing performances, playing so holy it transformed the *juke* joints into churches, and so sexy his music could "make women jump out of the window." Before each performance he used to say, "Let's call the children home." *Can I get a witness? Can I get a witness?*

K

KALEIDOSCOPE

An optical viewer that diffracts light into beautiful geometric shapes. The Scottish physicist Sir David Brewster modeled his 1817 invention on the telescope, calling it simply an instrument for observation of "rotating patterns of colored glass." Turning it around and around in his hand, and then in his mind, he finally arrived at its melodic-sounding name by joining the mellifluous Greek words *kalos*, beauty, *eidos*, shape, and *skopeo*, to see or view. The words combine to create a marvelous little verbal machine, "an observer of beautiful forms." Metaphorically, its adjectival form *kaleidoscopic* has come to mean an unexpectedly beautiful, playful, or fantastic display. Receiving a *kaleidoscope* as a gift from his publisher, Lord Byron appreciated not only its beauty but its metaphorical power, marveling at its "constantly changing patterns" in a letter from 1819. Describing his work habits, trumpeter Ornette Coleman said, "When I have them working together, it's like a beautiful *kaleidoscope*." A distant cousin would be *telepathy*, which combines *telescope* and *pathos*, to suggest turning the lens of the soul on one's "far-flung feelings."

KAVLA (TURKISH)

The ***thrill*** *of deal-making, the excitement of anticipation, the enjoyment of prolonged pleasure*. An ***untranslatable*** but desirable word for the delicious, held-breath moment between the end of haggling and the consummation of a deal, between the turn of the last lap and reaching the tape at the end of a race, between the inspiration for the painting and the ecstatic initialing of the artist's name, between the lifting of the loins and the climax in lovemaking. I caught this word in an article in *Smithsonian* magazine presenting the nefarious dealings of a looter of antiques, who described in near-erotic terms the *kavla* of the deal. The eponymic origins of the word go back to the city of the same name, *Kavla*, in ancient Greece, which was known for its rapturous customs for sealing a deal in its famed markets. Figuratively, *kavla* is now used for stretching out our most sensuous moments in order to make the pleasure of anticipation—rather than consummation—last as long as possible. Curious connection: *Kavla*, a Greek pop music group, retains a hint of the old meaning of the word in a few lines from the title song of its album: "Speaking and breathin' like crazy / Only the feelings remain … (It's *Kavla*)."

KENNING

*A figurative usage, usually a compound **metaphor**, mostly found in epic poetry.* Traditionally ill-defined as a circumlocution used where a good noun would do, a *kenning* is actually a noble member of the family of similes, metaphors, and riddles, what Seamus Heaney calls, in his ***translation*** of *Beowulf*, the "genius for analogy-seeking ... and compound-making," such as "word-hoard" for vocabulary. As epitomized by Norse-speaking Vikings and Anglo-Saxon bards, a classic kenning from *Beowulf* is "whale-road," which vividly depicts the migration path of whales across the sea. In *Grendel*, John Gardner's prose translation from the monster's point of view, Gardner writes, "Such are the tiresome memories of a shadow-shooter, earth-rim-roamer, walker of the world's ***weird*** roads." Examples include "battle-sweat" for blood, "enemy of the mast" for wind, "raven-harvest" for death, "moons of the forehead" for eyes, and "storm of sands" for battle. Thus, *kennings* are metaphorical phrases that allow the writer and listener to *know* a thing better by describing it not so obviously, but allusively. Fans of J. R. R. Tolkien might appreciate his work even more knowing that he worked on the OED for a year in his twenties; one of his proud contributions was "horse-whale," a vivid *kenning* for walrus. Speaking of which, it is well within our *ken*, our knowledge, to track its origin to the Old Norse *kenna*, to know, perceive, and the Germanic *kannian*, to be able. I am *keen* to try to keep this practice alive in my "wolf's joint," my wrist, so "Odin's lip-stream," my poetry, keeps running wild in my soul.

KERFUFFLE

An outburst, a commotion, a tempest in a tumult. Though the word is usually designated as obscure and unknown, a riffle through a Scottish ***dictionary*** reveals that it is an adaptation of *carfuffle*, derived from Scots *car*, which comes from Scottish-Gaelic *cearr*, wrong, awkward and *fuffle*, disheveled. Thus a *kerfuffle* is not only an outburst, but an awkward disruption, a badly motivated disturbance, a too-clever-by-half way of saying much ado about nothing. A CNET headline from summer 2009, "The *1984* Kindle Kerfuffle," played off the alliteration. The author seems to be asserting that the *rhubarb* over censorship was no more than a *kerfuffle* in a teapot.

KIBOSH (IRISH)

To put a lid on it, put a stop to, squelch. A kinesthetic verb that knocks on whatever it modifies. To take the lid off the mystery of this old Gaelic word we need to hop across the pond, as the Irish say, and revisit the Irish funeral practice of placing a *kibosh*, a black cap, on the deceased, a solemn form of saying farewell. Across the Irish Sea, in England and on the continent, a black cap was often worn by judges passing a death sentence. Thus, to put the *kibosh* on someone is declare them as good as dead. The Irish fairy tale collector Padraic Colum explains the word in a letter to etymologist and dictionary maker Charles Earle Funk: "*Kibosh*, I believe means the 'cap of death' and it is always used in that sense—'He put the kibosh on it.' In Irish it could be written *'cie bais,'*—the last word pronounced 'bosh,' the genitive of *bas*, 'death.'" A neoclassic citation comes from Crazy Joe DaVola in an episode of *Seinfeld*: "I know you bad-mouthed me to the execs at NBC, put the *kibosh* on my deal. Now I'm gonna put the *kibosh* on you. You know I've *kiboshed* before, and I will *kibosh* again."

KINEPHANTOM

An illusory motion, a kinesthetic word. This is one I've been looking for all my life, at least since noticing the weird phenomenon of the wheels of my boyhood friend Steve's bike appearing to spin backward as we were riding to Dynamite Park, in our little hamlet of Wayne, Michigan. Its origins are *kine*, to see, and *phantom*, illusion. The perception of the wheels of a vehicle moving backward when they are actually spinning forward is a familiar *kinephantom*. Speaking of spinning, *kinetosis* is an Old World word for motion sickness, from *kinesis*, motion, and *osose*, sick. If I'd only been able to pronounce it when I had to ask my dad to pull off to the side of the road in our 1960 Falcon, as we were driving to Lake Nipissing, Ontario, on family vacation. As a Grecophile, maybe he wouldn't have gotten so sick of hearing me moan, "I'm carsick."

KITE

An airborne toy made of the evergreen spirit in human beings to watch things fly. First recorded in 1664, a *kite* usually consists of a body of paper or cloth attached to a ribcagelike frame, and a tail of various materials. *Kite* is a doubly echoic word of a phenomenon commonly observed and admired by the folk for millennia—the soaring of a hawk called a *kite* since the Middle Ages. Deriving from Middle English *kyte*, from the Old English *cyta*, a hawk, *kite* is a word that soars. John Ciardi suggests that it echoes the call of the *kite*, as heard in the German *ciegan*, a piercing *ki-ki-ki*. In dramatic contrast, the rudely dismissive phrase "Go fly a *kite*!" reveals the diminishment of the modern imagination, as well as being dismissive of the body's natural desire to play, as if flying a *kite* were immature, something to grow out of. Consider the marvel of Benjamin Franklin flying his *kite* in a storm, or the exultant Afghan boy in *The Kite Runner.* To fly a *kite* is an act of joy, an emblem of freedom, an echo of the hawk in all of us. The prolific diarist Anaïs Nin captured the figurative meaning when she wrote, "Throw your dreams into space like a *kite*, and you do not know what it will bring back, a new life, a new country." Likewise, Lauren Bacall said in an interview, "Imagination is the highest *kite* one can fly." For a soaring companion word, the Scots say *skite*, to fly, in flight.

L

LABEL

A description, prescription, or depiction. Originally, from the world of heraldry and medicine, from Latin diminutive *labellum*, the little lip, depicted in old caricatures and graffiti. The Romans drew them as proto–word balloons hanging from the mouths of the figures in their wall frescoes and in chalk drawings to suggest what the character was saying. This appended *lip* received the name *labellum*, or *label*. The practice of writing "lip balloons" was carried over to the world of medicine by doctors who wrote on a piece of paper and tied or taped it to the *lip* of a phial; the term was even applied to the little ribbon attached to the sealing wax on old documents. By the early 14th century the Latin word and practice had been borrowed by the French as *label, lambel,* ribbon, fringe, and *lambeau*, defined by the *Collins French–English Dictionary* as "a strip, rag, shred, tatter," which should make us think twice about the tattered jerseys at the Green

Bay Packers' Lambeau Field. In case you were wondering, *record label* dates all the way back to 1907, described then as a "circular piece of paper in the center of a gramophone record." This in turn inspired the use of *label* to stand in generally for the record company, in 1952. *To label*, as a verb, dates back to 1601, and its meaning, "to categorize," to 1853. Thus, a *label* is a time-honored way to put words in someone's mouth, a way to describe, to give vital information.

LABYRINTH

A place of twisting passageways. Usually used interchangeably with a maze, which is designed to confuse with dead ends, a true labyrinth has but one path to the center. Famously mythologized in the popular story of Theseus and the Minotaur, which dwelled in the Knossos Palace on Crete. The twisty word derives from the Greek *labyrinthos*, a mazelike building with intricate passages, based on an earlier Lydian word, *labrys*, a two-edged axe, which symbolized royal power. The story goes that King Minos seduced an apparently irresistible cow, resulting in the birth of his monstrous son, half man, half ***bull***, which he hid in a *labyrinth* devised by Daedalus. The word entered English in 1548 in a figurative sense, to represent anything meandering or confusing, as expressed by *labyrinthine*, an adjective depicting a place of intricate and confusing passageways. Companion words include *labyrinthodonts*, a type of amphibian, and *labyrinthitis*, an inflammation of the inner ear, which is a maze of canals filled with fluid. Half of the ear's *labyrinth* is the snail-shaped cochlea, which conveys sound to the brain; the other resembles a gyroscope, which transmits information about the position of your head relative to the ground. If your gyroscope is thrown out of whack, vertigo can result. With incantatory cadences the mythologist Joseph Campbell wrote, "Furthermore, we have not even to risk the adventure alone. The *labyrinth* is thoroughly known. We have only to follow the path of the ***hero***." Thus, the *labyrinth* is the mythic map of the path of the soul as it meanders back and forth through the world.

Labyrinth

LACONIC

In a word. Brevity. Concision. Abruptness. To say more would mean less. During the Peloponnesian War, Philip of Macedonia (Alexander's father) sent a messenger from Athens to Sparta, the center of Laconia, warning, "If we attack Sparta, we will raze it to the ground; we will not leave a single stone unturned." The Laconian general looked him square in the eye and carefully measured his word. Then he replied, "If."

LADY

The woman of the house; a well-mannered, proper, and virtuous woman. According to linguist Owen Barfield, our English word *lady* derives from the "homely old Teutonic word *loaf-kneader.*" The connection provides remarkable insight into the central importance of bread in medieval households and the lives of those who provide it for others. In medieval England a lord was *hlaford*, earlier *hlafweard*, guardian of the loaf or loaf-ward. Similarly, as Coleridge cites, *lady* was *hlaefdige*, a woman who kneads, which consists of *hlaef*, bread, and *dige*, knead. Together, they provide a medieval word portrait; as Barfield writes, "So the *lady* kneaded the bread and the lord protected it." These leavening words gave rise to two everyday words in modern English: *hlaef* is the ancestor of "loaf," and *dige* gave us "dough." Companion words include *ladybird, lady's slipper, ladylike*, and *breadwinner* (*bread* being a euphemism for money), and "loaf of bread," which is Cockney rhyming slang for "head." In the parlance of East Londoners, "bread" rhymes with "head," so someone might say, "Use your loaf" when they mean "Use your head!" Circuitously, we come back to a *lady* being the real "head" of the household because she bakes the bread. The temptress Mae West said, "*Ladies* who play with fire must remember that smoke gets in their eyes."

LAGNIAPPE

An expensive word for a cheap gift given to a customer. This coinage comes from New Orleans, deriving from *la napa*, Spanish for "the gift," from the American Indian or Cajun word *yapa*, a present from a trader to a steady customer. The impulse behind this form of gift giving is alive and well in the form of tchotchkes and gewgaws such as T-shirts, pens, pads of paper presented as little gifts, reminders, gratitudes. Funk cites our greatest wordsmith, Mark Twain's, clever usage in *Life on the Mississippi*: "The English were trading beads and blankets to them [the Indians] for a consideration and throwing in civilization and whiskey 'for *lagniappe*.'"

LOGROLLING

A 19th-century American custom in which neighbors roll logs together into a pile for burning; a contest among loggers in which they balance on floating logs while trying to knock each other off. This terrific term passes the first ***test*** for the revival or spread of a word—it's terrifically *catchy*—and it's catchy because it's visual and fun to say. Furthermore, it is an American original. The contest is sometimes referred to as *birling* or *burling*, a game of skill among lumberjacks, which has its roots in the old Scottish word *birl*, to whirl round and round. Figuratively, *logrolling* refers to the tricky ability to keep your balance when everything is moving and slippery under your feet, but also, in politics, to the trading of votes or the scheming of legislators to slip a desired bill through without actually persuading fellow lawmakers about its merits—in other words, to knock them off the log. In an article published in 2003 in *Aquatics International*, Judy Hoeschler, who first learned how to *logroll* on water when she was 12 and won her first *logrolling* championship at 16, exulted, "Being a *logrolling* family is so much fun! It kinda blows people's minds when they see we're *logrollers* and none of us fit the Paul Bunyan image." The word also applies to making concessions to the other party (like your opponent on a whirling log) in conflict resolution.

LOUCHE

Of questionable reputation, in a raffish sort of way. An outlaw with a touch of class, a rake with a hint of glamour, a hipster in some neighborhoods, riff-raff in another, all might be described as *louche*. The word conjures the decadence of bohemians who want to live on the outskirts of society. Its origins provide a word picture. The Latin *luscus*, one-eyed, shady, disreputable, evolved into the French *louche*, for "cross-eyed" or "squint-eyed." Its evolution from rabble to raffish resembles the evolution of some outlaws' reputations; think of Bonnie and Clyde. The verb form, *to louche*, became popular in 19th-century Paris to describe the phenomenon of "clouding over," as when some *louche* characters poured water into their glass of anise-flavored drinks such as Pernod or ouzo, hence "the ouzo effect." In case you'd like to use it conversation, a poem, or song lyric, it helps to know that *louche* rhymes with baba ghanoush.

LOVE

The deep force that moves the sun, the moon, the stars, and the heart. An abiding affection. A word that transcends ordinary definition, and yet demands it, since it is often either misunderstood or trivialized. Etymologically it comes from loamy turf, the Proto-Indo-European *leubh*, which sired many progeny, such as German *liebe*, Dutch *liefde*, English *lief* and *liege*, dear or pledge, and even *libido*, strong desire. Many Western European words for "praise" come from the same source. The commingled meaning of "pleasing" and "praising," plus "satisfied" and "trust," all converge, as ancient poetry and modern psychology will attest, in our heart-swelling English word *love*. Where to begin with its innumerable uses? Why not at the very beginning, or near the beginning, in the single surviving line from Sophocles' play *The Loves of Achilles*: "*Love* feels like the ice held in the hand of children." Twenty-five hundred years later, in *Ulysses*, James Joyce wrote the following lines, which were inexplicably stricken in the original 1922 edition but restored in the 1980s. About to leave Ireland in "silence, exile, and cunning," Stephen Dedalus reflects, "Do you know what you are talking about? *Love*, yes. Word known to all men...." And later: "Tell me the word, mother, if you know now. The word known to all men. *Love*." Companion words include the ***murmurous*** *lovely* and the lamentable *loathed-loving*, another lost child from the first edition of the OED, referring to "hating oneself for being attached to somebody who is bad for you." When Pompeii was excavated in the 18th century, this touching piece of graffiti was discovered: "*Lovers*, like bees, enjoy a life of honey."

LULLABY

A nighttime song to lull children to sleep. One of the perennials on Most Beautiful Words lists, dating back to c.1560, a natural protraction of *lull*, from the Swedish *lulla* and Dutch *lullen*, prattle. Ultimately, a reassuring echo of the syllable *lu* or *la*, joined with a second element, perhaps from *by-by*, good-by. In the late 1960s, Lennon and McCartney of the Beatles gave us one of the loveliest of modern *lullabies* when they adapted "Golden Slumbers Kiss Your Eyes," a 17th-century poem by the poet and early ***dictionary*** maker Thomas Dekker. But rather than sing it themselves, they handed it over to Ringo to sing. His warmly avuncular version, which rounded out the *Abbey Road* album, has helped lull children and lovers to sleep ever since: "Sleep, pretty darlings, do not cry, / and I will sing a *lullaby.* / Golden slumbers fill your eyes." Companion *lullabies* include the incantatory Irish *"Tura lura lura,"* which "lures" our children to embark on a long, safe *tura*, or pilgrimage, across the Land of Nod, the world of sleep between dusk and dawn.

M

MEERSCHAUM

A mineral used for crafting tobacco pipes. Meerschaum has long been found on certain seashores in "rounded white lumps," and is believed by the folk to be petrified sea froth, as evidenced by the German *Meer*, sea, and *Schaum*, foam or scum (an early synonym for "foam"). This derives from the earlier Latin *spuma maris*, the spume of the sea, and before that, the Persian *kef-i-darya*. Easily shaped and sculpted, *meerschaum* is now synonymous with the frothy-appearing tobacco-pipe bowls carved by sailors with time on their hands. Brewer notes that when *meerschaum* is dug out of the shore, "it lathers like soap," which is exactly what it's used for by the Tartars to this day. Herman Melville's biographer, Laurie Robertson-Lorant, describes the famed author of *Moby Dick* in later life: "Most evenings he just sat in his rocker puffing his *meerschaum* pipe and watching the great fireplace swallow down cords of wood as a whale does boats."

MELANCHOLY

Overwhelming sadness, merciless moodiness, grief's house. Hovering on the edge of chapfallen, sullen, gloomy, and petulant. The word first appears in English in 1303, from the Greek *melancholia*, from *melas*, black, and *khole*, bile or gall, an excess of which was said to cause plunging fits of depression, or irascibility. Traditionally, *melancholy* was regarded as the result of an overabundance of this "black gall," a belief that's survived in the expression "You've got a lot of gall," suggesting someone who is rude, impertinent, or bitter. Medieval physicians believed the accretion from the spleen, one of the four "humors," led to depression, even insanity. Eventually, four types of melancholy were distinguished: *melancholia attonita,* gloomy*; melancholia errabunda,* restless*; melancholia malevolens,* mischievous*; and melancholia complacens,* complacent. And we might add a fifth, *melancholia romantica*, as in "Melancholy Baby," as sung by Judy Garland. Surprisingly, *down in the dumps* comes from *dumpin*, Swedish for melancholy; *dimba*, to steam, reek; and Danish *dump*, dull, damp, as in "to *damp* one's spirits." This was John Milton's sense when he wrote in *Paradise Lost*: "A *melancholy* damp of cold and dry, / to weigh thy spirits down," by which he is saying that *melancholy* damps, as in suffocates, the human spirit. Virginia Woolf wrote, in *Jacob's Room*, "*Melancholy* were the sounds on a winter's night." Van Gogh wrote to his brother, Theo, about his life of "active *melancholy*." On the walls of the Lion's Den pub in Greenwich Village we find: "Neurosis is red / *Melancholia* is blue / I'm schizophrenic / What are you?" Companion words include *moanworthy*, sad; *doleful*, full of grief; *lugubrious*, mournful; and *crepehanger*, a gloomy Gus, a pessimist.

METAPHOR

One thing that stands for another. A *metaphor* is a brief expression that compactly, often surprisingly, describes a thing as if it were something else. The word has survived almost intact from the Latin *metaphora*, a transferring of a word from its literal significance, in the fine definition of Skeats, and before that the Greek *metaphorein*, from *meta*, over, and *pherein*, to carry, bear across; hence, to transfer. The operative word here is *transfer*, whose modern sense dates from 1533, Middle French *metaphore*, to transfer from one context to another in a memorable way. Consider Raymond Chandler's description in *Farewell, My Lovely* of Moose Malloy, who "looked about as inconspicuous as a tarantula on a slice of angel food." Shakespeare's work fairly explodes with powerful metaphors, such as this one on aging, from Sonnet 73: "That time of year thou mayst in me behold / When yellow leaves, or none, or few, do hang / Upon those boughs which shake against the cold, / Bare ruin'd choirs, where late the sweet bird sang..." As a kind of scavenger after *metaphors*, I find Jorge Borges's reflections on "The Dark Night of the Soul," by Saint John of the Cross, very moving: "After he had an unutterable experience, he had to communicate it somehow in *metaphors.*" In 2004 the new Athens subway, called *Metaphoros,* was completed just in time to carry fans across town to watch the various Olympic competitions. Some of them also used "transfers."

MONDEGREEN

A mishearing of a song lyric that leads to a fresh new meaning, generally humorous, sometimes poignant. When she was a little girl the writer Sylvia Wright was listening to a mournful Scottish ballad, "The Bonny Earl of Murray," when she thought she heard: "Ye Highlands and Ye Lowlands / Oh Where hae you been? / They hae slay the Earl of Murray / And Lady *Mondegreen.*" Her mishearing of the last line, which is actually "And laid him on the green," has spawned a modern generation of malapropisms in its name. Wright became smitten with the common and often witty mishearings in songs, poems, and speeches, and eventually ***published*** an essay about them in a 1954 article. Common *mondegreens* include "round John Virgin" (for "round yon Virgin," from "Silent Night") and "You and Me and Leslie" (for "you and me, endlessly" from the Rascals' "Groovin' "). And from the Beatle's immortal "Michelle," submitted by my niece of the same name: "A Sunday monkey bored playing piano songs," her mishearing of the French *"Sont des mots qui vont très bien ensemble"* ("These are words that go together well.") For the record, *mondegreens* and word play do "go together well," in any language.

MUM

"Shush! Silence!" In Dr. Johnson's time a *mome* was "a dull, stupid blockhead, a stock, a post," an insult that derived from French *momon*, a game of dice played in masquerade in strict silence, from which comes *mum*, for silence. Eventually, we arrived at the marvelous injunction "*Mum's* the word." Or in Hamlet's famous *mummery*, "Words, words, words; the rest is silence." Its origins merge with that mythic Greek *mu*, closed lips, or as Skeats writes beautifully, "to express the least sound made with closed lips." Roy Blount Jr. adds, "Since it's not merely a sound, *mmmm*, but a word, to say it we have to move our lips." Thus, the difference between *mum* and *mmmm* is the effort to break our silence. An imitative word from the gentle sounds *mum* or *mom*, once described as "used by nurses to frighten or amuse children, at the same time pretending to cover their faces." Remarkably, most words for *mother* from around the world begin with exactly that *mmmm* sound, from a child's satisfaction with her mother's *mammary glands* and her earliest effort at baby talk, *mama*. Companion words from this *matrix* of mother-inspired words include *mumble; mummer,* a mask, buffoon, one who goes *a-mumming*; and *mummel*, a German bugbear. Typing all these *m*'s somehow summons "Hey, Baby (They're Playing Our Song)" by the Buckinghams, a Sixties love song with the infectious chorus "*Mmm-my-my-my* baby, *mmmm-my-my-my* baby, hey, baby, hey, baby…"

MURMUR

To speak softly; to grumble. One of the perennial favorite words on Top Ten Lists of the English language. Originally, however, it was an "expression of discontent by grumbling." Slowly it evolved from Old French *murmure* and Latin *murmurare*, a hum, muttering, rushing—which may be marvelously imitative of what's heard around a crackling fire, as evident in the Sanskrit *murmurah*. If you listen closely to *murmur*, you will hear traces and tones of "mother," "myth," "mystery," and those "crackling fires,"

Murmur (Grow, Grow)

all audible in the lowing sounds of the natural world, a babbling brook, a voice in an adjoining room, or, in the modern medical sense, the beats of an abnormal heart. The modern sense of "softly spoken words" is first recorded in 1674. My own first recollection of catching this word is from reading a book of essays by D. H. Lawrence in a bed-and-breakfast home in Dover, England, in 1980, and feeling the hair rise on my head when I read this: "I believe that a man is converted when first he hears the low, vast *murmur* of life, of human life, troubling his hitherto unconscious self." The savvy English commentator on modern mythology Marina Warner writes, "In an inspired essay on 'The Translators of *The Arabian Nights*,' Jorge Luis Borges praises the *murmuring* exchanges of writers across time and cultures, and points out that the more literature talks to other literatures, and reweaves the figures in the carpet, the richer languages and expression, metaphors and stories become." Companion words include *whisper*, as beautifully expressed in the Talmud: "Every blade of grass has its Angel that bends over it and *whispers*, 'Grow, grow.'"

MUSE

The personification of inspiration. According to Greek thought, when a human being felt a sudden infusion of inspiration or sensed a presence, it was the breath of a god or goddess. Every expression in the arts was personified by the *Muses*, one for each of the nine arts. When the first artifacts and books were collected, their new homes were called *museums*, such as the Alexandrian Library, which housed some 700,000 scrolls in its *Museion*, "The Place of the Muses." The nine Greek goddesses of the arts were daughters of Mnemosyne, the goddess of memory, from *mnemon*, mindful, and *mneme*, long memory. This is not so surprising, as Isaac Asimov points out, since all poetry was memorized in ancient times. Companion words include *music*, divinely inspired harmonies of sound, by which virtually all ancient Greek art and drama was accompanied; *mosaic*, pieces of memory; and *mnemonic*, the art of memory—all influenced by the flow of *mneme*, the continuing effect of past experience on an individual or the race. Memory's shadow words are disturbing, like *amnesia*, not-knowing, forgetting, and the French *oubliette*, a room whose only opening is a ceiling, where a prisoner is immured in order to be forgotten. Also, the ***quirky*** *Forgettery*, an invented word by Carl Sandburg, who recommended we build one so we wouldn't be plagued with remembering things that are best forgotten.

MYTHOSPHERE

The atmosphere of myth that surrounds and permeates our lives; the source of the sacred stories and images that tell how it all began. Coined by former *Time* magazine art critic, eminent mythologist, and all-around *bon vivant* Alexander Eliot, *mythosphere* is a brilliant invention, reflecting a lifetime of reflection about myth. "We're all aware," Eliot writes, "that [the atmosphere] surrounds, protects, nourishes, and energizes the world 'out there.' The *mythosphere* does all that too, but for the world 'in here.'" It was thousands of years in the making, he adds, and exists in our psyches as stories that "ineffably touch the heart." They are part of the cultural air that we breathe, and can help us reconnect to a dimension outside time and space. For this reason, myths have "shuddering relevance," and in most ancient

Mythosphere (Alex Eliot)

cultures *myths* have been regarded as truer than so-called fact. During the Renaissance, artist and scholars breathed deep from the *mythosphere* and helped revive Western culture. In the modern era, novelists, poèts, and film-makers have tapped the *mythosphere* to help liberate their creativity and explain the dynamics of their psychology. For these reasons, and many more, Thoreau said, "*Myth* may be the closest man has ever gotten to truth." By that he meant psychological truth, the mother of all stories, the truth of the soul. Again, Marina Warner: "Writers don't make up myths; they take them over and recast them. Even Homer was telling stories that his audience already knew." Companion words include *mystery, mystagogue, mythomania, mythopoeia, mythmaker.*

N

NEMESIS

Righteous retribution. We all have felt its sting; we even may have stung someone else with it. It's human nature, or should we say, superhuman nature? The word hails from the Greek *nemein*, to distribute, apportion, which gave rise to *lot,* and *allotment. Nemesis* was the goddess of vengeance, the daughter of Zeus and Hera who embodied something more than pure revenge, closer to karma. She represented indignation at the injustices of the world, and was depicted as the bitter relative who ruined so many weddings and relished so many funerals that the invitations stopped coming. In Greek myth she is the embodiment of the avenging spirit, a quality that arises from the depth of her bitterness at being treated like a second-class goddess. Thus, *Nemesis* was the "distributor" of justice, she who gave what was "one's due," their "lot in life," which came to mean "your number is up," as in allotment hunting, or in your fated death or punishment. By the 16th century *nemesis* came to mean "retributive justice," one's fate if one has lived dangerously or selfishly. *Nemesis* is the strange cousin in the attic of Narcissus, with his attendant narcissism, and gives birth to the psychological condition called *nemesism*, an obscure but valuable word that embodies inward negative feelings, a kind of cosmic soul rust. British novelist, short story writer, and playwright Brian Aldiss defined science fiction for all-time when he wrote that it is primarily the story of "Hubris clobbered by *Nemesis*."

NOCTAMBULATION

Night walking, studying; guiding one's way through the night. A gift for the young, a curse for the old. Nightly companion words are as numerous as the bats escaping caves at dusk: *noctiflorous*, blooming at night, not just flowers but night writers and night scoundrels; *noctuary*, a place for nighttime studies; *noctivate*; *nocta-collector*; *noctivagator*, one who wanders around at night; *noctiphobia*, fear of the night; *nightertale*, the nighttime, the whole night long; and the wondrously named *acronicta noctivaga*, the Night-Wandering Dagger, a dragonfly of British Columbia and the Yukon. Finally, consider the *night-blooming cereus*, a flower that blooms but once a year, in the middle of the night, when only the *lucubrators*, those working by candlelight, are still awake, relishing the darkness. Henry David Thoreau immortalized the feeling when he wrote, "I put a piece of paper under my pillow, and when I could not sleep I wrote in the dark." The Hungarian photographer Brassaï was a notorious nightwalker, shooting the gaslit Paris streets and its brothels, cabarets, and all-night cafés. His close friend Henry Miller wrote of his visit to the Hotel des Terrasses, where he pored for hours over the "nightly harvest of photographs which were spread about the pieces of furniture in Brassaï's room."

NOSTALGIA

Mythic homesickness. The word was coined in 1688 by Johannes Hofer, an Austrian medical student, who joined two Greek words, *nostois*, return, and *algos*, pain, to describe the longing for home of Swiss soldiers stationed in the mountains. But Homer used a version of it in the sense that many of the stories-within-stories of his epic poem, the *Odyssey*, were inspired by the *nostos*, the homecoming stories, or the *nostoi*, the popular tales of sailors' homeward bound journeys told and retold in ports all around the Mediterranean. His ***hero***, Odysseus, spurred on by the memory of Penelope's arms, the loyalty of his dog, the face of his son, defied the gods to "get home again" after the ten-year war against Troy: this panorama has been absorbed by English as *nostalgia*. Though often derided as sentimental, the real thing is a tidal pull of feeling, an undulating wave of emotions that can be triggered by a whiff of burning leaves, a ballgame on a radio, an accent, a taste of home cooking. As if derision weren't enough, in 1844 Dunglison reduced *nostalgia* to an "affliction produced by desire to return to one's country, commonly accompanied by slow wasting and [which] … may speedily induce death." Thus, a word as many-leveled as the ruins of Troy, the painful urge of a fierce desire to go home again. Who says you can't? We do it every time we feel *nostalgic*, whether for the past or, as physicist Stephen Hawking says, for the future, which is his definition of synchronicity. When we do get home, we'd best be ready, because as Will Rogers reminded us, "Things ain't what they used to be and probably never was."

NUMINOUS

Conveying divine power. A mystical word revived in our time by the German scholar Rudolf Otto, from the Latin *numen*, a divine power or spirit that brings life or guidance—a hint of the spirits that dwell in nature, and one aspect of its original and transcendent meaning of a "nod" of the gods. *Numen* refers to the spirits or geniuses that dwell in a place and have the potential to inspire creative efforts, and *numinous* refers to the sacred essence, the supernatural dimension, magical forces, in dramatic contrast to phenomena that can be apprehended by the senses. *Numinous* describes the otherwise inexplicable power emanating from a megalithic site in Brittany, or a painting of a storm at sea by

Turner, that reveals a *presence* in nature and that touches a *presence* in us. Figuratively speaking, Emily Dickinson's home in Amherst or the temples of Bali may be said to be *numinous* if they fire our imagination. In one of my favorite books, *The Star Thrower*, the anthropologist Loren Eiseley evokes the *numinous* without ever actually using the word: "As we passed under a streetlamp I noticed, beside my own bobbing shadow, another great, leaping grotesquerie that had an uncanny suggestion of the frog world about it. … Judging from the shadow, it was soaring higher and more gaily than myself. 'Very well,' you will say, 'Why didn't you turn around. That would be the scientific thing to do.' But let me tell you it is not done—not on an empty road at midnight." That's *presence;* that's *numinous*.

O

OBFUSCATE

To render obscure, darken, make unintelligible. A dusky word to suggest the murkiness around twilight, the witching hour, the time when the gates were locked all over the world for fear of what might come knocking. A 16th-century word that emerged from the Latin *obfuscare*, to darken, from *ob*, over and *fuscare*, to make dark. Figuratively speaking, from the camel markets of Beersheba to the hog markets of Wall Street, *obfuscation* is a timeless marketing ploy that allows things to be sold in a shadowy way, a deliberately befuddling manner. Confounding companion words on the dark side include *fusky*, darkened, and *obfuscatrix*, Alexander Theroux's terrific coinage to describe Gertrude Stein, writer of polysyllabic novels. The moral of this word story is simple: Sedulously eschew *obfuscation*.

OSTRANENIE (RUSSIAN)

To strangify. An invaluable word for a process most artists know well, the trick of making something ordinary seem extraordinary; something recognizable, unrecognizable; something dull, sharp. Have you ever stood before a painting and stared and stared at an object that seemed familiar—a horse, a curve in the road, a starry night—and felt a frisson, a shiver of unfamiliarity? As if you've never seen it before? This is one of the least understood but most compelling aspects of the creative process: the *strangifying* of the world so we can see it as if for the first time. The origins of *ostranenie* attest to as much, being from the Old French *estrange*, strange, and Latin *extraneum*, on the outside, foreign. Howard Rheingold refers to it as a "perceptual cleansing tool." Companion words include *defamiliarize* and the Old English *estrange*, "the making strange," which brings us full circle. Consider the peculiar last moments of Robert Louis Stevenson as he lay dying in Samoa, his words echoing the pathos of his novel *The Strange Case of Dr. Jeckyl and Mr. Hyde*: "What's the matter with me? What is this *strangeness*? Has my face changed?"

P

PANACHE

Effortless style, easy swagger. If you can picture José Ferrer in the classic black-and-white movie version of *Cyrano de Bergerac*, leaping across the battlements of the castle, flashing his sword, and flourishing the white plume in his hat, you can begin to appreciate the connection between poetry and *panache.* The play's author, Edmond Rostand, explained his use of the word to the French Academy: "A little frivolous perhaps; a little melodramatic certainly, the *panache* is no more than a charming gesture. But this charming gesture is so difficult to make in the face of death and supposes so much strength that it is a charming gesture I would wish for all." The first historical reference is 1553, when it is mentioned as "a tuft or plume of feathers," from the Middle French *pennache.* Figuratively, it means a style infused with flair, élan, dash—pleasingly flamboyant, like Myrna Loy and William Powell in the *Thin Man* movies.

Curious companion words include *aplomb*, cool, classy self-confidence, from "true to the plumb line," and *sprezzatura*, the art of performing a task effortlessly. In a review of the 1937 movie *Toast of the Town*, Donna Moore describes an actor who embodies all of the qualities above: "Cary [Grant] plays the charmer," she writes, "with his usual *panache* and is a sight for sore eyes in his top hat and tails."

PERIPATETIC

Walking and talking, in the interest of philosophy as much as exercise. After the *Peripatetic* School of the Lyceum, founded by Aristotle, whose custom was to teach and dispute while meandering around Athens. His students became known as *peripatetics*, from Greek *peripatetikos*, given to walking about while teaching, from *peri*, around and *patein*, to walk, plus *patos*, a path, and the expression *peripatikou*, "I walk about." Likewise, *peripatos* means "covered walk." Since the 17th century, *peripatetic* has described a person who wanders all over, the Western equivalent of the Native American elder as one who "walks his talk." Not so obscure a word that it couldn't be tapped by lyricist Edward Kleban for "One," the hit song from *A Chorus Line*: "She's uncommonly rare, very unique, / *peripatetic*, poetic and chic." Curious companion words include *gyrovagus*, an Irish pilgrim, from *gyro*, circle, circuit, and *vagus*, wandering, roving. Walking our talk here, as our Native American elders say, we come to the marvelous speculation that our word *vague*, meaning "unclear, vacillating, rambling," from the Middle French *vague*, might just be a kind of folk memory of wanderers, rovers, ramblers, and vagrants. Other familiar forms of *peripatetic* souls include *pellegrino*, Italian for "pilgrim, wanderer"; *gallivanter*; and *rolling stone*, which inspired the naming of the band and the Dylan song.

PETRICHOR

The smell of rain rising from the earth. A niche-filling word to describe the seemingly ineffable smell of rain as it wafts off the ground, particularly after a long spell without rain. Coined in 1964 by I. J. Bear and R. G. Thomas, two Australian anthropologists, in an article titled "Nature of argillaceous odour" published in the journal *Nature*. Wisely wanting to avoid the clunky technical word for smells coming out of the *argillaceous*, clay, they borrowed the Greek words *petros*, stone, and *ichor*, blood of the gods, and provided us with a rainy-day word for all seasons. Since there isn't a common word for the head-reeling, swoon-inducing smell of rain wafting off a paved road, I hereby nominate *pluviaroma*, from the Latin *pluvia*, rain, *via*, road, and *aroma*. Hence, *road-rain-smell*. Fellow words include *Jupiter Pluvius*, the god of rain; *pluviograph*, a rainfall gauge; and *interpluvial*, the period between rains, a vitally important calculation in drought-ridden areas of the world. For fans of new words, consider the estimates of the number conjured up by Shakespeare, which range from 1,700 to

21,000 words. What follows is a partial list: *accommodation, advertising, besmirch, castigate, champion, dextrous, dialogue, dishearten, ladybird, love-letter, lustrous, moonbeam, radiance, undress, whirligig,* and *zany.*

PHANTASMAGORIA

A flickering series of phantoms, apparitions, visions, or illusory images. From an ancient Greek word, *phantasma,* to show, to display, to shine, that later illuminated such words as *Pharos,* the famous lighthouse at Alexandria, Egypt, and ***epiphany***, the shining forth of divine light. Soon after the French Revolution, the showman and entrepreneur Etienne Gaspard Robertson opened a *son-et-lumière* show in Paris he called *Fantasmagorie,* from the Greek *phantasmagoria,* and introduced a new kind of "magic lantern" show with a new projector, the *Fantascope.* In 1801 the word reappeared in the French *phantasmagorie,* courtesy of the French dramatist Louis-Sébastien Mercier, who combined *phantasma,* image, with *agora,* assembly, marketplace. Thus, *phantasmagoria* truly means "a showing of fantastic images in public." The next year, it was borrowed as the name for a magic lantern in a Paris exhibition. In 1822, five years after Brewster's invention of the ***kaleidoscopic***, the meaning of *phantasmagoria* becomes more dynamic, more modern; now it means "a shifting scene of many elements." Companion words include the indispensable *fantasy,* a shining vision. The English critic Marina Warner writes, in *Phantasmagoria*, a collection of essays about spirit visions, horror films, and dreams, "Whereas the dioramas and panoramas concentrated on battles, modern cityscapes, or exotic scenery, customs, and people—they are the forerunners of the wide-screen epic films—the *phantasmagoria* shadows forth the great silent movies like F. W. Murnau's *Nosferatu* [1922] and Robert Wiene's *The Cabinet of Dr. Caligari* [1920]."

PHONY

Calculatingly false, unctuously insincere. A robust example, as Cassidy claims, of how an honorable word from classical Irish, *fainne*, devolved into street slang of the English-speaking empire. *Fainne*, ring, was corrupted to *fawney*, a fake gold ring, which inevitably became *phony*, street slang for "fake or sham" anything, from gold rings to politicians. As the story goes, the use of the word by Irish immigrants in Britain filtered down to "thieves and swindlers" in need of "secret code words." These no-goodniks sold the spurious gold rings as if they were 24 karat, but they were really imitative. When I started teaching screenwriting at the American Film Institute, in the early 1980s, I was warned by one of my fellow instructors not to take the movie business too seriously. "Behind the *phony* tinsel of Hollywood," he said, forgetting to tell me that he was quoting Oscar Levant, "lies the real tinsel."

POCHADE (FRENCH)

A quick sketch; a rapidly done watercolor. A concise and useful loan word, inspired by the practices of artists like Matisse who made the *pochade* one of their daily rituals. Sitting in his customary seat at a Paris café, Matisse set himself a daily challenge to quickly sketch (from Dutch *schets*, things rapidly done) or paint a few pedestrians in the time it took them to pass by his table. Originally, *pochade* just meant "pocket," but soon it stood for "a pocket painting," like the City Lights pocket paperback series, or medieval *vade mecums*, pocket prayer books. The American Society of Portrait Artists defines a *pochade* simply as a "hasty sketch." More broadly, it is a small painting done quickly on location, either for its own sake or for later reference back in the studio for a large-format work. I first caught up with the word from an old friend, the New York painter John O'Brien, who lived and worked in Paris. He regarded the act of painting as having three acts, a complete dramatic structure, the first act being the *croquis*, a quick sketch by pen or pencil as a reminder of a scene, the second act the *pochade*, which adds color atmosphere, and the third and final act the culmination, the *portrait* or *landscape*, which included the details, faces, gestures, shadowing, and so on. Typically, after an inspired morning of work *en plein air*, outdoors, the artist would retreat to the studio, where he or she placed the sketchpad or canvas on the *easel*, from the Dutch *ezel*, donkey, that old reliable beast of burden that had been used for centuries. .The word has lumbered on for four centuries, losing the memory of the donkey but retaining the image of the steadfast *easel.*

POLTROON

A good-for-nothing coward. Its 16th-century roots paint a not so pretty picture. The Middle French *poultron* is a rascal, from Italian *poltrone*, a sluggard, a lazy fellow, and possibly *poltro*, an unbroken colt, and even *poltrare*, to lie in bed. Together, they become *poltroon*, a word that filled a niche in English for a lazy kid who won't get out of bed, won't get his hands dirty in the real world, like the colt that hasn't been broken (initiated) yet. Thus, within a single word we find both a rich etymology and the plot for a melodrama that could be called "A Coward Is Born." Tangentially, Dr. Johnson passed on the old chestnut that *poltroon* derives from an Italian punishment called *truncato*, which means "thumbs cut off," based on a practice of cowards who cut off their own thumbs so they didn't have to serve in combat. Speaking of which, *coward* derives from the Old French *couart*, from *coe*, meaning "tail" (which gave us *coda*), as in the *lion couard*, the "cowardly lion," illustrated in medieval heraldry as having its tail between its legs. Now, there's a vividly painted word. Coming full circle, NPR's Nina Totenberg once said, "Every moment of the fashion industry's misery is richly deserved by the designers … and magazine *poltroons* who perpetuate this absurd creation." Companion words include the dubious *chucklehead, jackanapes, craven,* and ***dastard***.

PORTMANTEAU

A made-up compound word. Originally, a large suitcase or ***travel*** trunk that opened into two compartments, from *port,* to carry, and *manteau*, coat; it was cleverly appropriated to describe how two words can also be folded into one. The ingenious Lewis Carroll borrowed this idea, in the spirit of Humpty Dumpty, who said, "There are two meanings packed in one word," and created a locker full of doubled-up words. As if packing for a very long voyage, Carroll folded together "***fury***" and "furious" to create *frumious*; "chuckle" and "snort" to form *chortle*, and "gallop" and "harrumph" for the glorious *galumph*. If you look up *portmanteau*, you'll eventually catch sight of the word *luggage*, which makes me think of the ballplayer Yogi Berra's assessment after leaving one particularly hospitable hotel: "The towels were so thick there I could hardly close my suitcase." All card-carrying word lovers have their own favorites, such as the lovely *spindrift*, from *spin* and *drift*, to reflect the actual movement of sea spray when it hits rocks on shore or the side of a ship. One of mine is the Appalachian *bodacious*, from *bold* and *audacious*, as in "I'm bodaciously ruin't." And who hasn't smiled as wide as the sea after reading e. e. cummings's hyphenated *portmanteaus*, "The world is / mud-luscious and / puddle-wonderful."

PREPOSTEROUS

Absurd, ludicrous, insane. A marvel of a word, both literarily and pop culturally. Every time I come across it I can't help but hear Snaggletooth's lisping voice in the old Warner Brothers cartoon: *"Pre-pos-ter-ous!"* His mincing pronunciation actually helps us break it down so we can appreciate its surreal meaning even more. It derives from the Latin *prae*, before, and *posterus*, coming after. Something is *preposterous* because it seems "bass-ackwards," as my Uncle Cy used to say. Skeat says, "hind side before," which lends an image of an animal walking backward into an onlooker. So something that is preposterous can seem as if it's already happened and is bound to happen again. To say it another way, if you don't know whether you're coming or going, you're in an ***absurd***, or *preposterous*, situation. Herman Melville wrote bitingly, "Of all the *preposterous* assumptions of humanity over humanity, nothing exceeds most of the criticisms made on the habits of the poor by the well-housed, well-warmed, and well-fed." Kurt Vonnegut Jr. wrote, "Any reviewer who expresses rage or loathing for a novel is *preposterous.* He or she is like a person who has put on a full suit of armor and attacked a hot fudge sundae."

PRETZEL

A bagel with its knickers in a twist. Abbots have always had a problem disciplining their monks. Many a monastery has been rent asunder by the sound of snoring friars. Eventually, one abbot, it is said, promised he would bake his somnolent monks a special piece of bread, and shape it in their honor. He called it a *pretiola*, Latin for "praying," and it was offered to them only if they could stay awake during prayers. His innovation was this: he took some bread strips and folded them across each other to resemble the folded arms of a praying monk. Ever since, *pretzels* have been marketed as a reward, a comfort food, for one good deed or another, such as sitting still in front of a television with a football game on. Competing etymologies come from the German *Prezel*, from Latin *brachitellum*, a baked biscuit in the shape of folded arms, from *bracchiatus*, with arms. It's not for nothing that a *pretzel* is called a *snack*, which comes from *snatch*, Lowland Scottish for "a sudden snap of the jaws." In ***jazz***, *pretzel* is a nickname for a French horn. Fellow words include *bagel*, a New York invention and delight, heartily described as a "donut with a college education." The *croissant* was born one night in Vienna in 1656, in honor of the Austrian army's turning back the hordes under a crescent (*croissant*) moon.

PROTEAN

Shape-shifting; capable of change. After *Proteus*, the sea god, son of Poseidon. Homer writes that after the sack of Troy the Greek general Menelaus and his soldiers meandered across the sea for many years trying in vain to get back to Greece. Finally, they heard tell that the squirmy, shape-shifting *Proteus* held the secret to their reaching home again. They found him ***floundering*** on a rock off the coast of Africa, but every time they tried to seize him he changed shape, as a chameleon changes colors, from "lion to panther to

Protean (Shape-shifting)

serpent." Finally, *Proteus* relented and revealed the necessary sacrifices the woebegone sailors needed to perform for a favorable wind to blow them home again. Ever since, his name has served as a colorful adjective for anything that freely changes shape, from opinions to bodies. A marvelous companion word, worthy of revival, is *shape-smith*, an old term for "body builder." American computer scientist and futurist Alan Kay grabs hold of the ancient and slippery word and updates it: "The *protean* nature of the computer is such that it can act like a machine or like a language to be shaped and exploited."

PUBLISH

To go public with print. Johnson's *Dictionary* says it best: "The act of notifying to the world; divulgation; proclamation." During the halcyon days of the Roman Empire public officials made regular announcements about state decisions, an act called *publicare*, to make public. The word moved from Latin to old French *publier* and ultimately to medieval English as *publish*, though it endured scores of different spellings. As *publish*, it has come to mean the dissemination of announcements or pronouncements, ranging from wills to weddings, laws to royal decrees. With the invention of Gutenberg's press in the late 15th century, *publication* became synonymous with printing and distributing books or engravings. In *Why We Say It*, Webb Garrison cites one of the first *self-publishing* pronouncements on record, that of Sir Thomas More, who felt reduced (as opposed to Walt Whitman's sense of feeling expanded) by its necessity: "I am now driven to the business of *publishynge* and puttynge and boke in prints my selfe." My love of *publishing* goes back to my first job on the hometown newspaper when I was a 16-year-old cub reporter, but I caught a novel version of the word and the idea at a 1980 poetry reading by Allan Ginsberg. That night he exhorted all in the audience to remember the original sense of the word when he said that every public reading of a poem was a ***bona fide*** form of *publishing*, taking the good word to the people. For the last word on getting *published* let's turn to one of the least recognized, in her own time, of all great writers, Emily Dickinson, who said, "Publication—is the auction of the Mind of Man." Of her 1775 poems, only seven were *published* in her lifetime, which flies in the face of the academic exhortation to "*publish* or perish." Dickinson rarely *published*, but her poetry is imperishable.

PUN

A play on words. For some, a *pun* is the height of cleverness, for others a punishment, like having one's ears pounded—no mere coincidence, as that's exactly the derivation. *Pun* devolves from the Anglo-Saxon *punian*, to pound. Skeat writes, as if mortally offended, "Hence, to pound words, beat them into new senses, hammer at forced similes." To paraphrase Shakespeare, the lad doth protest too much. The bard couldn't help himself; he *punned* precisely 1,062 times in his works. The technical term is *paronomasia*, but ***slang*** words proliferate, such as *liripoop* and *quip*. Everyone has their favorites, such as the "unspeakable" *pun* by Confucius: "Seven days on ***honeymoon*** makes one whole week." In his risible handbook *Stop Me If You've Heard This*, Jim Holt writes, "Shakespeare's puns, while chucklesome, are invariably bawdy, even when they are being made by clowns: *Hamlet:* "Lady, shall I lie in your lap?" *Ophelia*: "No, my lord." *Hamlet:* "I mean my head upon your lap." *Ophelia*: Ay, my lord." *Hamlet*: "Did you think I meant country [cunt-try] matters?" My punster father used to love to quote the famously droll Dorothy Parker's "You can lead a horticulture but you can't make her think," which she thought of when challenged to use the botanical word in a quipping contest at the Algonquin Club. Her notoriously quick wit was the mirror image of ***esprit de l'escalier,*** what we might call *esprit de table*, the spirit of the table. Companion words include the querulous *quibble*, originally meaning to *pun* or play on words, and only later to have reservations about them.

PUSILLANIMOUS

In a word, *cowardly*. Possessing little courage, less moral fiber, hardly any strength, and almost no resolution. In a phrase, a cowering soul. The roots tell us what the word was originally trying to convey. The Latin *pusillanimis*, from *pusillanus*, narrow, and *animus*, soul, evolved from the Greek *oligopsychosos*, small-souled, from *pusillis*, very weak, and *animus*, spirit or courage. A *pusillanimous* character is one who isn't animated because their soul has shrunk, so they're *cowering*, hence a *coward*, one lacking any semblance of courage. Several old European words complete the picture: old French *couard* and the Italian *codardo*, a hare, a skittish animal, and the Swedish *kura*, to sit quiet, all hunched up. Thus, to be *pusillanimous* is to be skittish, to shrivel in the face of danger, because one's soul, the source of moral and physical strength, can't catch up or is trapped—thus, a spiritless coward who doesn't have the heart to face life. History is chock-full of infamous cowards who fully embody the word, even the lovable Cowardly Lion, from *The Wizard of Oz*. Jack London wrote, "Why, you *pusillanimous* piece of dirt, you'd run with your tail between your legs if I said boo." Companion synonyms include *chicken-hearted*, *craven*, *faint-hearted*, *lily-livered*, *unmanly*, *shrinking violet*, all words with a tint of contempt because of the deep human desire to embody their opposites of strength, courage (heart), and ***wit*** (brains).

Q

QUICK

Alive, enlivening, ensouled. MacKay clarifies the older meaning of the word, "alive," in what he calls the "fossilized phrase" from scripture: "The quick and the dead." "Look alive" is also synonymous with "be quick," or *quicken*, from the Middle European "to become alive" and the earlier Anglo-Saxon *cwic*, alive. By the Middle Ages, *quick* became the *quickening*, a theological term for the moment the soul enters the body—by tradition, in a spiral motion through the whorls in the top of the head. By some arcane form of reasoning, the Church ***calculated*** this mystical moment as occurring at precisely forty days for a male fetus—and eighty days for a female. When I pointed this out during a reading for my *Soul: An Archaeology*, in Berkeley in the 1990s, a woman called out from the back of the room, "That's because women take longer to warm up!" In "Messenger," Mary Oliver writes: "Here the *quickening* yeast; there the blue plums. Here the clam deep in the speckled sand..." To be *quick* is so aligned with the life force that the expression "cut to the *quick*" came to meaning cutting to the living core of a person. Figuratively, if you say to somebody "You cut me to the *quick*," it means "You've wounded me, you hurt my feelings." Thus, *quick* means speed, soul, spirit, essence; to be *quick* means to *move* from your very center, a sense perfectly captured by *Sports Illustrated*'s consensus for the greatest coach ever, John Wooden, who admonished his players, "Be *quick*—but don't hurry!"

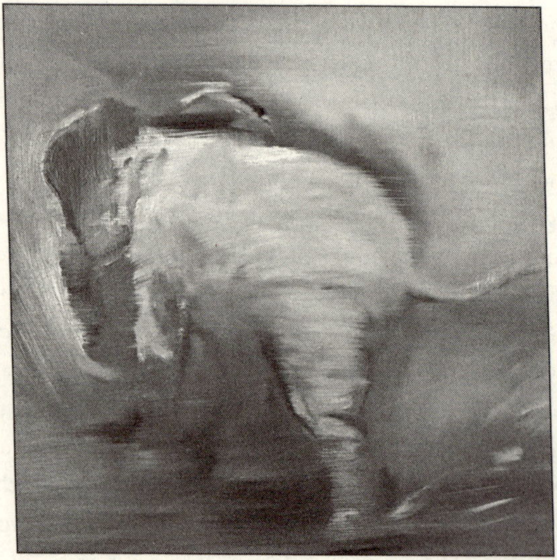

Quick

QUIRKY

Peculiar, shifty, tricky, a hint of kinky. By any measure, *quirky* is eccentric, which originally meant "off-center," or "out of orbit." Old reliable Mackay defines a *quirk* as "An unfair turn in an argument; an evasion or twisting of the truth." The word originates from the Middle Dutch *kuerken*, a cunning trick, and the earlier *kure,* a whim, or a cure, and from the German *quer*, twisted, possibly from unusual techniques in weaving. By the 1960s, *quirky* was no longer something to be avoided, but embraced, in the modern sense of *idiosyncratic.* Thus, to be quirky is to act differently, eccentrically, cunningly, as a way to cure yourself. So you could say Alfred Hitchcock was a *quirky* character in the pejorative sense of ***weird***, or you could be more compassionate and say that Hitchcock's *quirky* obsessions with guilt and innocence, police and pretty blondes, was his way of staying sane. One of the *quirkiest* actors in movies, William H. Macy, says, "Stephen King writes a lot of things that are really charming and *quirky*, and that are more ironic than horror."

QUIZ

A ***test****, a question, a mystery word.* *Quiz* is of obscure origin—but stories abound. So we can approach the word in its own spirit, *quizzically:* When is the first mention of the word? 1847. What are the roots? The first Latin question, *Qui es?* "Who are you?" asked in traditional grammar schools.

What about that old chestnut, the Dublin bar bet? There is a popular though undocumented story that dates back to around 1836 about a man named Jim Daly, the manager of a Dublin theater, who laid down a wager in a local pub that he could coin a new word and render it famous within twenty-four hours. According to the legend, he won the bet by stenciling, as Brewer writes, "four mystic letters," *Q-U-I-Z*, all over town, which prompted the indignant question, "What is this?" To which Daly was happy to answer something to the effect of, "*What is this?* Why, it's Latin for 'What is this?!'" Speaking of questions, the story goes that the question mark itself [?] is a kind of collapsed version of the letter "Q," short for "question." *Quiz* is also slang for an "odd character." Irony of ironies, Charles Van Doren, the Columbia University English professor implicated in the scandal to "fix" the 1950s television *quiz* show "Twenty-One," told a grand jury through his lawyer, "It is silly and distressing to think that people don't have more faith in *quiz* shows."

R

RANKLE

To bother, to fester, to burn with hurt. That long, hard *a* takes a great "bite" out of anyone who uses the word, for a good reason. Look it up and track it all the way back to the beginning and you'll find a "dragon's bite" lurking inside the dark cave of its distant origins. *Rankle* is rooted in *drakos*, Greek for "eye," close cousin to *drakon*, serpent, because of their burning red eyes. The Romans borrowed the word, changing it slightly to become the Latin *draco*, with its diminutive *dracunculus*, little dragon, which shape-shifted like a Druid priest into the Old French *draoncles*, a festering sore that resembled a coiled serpent, then *rancler*, an abscess or burning ulcer, and finally into the English *rankle*. Thus, *rankle* carries an echo of the folklore about the venomous and fiery bite of dragons, remembered with an insult or a slight from someone whose "bite" feels poisonous. Trusty old Ben Franklin wrote, "If you argue and *rankle* and contradict, you may achieve a temporary victory—sometimes; but it will be an empty victory because you will never get your opponent's good will." And here is a piercing reference from Mary Shelley's *Frankenstein*: "Farewell! I leave you, and in you the last of human kind whom these eyes will ever behold. Farewell, Frankenstein … Blasted as thou wert, my agony was still superior to thine; for the bitter sting of ***remorse*** will not cease to *rankle* in my wounds until death shall close them forever."

Rankle

RASA (HINDU)

The aesthetic, spiritual, or emotional *essence of a work of art. Rasa* is the core of a work that is to be relished and tasted, its flavor, perfume, mood experienced through immediate perception rather than rational apprehension. This is art appreciation through synesthesia, the belief that art is so complex it needs more than our five senses to fully comprehend it. For centuries Hindu artists and philosophers have studied this phenomenon and arrived at nine levels of spiritual ecstasy, from the Sanskrit *rasa*, relish, taste, flavor, sentiments. According to the French essayist René Daumal, the nine essential *rasas*, or savors, are "simple, like the taste of a complex dish," and "direct apprehensions of a state of being." Daumal goes on to say that *rasa* or savor is "a moment of consciousness provoked by the mediums of art and colored with a particular pathos." Traditionally, the nine rasas are: *Shringara*, the erotic; *Hasya*, the comic; *Karuna*, the pathetic; *Raudra*, the furious; *Vira*, the heroic; *Bhayanaka*, the fearsome; *Bribhatsa*, the odious; *Adbhuta*, the supernatural; and *Shanta*, the serene or tranquil. *Rasa* also refers to the limitless pleasure one can experience in painting, sculpture, poetry if appreciated through these nine tastes or moods. Ananda Coomaraswamy wrote, in *The Divine of Shiva*, "The 'nine *rasas*' are no more than the various colorings of one experience, and are arbitrary terms of rhetoric used only for convenience in classification: just as we speak of poetry categorically as lyric, epic, dramatic, etc., without implying that poetry is anything but poetry. *Rasa* is tasted—beauty is felt—only by empathy … that is to say by entering into, feeling, the permanent motif; but it is not the same as the permanent motif itself, for, from this point of view, it matters not with which of the permanent motifs we have to do."

REBATE

To reclaim; to call or beat back. From two senses of the Old French verb *rebatre*, "to blunt a sword's edge," and "bringing back a bating hawk," both emerging from *re*, back, and *batre*, to beat, bring. Thus, the *rebate* for the falconers of old referred to bringing back a hawk that left its perch on the gauntlet before being commanded to do so. The falconer who called the hawk back was "reclaiming" it, from the Latin *re*, back, and *clamo*, call. Similarly, the craft of the smith over the forge was usually to hammer the rough edges of a sword, but in certain cases, as when creating a practice sword, the goal was to "beat back or down" the sharp edges so no one got hurt. Taken together, the English sense of *rebate* emerged as claiming a discount so as to blunt the edges of the expenditure, to ease the pain caused by high prices. Filed under the category Unnecessary Quotes is this ad from the *Kansas City Star*: "When our Kansas City Chiefs shutout [sic] the hated Raiders on Sunday, September 9th, you will receive a *rebate* of all purchases $599 and up, thru Saturday only or until qualifying purchases reach $1,000,000. No purchase necessary." As the *New Yorker* says, "Block that metaphor!"

RED-HANDED

Guilty. Originally, a 15th-century Scottish legal term based on the vivid image of a criminal caught with blood on his hands. Thomas Blount, in his *Law Dictionary and Glossary* of 1717, claims it derives from the term "bloody-hand," which was one of the "four kinds of offences in the king's forest, by which the offender is supposed to have killed a deer." He adds, "In Scotland, in suchlike crimes they say, 'Taken in the fact, or with the red hand.' " Sir Walter Scott uses the term in *Ivanhoe*, in 1819. In modern times, the phrase refers to the travelers' custom of dusting the locks of suitcases with ninhydrin (nin) protein dye that turns bright red on contact with the skin of any thief trying to break the locks. Thus, one who is "caught *red-handed*" has been busted, caught, guilty. Today, the phrase is virtually synonymous with *in flagrante delicto*, Old Latin for a "blazing misdeed"—in other words, caught with your pants down. The Urban Dictionary website updates the phrase as "to quote *red-handed*," as "when someone comes out with a witty comment or funny line which they have taken from a film or television show. The embarrassment comes when they are caught out, and someone reveals to the rest of the group that what was just said was not their own wittiness or quick thinking." Thus, to be caught *red-handed* today is to be caught with blood on your quotes if you quote *The Sopranos* without crediting the show. Ah, *fuhgeddaboudit!*

REMORSE

Anguish caused by guilt. The ancients personified the powers of conscience and *remorse* as the three Erinyes, a trio of sisters who relentlessly pursued guilty mortals. Those they caught were fated to suffer "lifelong misery," as Isaac Asimov writes, for wrongs they'd committed. The career of this word began with the Latin *remorsus,* from *remordeo,* which splits into re, back, and *mordeo,* bite. Your conscience "bites" you "back." Samuel Coleridge wrote, in his play *Remorse,* "It is as the heart in which it grows: If that be gentle, it drops balmy dews of true repentance; but if proud and gloomy, it is the poison tree, that pierced to the inmost, weeps only tears of poison." Novelist George Moore adds, "*Remorse* is beholding heaven and feeling hell." Thus, a painful word picture emerges: our inmost nature, our conscience, has a kind of *mordant* sense of humor, taking a bite of our soul to remind us when we are making bad.

RHAPSODY

A beautiful tribute. The sound, act, and triumphant feel go all the way back to the Greek custom of taking "loosely sewed pieces or rags, strung together, Greek *rhapsodia, rhapto,* sew, ode, song." Its earliest sense in modern Europe, recorded in 1542, was "epic poem," from Middle French *rhapsodie,* from the Greek *rhapsodios,* a reciter of epic poems, gifted in *rhaptein,* the ability to stitch together the odes, from *oide,* song. Over the centuries this ability to remember, sing, and inspire was so admired that *rhapsody* came to mean any exalted feeling or expression, a meaning that dates back to 1639. By the mid 1850s, it was used to describe "sprightly musical compositions." Snarky times are suspicious of lofty expressions of art, and so *rhapsody* has devolved into *rhapsodic*, which in some circles can mean exaggerated ***enthusiasm***. So if the meaning is still obscure, I recommend listening to Rachmaninov's *Rhapsody on a Theme of Paganini*, a work that stitches together the Russian's passion with the Italian's exaltation. In her essay "Building the House," poet Mary Oliver writes, "Privacy, no longer cherished in the world, is all the same still a natural and sensible attribute of paradise. We are happy, and we are lucky.... We make for each other: companionship, intimacy, affection, *rhapsody*."

RIVAL

An opponent in a contest. During the Roman Empire a man who had water rights to the same stream as another was a *rivalis*, from *rivus*, stream or brook. Since competitions often arose, *rivalis* took on the meaning of competitor. People living across a stream from each other, or near each other on the same side, have often quarreled about fishing rights, the right to build a dam, or other privileges. Our English *rival* commemorates such competitiveness. In modern terms it refers to the competitiveness of neighbors, as do *rivalry* and *rivalrous*. Al Gore writes, "The heart of the security agenda is protecting lives—and we now know that the number of people who will die of AIDS in the first decade of the 21st century will *rival* the number that died in all the wars in all the decades of the 20th century." Seven-time Tour de France champion Lance Armstrong: "Anyone who imagines they can work alone winds up surrounded by nothing but *rivals*, without companions. The fact is, no one ascends alone." Companion words include *nival*, which rhymes with *rival* but derives from the Latin *nivosos*, for snow. Its ***murmuring*** meanings include the tenacious power of certain plants or animals to survive underneath a pack of snow. It's uncertain whether the word can also refer to people with the same capacity.

S

SALARY

Wages, recompense. After the custom in the Roman army to pay a portion of the wages to its legionnaires in the form of a daily handful of salt, *salarium*, from the Latin *sal*, an allotment known as their "salt allowance." For the salt-crazed Romans, who constructed their towns near salt supplies and fought wars to protect them, *salary* came to mean wages in general. Look it up and you'll discover the phrases "salt away," an echo of storing salt as some might stuff their pillows with cash, "worth his salt," for someone who has earned what he's been paid, and "salt of the earth," an unaffected, natural person. The *Via Salaria* was the first imperial road built, to convey salt from the port of Ostia. The Roman Pliny wrote in the 31st volume of his *Natural History*, "[In] Rome … the soldier's pay was originally *salt* and the word *salary* derives from it …" Regarding the money she made as a writer, Dorothy Parker said, "*Salary* is no object; I want only enough to keep body and soul apart." Two-time baseball MVP Frank Robinson said, in 2002, "We keep talking about the *salaries* escalating, and how they affect the future. Well, they're still going up. It's still up to the individual if he wants to stay around. Players have to be healthy and continue at a high level of hitting home runs. That's what it is going to take, and I don't know how many are willing to do that."

SARDONIC

Humorous in a bitter, biting, or mocking way; smiling grimly. This contemptuous word stems from the French *sardonique,* adapted from the phrase *ris sardonien*, a forced or careless mirth, as Cotgrave (1611) defines it. It derives in turn from the Greek *sardonikos*, a bitter laugh. If this seems like an *oxymoron* ("sharp dullard or fool"), remember that it comes straight from a folk memory about the nature of bitterness itself. The *herba sardonia* plant from Sardinia is so foul-tasting that it caused "a convulsive movement of the nerves of the face, resembling a painful grin," as Virgil described its effect in the *Eclogues*, enough "to screw up the face of the eater." Companion words include *sardine*, plus *sardis* and *sardonyx*, two precious gems found in Sardis, in Lydia (Asia Minor), resembling, as Pliny writes, the onyx in fingernails. A close cousin of *sardonic* is *sarcophagus*, a carved stone coffin, from *sarco*, body and *phagein*, to eat, a visceral word picture of "flesh-eating" stone, no doubt influenced by close observation of the effects of time on entombed bodies. We find a close cousin to the bittersweet *sardonic* in Byron's "Corsair." Of the corsair, who hailed from Sardinia, he wrote, "There was a laughing devil in his sneer"—*sneer* being from the Old German *snereen*, to cause a hissing noise, and Danish *snaerre*, to grin like a dog, show one's teeth, which brings to mind the acrid response to eating *herba sardonia.* Somerset Maugham once said, rather bitterly, "Money is the sting with which a *sardonic* destiny directs the motions of its puppets." And from Anne Sexton: "Either I'm just too paranoid or this is just my way of now playing the *sardonic* court jester instead of the 'angry young man.'"

SAUDADE (PORTUGUESE)

The constant desire that hurts, the irrepressible ***yearning*** *for something that may not even exist.* This ***untranslatable*** but indispensable Portuguese word describes in two syllables what English can't do in anything shorter than a dissertation: the longing for perfect ***love***, the complete utopia, a perfect work of art, even a person who has gone missing, in war or tragedy. Still, the memory is deeply felt in the heart, though others would demean it as indolent dreamy wistfulness. When *fado* is consciously evoked in music, poetry, dance, and film, the feelings of excitement and passion live on as *saudade*, lingering like perfume, moving outward like ripples in a pond, which creates *saudade*, "a resigned, bittersweet, existential yearning for something we would like to change or experience, but over which we have no control." A companion word in English would be the *blues*, a fiercely honest musical expression of joy–pain and sweet–sorrowful, transformed by the artistry of a Ray Charles or Billie Holliday into a triumph, however momentary, over the inevitable sorrows of the human condition. The *fado* singer Katia explains, "*Saudade* is a very deep feeling. It's when you miss someone or something or a place very, very hard. *Saudade* is the only Portuguese word that doesn't have any synonym in any other language. *Saudade* makes us feel good and sad at the same time."

SAUNTER

To walk without a care. A Sunday stroll of a word. One of the most relaxed verbs in English, it comes by way of the French *sauntrer*, gloriously defined by Skeat as "to adventure oneself," based on the Old French *aventurer*, to adventure or venture forth. *Saunter* stretches back much farther, to the 1,700-year-long tradition of walking to *la Sainte-Terre*, the Holy Land, in the footsteps of Helena, Emperor Constantine's mother, who was in search of the Holy Cross. Her visit to Jerusalem is considered the first Christian pilgrimage, which sparked untold thousands of others to follow along the "glory roads." During medieval times the route to the *Sainte-Terre* was steadily smoothed, like a pilgrim's sandals, to become our gently swaying verb *saunter.* By Henry David Thoreau's time at Walden, in the early 19th century, it was a rather suave way of describing a ***contemplative*** walk. Thoreau wrote, in his journal, "The really efficient laborer will be found not to crowd his day with work, but will *saunter* to his task surrounded by a wide halo of ease and leisure." Uncharacteristically, Grosse snipes at the very idea of those *saunterers*: "An idle, lounging fellow … applied to persons, who, having no lands or home, lingered and loistered about … [in] the Holy Land, Saint Terre, as waiting for company." The ultra-long-distance walker and early environmentalist John Muir writes of his adventuring through the American Holy Land of Yosemite, in California: "The last time I *sauntered* through the big cañon I saw about two [rattlesnakes] a day." Companion words include the Spanish *paseo*, a leisurely walk, and "*suave around*," the Red Sox slugger Ted Williams's surprisingly elegant description of the way that classy ballplayers moved on the field.

SCAPEGOAT

Someone who is blamed for the sins of others. Traditionally, a real goat, one that was allowed to *escape*, symbolically shouldering the sins of the community. Ancient annals tell us about the custom of the Day of Atonement, in which the sins of the people were ritually transferred to a goat that was then banished to the wilderness. Meanwhile, a second goat was sacrificed to the Lord, as the "sin offering." Thus *scapegoat* came to mean a person who likewise shoulders the blame (from *blaspheme*, to speak ill of)—the sins of someone else—an echo of the apparently universal impulse to look for other people to slur, denigrate, or accuse for troubles we ourselves have caused. The terror of being thus accused is expressed well by none other than Rod Serling. "The tools of conquest," he intoned, "do not necessarily come with bombs, and explosions, and fallout. There are weapons that are simply thoughts, ideas, and prejudices to be found only in the minds of men. For the record, prejudices can kill and suspicion can destroy. A thoughtless, frightened search for a *scapegoat* has a fallout all its own for the children unborn. And the pity of it is that these things cannot be confined to The Twilight Zone."

SCHEDULE

A timetable; a wish list of things to do. As Wilfred Funk reminds us, most of the words connected with writing have their roots, so to speak, in the bark of a tree, the surface of a stone, or in some cases, the leaves of plants. Modern usage prosaically refers to inventories and supplements, which hardly captures the word's redolent essence, with its smells of the Nile, the Aegean, and French cafés. Our use of *schedule* arrived right on time in America, like a locomotive chugging into a station, during the punctuality-obsessed 19th century. What it carried was a train of associations, from the Old French *cedule*, a scroll, which came from the

Latin *schedula*, a small slip of paper, and *scheda*, a strip of papyrus, and the earlier Greek *skede*, a cleft or cleaved piece of wood. Thus, a *schedule* is a timetable written on a small piece of paper that we cleave to. The wonder-tracking naturalist Annie Dillard writes, "A *schedule* defends from chaos and whim. It is a net for catching days. It is a scaffolding on which a worker can stand and labor with both hands at sections of time."

SCOOCH OR SCOOTCH (SCOTTISH)

To move closer, closer, closer...to the edge. Scootching up to this word in a handful of ***dictionaries*** only provided me with the pallid meaning "to slide on over," usually to make room for someone or something else. But serendipity struck recently on a visit to Ansel Adams's cabin in Yosemite, where I plucked the memoirs of naturalist and legendary hiker John Muir off the bookshelves. By chance, Muir mentions a game he grew up playing in the north of Scotland called "*scootchers*." According to Muir, it was a game in which kids challenged each other to *scootch* closer and closer to the point of danger, to advance slowly on a dare. In his case he and two friends *scootched* to the edge of a rooftop. Echoic of an action, possibly deriving from *scoot*, to move swiftly, possibly from *scout*, to seek out. Close cousins would be *scrooch* or *scrootch*, to hunch down, crouch. The episode of *The Simpsons* called "Insane Clown Puppie" features a hilarious Christopher Walken reading menacingly to a group of cowering school kids: "Goodnight moon, goodnight, *moon*, goodnight cow, jumping over the moon. Please children, *scootch* closer. Don't make me tell you again about the *scootching*. You, in the red, chop-chop!"

SCRUTINIZE

To search carefully. An easy enough definition, but one that only begins to describe the tactile pleasure of looking closely, whether at ***dictionaries***, advice, or cloud formations. *Scrutinizing* originally referred to looking closely at rags that could be pulped into paper, which brought a few pennies for the ragpickers. The word comes from the Latin *scrutinium*, a careful inquiry, and *scrutari*, to examine carefully, and *scruta*, broken pieces, trash, rags. Thus to *scrutinize* is look at virtually anything carefully, closely, like Calvin, in *Calvin and Hobbes*, who believes "there's treasure everywhere." Compare *speculate*, to hold a mirror up to. Paleontologist Stephen Jay Gould wrote, "The most erroneous stories are those we think we know best—and therefore never *scrutinize* or question."

SEEKSORROW

One who looks for trouble, sees sorrow everywhere. A classic ***portmanteau***, from *seek*, strive, and *sorrow*, to be sick with grief, which implies a curious pessimist, an adventurous glutton for punishment, or possibly someone who feels the necessity of enduring the dark night of the soul. Dr. Johnson defined it as "one who continues to give himself vexation." A candidate for one of the top ten words that need reviving. Who hasn't felt oneself to be one's own worst enemy? We've all known someone, perhaps a co-worker, who seems to go looking for trouble, but one word is swifter than five. One of the most heartrending usages is one of the earliest, in the 5,000-year-old Sumerian story of the king of Uruk, after his closest friend, Enkidu, has died: "Why, Gilgamesh, do you ever *[seek] sorrow*?" cries out the wise old man Utanapishtim. More recently, Edith Wharton wrote, "There's no such thing as old age, there is only *sorrow*." Composer Franz Schubert once reflected upon the deep-seeking sensibility in his work: "When I wished to sing of love, it turned to sorrow. And when I wished to sing of sorrow, it was transformed for me into love."

SHANGHAI

To kidnap and secret away aboard a ship. A clandestine word conjured up in San Francisco's Chinatown during the Gold Rush years. The story goes and goes that ships docking in San Francisco Bay had usually been away at sea for years, leaving their crews depleted. The solution for many a captain was to walk from the wharf up Broadway to Grant Avenue and into Chinatown, where they stopped at bars called "deadfalls." In collusion with the bar owners, the captains plied sailors on leave with free drinks, often with a "Mickey

Finn" dropped in for good measure. The unsuspecting Jack-Tars were then led to trap doors that dropped them into perilously dark basements, where they were bound and tied until the next morning. Then, usually still drugged, they were frog-marched to the harbor. As if in a bad movie, the hungover sailors woke up days later to find themselves halfway to Shanghai. Thus, to be *shanghaied* means to be fooled, with desperate consequences. Companion words include *press-gang*, a group of mercenary sailors who trawl

Shanghaied

the docks and back alleys for men they can strong-arm into maritime work. Surprisingly, *crimp*, from Dutch *krimpe*, meaning "a confined place for fish till wanted," has similar origins. Smyth wrote in 1867 that ship agents loaned money to sailors on leave, a practice that "indebts the ***dupes***, and when well plied with liquor are induced to sign articles, and are shipped off, only discovering their mistake on finding themselves robbed of all they possessed."

SKEDADDLE

To run away. No one knows for sure; the true origins themselves have *skedaddled* into the shadows of linguistic history. Speculation has it that the word was minted during the American Civil War as military ***slang***, possibly from Scottish-Irish immigrant soldiers' use of the old Gaelic *skiddle*, to spill, scatter; this may be connected to an earlier use in northern English dialect, *sket*, rapidly, and *daddle*, to walk unsteadily. Thus, a word picture emerges of a terrified or disgruntled soldier "lighting out or leaving in a hurry," and then, as the war dragged on, "breaking away and running from battle." Companion words include *scat*, *scoot, skidoo*, as in "23-Skidoo," probably from *skedaddle*. Medieval folklore ascribes *skedaddle* to "the wasteful overflow of milkmaid's milk," from Gaelic *squit*, wander, and *allta*, wild. Other memorable Irishisms of the period: *so long*, from the Irish *slan*, farewell, and the rambunctious *shenanigans*, which Robert MacNeil in *The Story of English* playfully traces back to the Irish "I play like a fox." The explosive *smithereens* is rooted in *smither*, small fragment, the result perhaps of a few too many donnybrooks. Uncertainty never sounded so uncertain as it does in *swither*, as in "That put me in an eerie *swither*," or the *swithering* factor in a hotly contested election in which the voters are unable to make up their minds, from Scandinavian *swidder*, uncertain.

SKEW

To make oblique, slanting, distorted; to twist and turn; to shy away from. To discover the roots, this is the route we have to take. *Skew* derives from the Middle English *skewen*, to turn aside, which came from the Old High German *sheuen*, to avoid, and its adjective, *sheu*, shy, as in timid, but also "to shy away from." In Middle English *shey* is "a shy horse." Thus to *skew* is to turn aside, out of fear, like a *shying* horse, or to distort out of recognition. The modern sense appears in a December 2009 edition of the *Hollywood Reporter:* "Advance ticketing for James Cameron's sci-fi actioner *Avatar* is *skewing* heavily toward male moviegoers, but sales are going so strongly that it shouldn't represent a problem." Companion words include the whimsical *slantandicular*, a *posilutely* vibrant synonym for *perpendicular*.

SKYLARKING

An old nautical term to describe an English sailor's game of climbing the rigging to the masthead, and then sliding down the backstays for the sheer fun of it. Once deemed a sport for "English ***thrill***-seeking sailors," *skylarking* has slid down the language to become one of our most vivacious verbs, generally referring to a pleasant jaunt, a getaway. Originally, it was *skylacing.* First recorded in 1809, *skylacing* was "wanton play about the rigging, and tops," later corrupted to *skylarking,* a compound of *sky* and *lark*, an old English word meaning "to frolic or play." Metaphorically, it now encompasses the modern European sense of the songbird, from Middle English *larke* and Old English *lawerce*, though there is also evidence of a Greek proverb, "With even the unmusical, the *lark* is melodious." The old English phrase "to rise with the lark," meant to get up early in the morning. Nowadays, a *lark* is a "spree or frolic or pleasant jaunt." Companions include: "To a *Skylark*," a poem by Shelley, Skylark, a popular Buick from 1953–1972, and "Skylark," the love song written by Hoagy Carmichael and Johnny Mercer in 1941.

SLANG

Street talk, abusive language, a colorful rap. Uncertain origins, but most scholars agree it appears first in secret language of the underworld in the 18th century. John Ayot argues that *slang* is the direct descendant of ***cant***. The most vivid theory takes it back to the early Icelandic *slyngva*, to sling, which influenced other words across Scandinavia such as the Norwegian *sleng*, to throw around offensive language, and *slengja*, to toss abuse, from *slengjakjeften*, to sling the jaw. Thus, *slang* is the tossing around of wild words, insults, hipster talk—what is sometimes called in American *slang* "jaw-boning." Leave it to Robert Frost to give it a modern twist. "*Slang*," he said, is "a language that rolls up its sleeves, spits on its hands, and goes to work." Companion words include *slang-whanger*, a nickname for the English essayist William Hazlitt. In his classic work *American Slang*, H. L. Mencken writes, "College *slang* is actually made by the campus wits, just as general *slang* is made by the wits of the newspapers and theaters." Companion words include *argot*, an old French synonym for *slang* that meant "to tear, from beggars' clothes"—an effective way to describe how educated people rip—borrow—so many colorful words from people reduced to living on the streets and *sling* them around in their music, poetry, movies, dissertations.

SLOGAN

A saying, advertisement, a shout to the sky. In ancient Scotland and Ireland *sluagh-ghairm* was the war cry of the army, the host-cry, or gathering word of a border clan; "a war cry, meaningful one, perhaps name of chief of clan, or place, so a rallying cry or password by Highlanders and Borderers." In 1808, Sir Walter Scott introduced the word into English use in his novel *Marmion*: "The Border *slogan* rent the sky, A Home! A Gordon! Was the cry!" First an Indian, then a cowboy, always a brilliant Cherokee comedian, Will Rogers got the contemporary sense of it right when he quipped, "You shake a *slogan* at an American and it's just like showing a hungry dog a bone." Companion words include the modern *sloganeering*, which generally means reducing complex ideas to whatever can fit on to a placard. A popular synonym is *brand*, compressing the qualities of a product to a *slogan* or tagline that stands for *the brand*.

SNEAK

To creep along; to move stealthily. The furtive verb has slithered along the linguistic path from the Irish *snighim*, "I creep." Other crawling derivations include the Anglo-Saxon *snican*, to creep, from the Middle English *sniken*, to crawl, a close cousin of the Old English *snican*, to desire, reach for, and Old Norse *snikja*, related to snake. On the island of Guernsey the old Gurns say *snequer*, which means "to rob slyly," and in Iceland *snik-inn*, which means "to hanker after." Thus, to sneak is to creep along and reach for something you deeply desire or hanker for, even if you have to steal it. That illicit aspect of the word can be heard in the long "ea," which sounds creepy, like a loose board in the attic. Companion words include *Sneaky Pete,* a personification of cheap booze, from 1949; *slink*, to creep, crawl, from Anglo-Saxon *slincan*; and the Dutch *slinken*, to shrink, shrivel. The sexy *slinky*, as in a sinuous and slender woman or the clothes she slid into, slithers into the lexicon in 1921. The *Slinky* toy became all the rage in 1948. Companion quotes include the Milwaukee Braves' first baseman Joe Adcock's "Trying to *sneak* a fastball past Hank Aaron is like trying to *sneak* the sunrise past a rooster."

SORCERER

A wizard, a reader of fate, foreteller of the future. Originally, one who predicted the future by drawing lots, so *sorcery* is rooted in the lore of the Roman god Sors, the god of chance. Lucky for us, because Sors inspired the Latin *sors*, lots; *sortes*, the responses made by oracles; and *sortarius*, caster of spells. Ultimately, our everyday phrase "sorting out" derives from *sortilege*, which combines *sors*, lot, plus *legere*, to read. Coming full circle, as word hunts often do, *sorcery* cast its own spell when it was taken into Old French as *sorcier*, which became the English *sorcerer*. It pours through the language in "To read one's lot in life," and in "to accept one's lot," "to trust in the luck of the draw," "Sort it out!" and "all sorts," literally "the dregs," "the "drippings" in the bottom of beer mugs, to be sold later at a lower price to the poor and undiscerning. Thus a *sorcerer* is someone who "sorts out" all the conflicting messages about the future and seems to cast a spell when explaining how the fates have arranged for things to unfold. Companion words include *soothsayer*, one who tells the truth, figuratively, about the future, from *sooth*, from *southe*, to assent, confirm, prove to be true. And a *sorcerer's* apprentice of a word, which Helen Keller used audaciously: "Smell is a potent wizard."

SPOONERISM

Corkscrewing words; words turned inside out. A *spoonerism* is what happens when you get your "turds wurned around." Named after William Archibald Spooner (1844–1930) dean of New College, Oxford, for whom language often inverted itself as it came out of his mouth. Here are three of his classics: "Our Lord is a shoving leopard," for "Our Lord is a loving shepherd," "Let us raise our glasses to the queer old dean," for " …the dear old queen," and "It is kisstomary to cuss the bride," for "It is customary to kiss the bride." Companion words include *malapropism,* from *mal*, bad and *proper*, word usage—a coinage from Dickens, "Mrs. Malaprop," who is lampooned for using the wrong words at the most inappropriate moments. Also *Bunkerisms*, after Archie Bunker in the 1970s television show "All in the Family." Finally, a noteworthy anecdote reminding us that even reading dictionaries can be dangerous, from the story of Omai, a Tahitian brought back to London by Captain Cook. After reading Johnson's *Dictionary*, Omai confused "pickle" with "preserve" when introduced to Lord Sandwich. "May God Almighty pickle his Lordship to all eternity," he said.

STIGMA

A mark, a brand. The Greek *stizein*, to tattoo, seared its meaning into our *stigma*. An obsolete meaning refers to a scar left by a hot branding iron, probably in reference to a mark of shame left on a thief, prostitute, coward. Companion words include *stigmata*, a religious phenomenon in which bodily marks resembling the wounds of the crucified Christ appear, and the botanical term *stigma*, the part of the pistil of a flower that absorbs pollen. Alexander Theroux writes, in his beguiling *The Primary Colors*, "It takes 200,000–400,000 dried *stigmas* of the violet flower to make two pounds of saffron. And moreover each flower only has three stigmas, which must be picked by hand at dawn before the sun gets too hot." He adds that the ancient roads of Rome were strewn with saffron whenever emperors or statesman passed over them. Brewer adds the Latin phrase *Dormivit in sacco croci*, "He hath slept in a bed of saffron," meaning "light-hearted" because of its exhilarating effects. Thus, *stigma* is a deep mark, ranging from a brand to a tattoo to a subtly beautiful flower.

STORY POLES

The sticks that mark out the foundation of a house-to-be. Story poles are an ancient custom to remind the builders what is actually to be constructed, but also to signal to the community what is about to change. Synchronistically, across the street from the North Beach café where I'm writing at this very moment, *story poles* are being raised to inform the neighborhood where the new library—and a new story—will be erected. Figuratively, stories are the foundation of our lives. For me, a significant *story* is an account of something worth telling, a narrative telling how things happen. The oldest version of the word comes from Latin *historia*, an account, and the Middle English *storie*, and Old French *estoire*, a tale. The longest example may be the Hindu epic the *Mahabarata*; the shortest story may be Sandburg's "Born. Played. Died." Companion words include *storiation*, the architectural feature of narrative images carved into the side of a building. *Confabulation* is psychology-speak for the "generally unconscious, defensive 'filling in' of actual memory gaps by imaginary experiences." The Irish *banaghan* refers to someone who tells terrific stories. A *taleteller* is a *storyteller* nonpareil, someone hired to "tell wonderful stories of giants and fairies, to lull their hearers to sleep." A *talesman* is the author of a story or report; a *tale bearer* is a mischief maker, the incendiary in the family. Of story tributes there is no end. Ray Bradbury said, "Don't you know, it was my *stories* that led me through my life?" Of his role as choreographer for *West Side Story*, Jerome Robbins observed, "What are they dancing about? What's the *story*? You danced to fit the character."

SULKY

A lightweight, two-wheeled harness-racing vehicle; a sullen, ill-humored, aloof person. If you can visualize a carriage with room for one and only one person, or a horse trap, you can learn, by what word mavens call "back-formation," the inner meaning of its root word. Searching for *le mot juste* for the one-seated vehicle, someone's mind alighted on the image of a loner, a brooder, one who goes it alone, suspiciously solitary. In a word, a *sulker,* one who *sulks,* acts petulantly, broods in an obstinate way. Originally from the Old English *solcen,* slothful, idle, remiss, disgust, languid. The 1913 edition of *Webster's Revised Dictionary* provides an obscure but useful origin for *sulk* as deriving from the Latin *sulcus,* a furrow, and possibly Old English *sulke,* sluggish. The usage we recognize is "to mope or brood, to be sullen, resentful silence, out of humor, as reflected in the *sulker's* furrowed brow." William Blake puts it in perspective: "When I saw that rage was vain / And to *sulk* would nothing gain, / Turning many a trick and wile / I began to soothe and smile." Companion words include *sullen,* morose, but originally meaning "solitary, hating company," as in *The Sullen Art,* Colin Wilson's book about the lone, brooding pursuit of poetry; ***boudoir***, a place to *brood* in, from French *bouder,* to *sulk,* perhaps also from English *pout*; and *glouping,* a splendidly sonicky word for "sullen and brooding."

SUTURE

To sew; a seam, a thread. This venerable word refers to the ties that bind us, whether it's in the *sutras*, the sacred Hindu writings, or the surgical stitches after an operation. If you follow the *thread* of the word from its origins in the Proto-Indo-European *syu-* or *su-*, to bind or sew, you will come to the Latin *sutura*, a sewing together, and eventually to the English *seam* and *seamstress.* Similarly, a *stitch* is "a passing through stuff of a needle and thread." Centuries of drawing out these threads gave us the Old English *spinnan*, to *spin,* as in the spinning of *yarns* by sailors while mending their nets, and the expressions "three sheets to the wind" and "know the ropes." *Gray's Anatomy*, first published in 1858, defines *sutures*: "The bones of the cranium and face are connected to each other by means of *Sutures.* … The *sutures* remain separate for a considerable period after the complete formation of the skull. It is probable that they serve the purpose of permitting the growth of the bones at their margins, while their peculiar formation, together with the interposition of the *sutural* ligament between the bones forming them, prevents the dispersion of blows or jars received upon the skull." In the fall of 2009, at a dinner in San Francisco, Deepak Chopra told me that ancient Hindu sages taught that "the *sutras* stitch together consciousness, and every sutra is a reflection of all the threads of the universe." Metaphorically, *sutures* not only tie things together, they also expand to allow growth, to connect us to ourselves and to each other.

SWAFF

To come one over the other, like waves upon the shore, like waves of sleepiness upon a man who has been up for three days, like waves of nausea upon someone on a ship in heavy seas. "Drenched with their *swaffing* waves," in the wondrous phrasing of *Taylor's Works,* 1630. *Swaff* is also a noun in English dialect for the amount of grass a scythe cuts with one bold stroke. A plangent word worth reviving, a word that sighs and soughs. Companion words include the Scottish *dwam*, the trancelike feeling that washes over a person, rendering them unaware of what's occurring around them. Similarly, a *fugue* is a flight of consciousness, from the Italian *fuga*, for flight, a wavy, dreamlike state of altered awareness that may stretch for hours or days with little memory of what happened.

T

TABOO

Forbidden, prohibited, out of bounds. A complex series of prohibitions related to things holy or unclean; an ancient Polynesian practice to protect and ensure the sacred. Captain Cook wrote in a journal entry from 1777 that the word "has a very comprehensive meaning; but, in general, signifies that a thing is forbidden.... When any thing is forbidden to be eat, or made use of, they say, that it is taboo." In the spring of 2009 I caught sight of the word while walking along a beach in Samoa. Written in bright white paint on a towering palm tree was the word TABOO. Beneath the warning was a strip of yellow police tape that stretched to the next tree about ten yards away and to the tree beyond it. Then I saw the reason for the warning. Within the semicircle of towering palms was a small flotilla of outrigger canoes. Clearly, intruders, strangers, nonsailors, were meant to keep away. This bold word has meant exactly that for millennia throughout Polynesia, to prevent the desecration of sacred objects such as sailing vessels, or virtually anything that the tribal kings had touched. "Furthermore," wrote Margaret Mead of her time in Samoa, "among true *taboo* prohibitions, those whose breach is followed by automatic punishment, there are in Polynesia two main classes: *taboos* associated with the inherent sanctity of the gods, chiefs, and priests, and *taboos* associated with the inherent uncleanness of certain occurrences, such as menstruation, [childbirth], bloodshed, and death."

TEST, TESTAMENT

*A **quiz**, an exam, a questioning.* In Roman times a man would swear to the truth by tugging his beard, crossing his heart, or making a vow on the lives of his family or ***fortune***. Or—he would grasp his own *testes*, testicles. (Some say it was those of the man to whom the oath was made.) The word picture gets curiouser and curiouser, as Lewis Carroll said, in the Latin word for "witness," which is *testis*, and for "testifying," which is *testificari*, to bear witness. These words led to *testament*, from *testis*, witness, and *facere*, to make—meaning both the written record of a statement and "an open profession of one's faith and devotion," in 1526, or "publication of a will," from *testamentum*. In its annual contest for the most humorous malapropisms, the *Washington Post* reported that one contestant defined *testicle* as "a humorous question on an exam." Companion words are legion: *testimony,* evidence; *testudo,* tortoise; *textile*, from *textere*, to weave; and *test tube*, a vessel for conducting simple chemical tests. *Test-tube baby* is recorded from 1935; *test drive* is first recorded in 1954. Thus, a *testament* reveals your deepest truth, what you would swear to. To which the soul man, Motown singer Marvin Gaye, sang, "Can I get a witness?"

THESAURUS

A treasure trove of synonyms. An upside-down ***dictionary***; whereas a ***dictionary*** provides meanings for words, a *thesaurus* provides words for meanings. While ruin-hunting in Olympia, Greece, after the 2004 Olympics, I was startled to see the original use of the word *thesauros* on my map of the ancient grounds. There in black and white was the Greek word for the six buildings that lined the path leading to the famous stadium (from *stadia*, a 200-meter running track). For centuries, visitors and dignitaries attending the Olympics would contribute spectacular gifts—*treasures*—from their cities or homelands, which were housed in a newly constructed *thesauros*, from the root of *tithenai*, which later gave us both *treasure* and *tithe*. The term *Thesaurarie* was used by compilers of ***dictionary*** as early as 1592, for a collection of rich information about words. In 1823, *thesaurus* made its first appearance as an English word, around the time an eccentric British physician, inventor, and lexicographer,

Peter Mark Roget, known for his discovery of the "persistence of vision," began a lifelong project of collecting his "treasure house of words." First published in 1852, Roget's *Thesaurus* was originally titled *Collection of English Synonyms Classified and Arranged*, and proved to be so popular it was reprinted twenty-eight times during his life, expanded by his son John in 1879 and again in 1911, and reprinted and expanded more than a hundred times since then, in many languages. Curiously, his *Thesaurus* was long considered a "difficult book"—at least until the crossword puzzle fad transformed the book into an indispensable prompt. And the 1550 term *treasure trove*, from the Anglo-French *tresor trové,* via the Latin *thesaurus inventus*, found treasure, which refers to the old custom of rendering to the lord of the land or the king any *treasure* that is found on his land.

THOLE

To suffer, abide, to tolerate without complaint. "Endure," according to Coleridge's *A Dictionary of the First, or Oldest Words in the English Language.* As they say in the Highlands, 'Ye'll just have to *thole* it." A "lost beauty," a missing link, or a word we miss and don't even know it. *Thole* is of Anglo-Saxon heritage, immortalized in the 10th-century epic *Beowulf.* Obscure but still used in pockets of Gaeltacht country, as in "To *thole* the *dool* (doldrums)," which means to bear the evil consequences of something. When Seamus Heaney was translating *Beowulf*, he turned to his own family in Northern Ireland, who still used the word. His aunt used to say of those who were grieving, "They'll just have to learn to *thole*." In his classic *Lost Beauties of the English Language*, Charles Mackay regrets the way that the deeply mournful Old English and Scottish *thole*, with its long *o*, "was wrongly thrust out of the English to make room for modern substitutes from the French," such as the weaker expression "to bear." Companion words include the Old English *tholemod*, long-suffering; *untholandlik*, unendurable; *untholeable*, intolerable, not to be tholed or endured. Finally, a Scottish proverb that rolls around the heather of the heart: "He who *tholes*, endures."

THRILL

To vibrate, to excite; originally, to pierce, to make a hole. One of the most penetrating words in the language, *thrill* has its roots in the sound and ***fury*** that a tool makes when it creates a hole, or an arrow when it hits its target. It comes from the Middle English *thrillen*, from *thryel*, hot, and *thurh*, through, meaning "to pierce." By 1592, it had evolved to mean "a shivering, exciting feeling," as when someone is "pierced by an emotion," a distant echo of the heart-puncturing arrows of Eros. Metaphorically, *thrill* has developed into the sense of being filled with a quivering pleasure, as when listening to B. B. King's "The *Thrill* is Gone," or reading an Agatha Christie *thriller.* Cole Porter captures both senses when he writes: "I get no kick from champagne / Mere alcohol doesn't *thrill* me at all. / So tell my why should it be true / That I get a kick out of you?" And on a poignant note, when Ishi, the last Yahi Indian, died, he was buried, as the newspapers said, "with some things of a personal nature," including five of his own handmade arrows. To me, a *thrilling* detail.

TOPSY-TURVY

Upside down, ***crazy****-making.* The word is a brilliant example of a common but intimate daily practice metamorphosing into a colorful ***metaphor***. The reeling expression comes from the old-fashioned hearths of rural Ireland where peat or turf was burned by the local *bogtrotters*, and refers to the way that it was stacked to dry. As Joseph Taylor defined it, in his 1819 ***dictionary*** *Antiquitates Curiosae*, the common practice was to stack turf "the top-side-turf-way," which meant the wrong side upward. As W.B. Yeats might have said, "It's all in a *darg*," meaning "a day's work," Old Irish for completing the task of peat-cutting and carrying it back home in a wheelbarrow, as immortalized by Halliwell in his 1811 dictionary. Philosopher William James, ever wrestling with the unpredictability of the human mind, wrote, "Men's activities are occupied into ways—in grappling with external circumstances and in striving to set things at one in their own *topsy-turvy* mind."

TRANSLATION

Carrying meaning from one language to another. A relic of a word. The derivation is from the Latin *translatus* and *transferre*, carry across, from *trans*, across, and *latus*, carry, borne, which easily slid into the English *transfer*, capturing the sense of movement of words across the borders of incomprehension and misunderstanding. But its earliest meaning is cultural and spiritual, anchored in the "transfer of relics" from one cathedral to another during medieval times. There is a curious connection between the *translation* of a relic, say the femur bone of St. Francis, and the *translation* of Chekhov from Russian into English, and here it is. For a site to qualify as a cathedral, a genuine relic was needed as proof of the holiness of the site. Inevitably, a brisk business arose in the transfer, or *translating*, of relics from one church to another, like soccer players switching clubs. Thus, to *translate* is to carry the meaning of one language across the great divide between cultures to a second language on the other side. Tragically, Henry VIII chose to publically burn thousands of those *translated* relics—the bones of saints—whose ashes eventually gave us the word *bonfire*, from "bone-fire." In the *Sunday Telegraph* in August 2009, Alain de Botton reviewed the new *translation* of Marcel Proust: "The greatest praise one could pay this new edition of *In Search of Lost Time* is therefore to say that it allows us to forget both that we are reading the work of many different *translators* and, for long sections, that we are even reading anything that began in a foreign language at all. Like the best *translations*, it lets the author speak." Amen.

TRAVEL

To take a journey; a trip. A universal practice with universal features—departure, encountering obstacles, returning home—all of which are reflected in the story of the word. Our English word dates back to 1375: "to journey," from Early French *travailen*, to toil, labor, work hard. The earliest references to the word don't have our—(sigh)—romantic associations; they refer to "pains; labor, toil, suffering, childbirth pains," as James Murray defined it for the OED. The French verb gave us travail, hard work, but also a farrier's (blacksmith's) frame for unruly horses, and the earlier *tripalium*, a medieval three-paled (-spiked) instrument of torture. Tied together, the notion here is of embarking on a difficult journey, which will either torture you or *stretch* you. Historian Daniel Boorstin writes that the *travel*–travail connection evolved during the Middle Ages owing to the fact that "traveling entailed hard work such as learning the local language, studying its history, risking different cuisine, in contrast to tourism, where the guide does all the work for you. *Travels* as "an account of journeys" is recorded from 1591. *Traveled* as in "experienced in *travel*" is from 1413. *Traveling salesman* is attested to in 1885. *Travelers' tales* are stories brought home by survivors, pilgrims, adventurers, and poets. Companion words include the lapidary *trip*, which can refer to a short journey, a clumsy fall, a slip of the tongue, and a bastard. Grosse pounds out a triple ***pun***: "She has made a trip; she had a bastard." And why, other than for diversion, do we hit the road? Hear out Mark Twain: "*Travel* is the death of prejudice."

TRIVIA

Useless but fascinating facts. Trivia is the kind of thing you pick up or learn at a crossroads, and the derivation is exactly that, from the Latin for *crossroads*, from *tri*, three, and *via*, way or road. This allusion is potent, because in ancient times a traveler arriving at an intersection of three streets in Rome or elsewhere in Italy would have encountered a type of kiosk where a wide range of information was listed. If you were a novice, all of it would be valuable; if you were a veteran traveler, it would seem old hat, twice-told tales—ultimately, *trivial talk*, mere gossip, at the crossroads. At universities during the Middle Ages, educators taught the Seven Liberal Arts, known as the *trivium*, the three ways or three roads of learning believed to form the foundation of learning, ***grammar***, logic, and rhetoric, followed by the *quatrivium*, arithmetic, astronomy, geometry, and music. Companion words include the board game phenomenon Trivial Pursuit, which transforms the idea of *trivia* into must-know facts about pop culture.

TROPHY

A monument to victory. In ancient Greece a triumph in war was marked by hanging the spoils or prizes of war—weapons, shields, even body parts—in a tree near the battle site. These monuments were called, in Greek, *tropaion*, defeat, from *trope*, a rout, in the sense of turning back the enemy. By the early 15th century, the *trophy* had been awarded to the Romans, where it became the Latin *trophæum*, a signal of victory, a monument; it was then given to the French, among whom it become *trophée* by the 16th century. Figuratively, *trophy* first was recorded 1569 in English to mean any token or memorial of victory, a physical manifestation. By 1984, the phrase *trophy wife* was popular, according to my *Dictionary of American Slang*. Companion words include *trope*, a figure of speech. Thus, a *trophy* symbolizes the vanquishing of the enemy and a celebration of victory, but is also something to hang above the mantel, as our ancestors hung theirs from a tree. Soccer star David Beckham once said, "With United, we'd all grown up together, we all wanted to win the biggest *trophy* in football. We did it together." Regarding the difference between art and reality, singer Rufus Wainwright remarked, "Life is a game, and love is the *trophy*."

U

UNTRANSLATABLE

A word in one language that has no direct equivalent meaning in another, but strikes a chord and invites paraphrase. Let's start with a word from the Fuegian language of southern Argentina, *mamihlapinatapa,* which means "a meaningful look shared by two people, expressing mutual unstated feeling," listed by the *Guinness Book of World Records* as the 'Most Succinct Word in the World.' Another award-winner, voted 'Most Untranslatable Word in the World,' is the Congolese *ilunga*, which describes a person who is ready to forgive any transgression a first time, willing to tolerate it a second time, but cannot abide it a third time. In German a euphemism for "coward" is *Handschuh-schneeballwerfer*, defined as a person who "wears gloves to throw snowballs." The Flemish language provides us with *iets door de vingesrs kijken*, a phrase to describe the embarrassing behavior of looking through your own splayed fingers; figuratively, looking the other way. The Russian *pochemuchka* describes a person who asks too many questions. Running your fingers through your lover's hair in Brazil is called *cafune* in Portuguese. To wipe your plate of pesto clean with bread, in Italy, is called *faccio la scarpetta,* literally "to wipe one's shoes." *Mokita*, from New Guinea, means a truth everyone knows but no one dares to speak. The Kiriana language of New Guinea provides us with *Biga Peula* which refers to potentially "unforgivable, unatonable, unredeemable words," which we better think twice about uttering. Pidgin gives us *wantok*, "one talk," meaning "we're in this together because you belong to the village and the village has some responsibility to you and you to it." An *untranslatable* Czech example is *litost*, a sudden insight into one's own misery. A student at the 2009 Book Passage Travel Writers and Photographers conference shared one of her favorite words with me: "The word is 'remolino,'" she wrote to tell me. "My brother recalls it translating as 'windmill'—as in a little windmill on the back of the head, but we couldn't find anything like that in the online Spanish-to-English dictionaries. You'll find it translating as a whirlwind, whirlpool, spiral, swirl, and cowlick. I'm afraid 'cowlick' is the mundane word they're giving for it. When he lived in Spain, he was close friends with a man from Chile, and in the Spanish Wikipedia I found that in Chile they call windmills 'remolinos,' while in other Spanish-speaking countries they're generally called 'molinos.' So I guess that's where he got the windmill idea." Another personal favorite of mine is the Eskimo/Inuit word *eyecheektakok.* One of the myriad words for snow in the Arctic, this one refers to the "crack in ice that is pulsating or opening and closing." Finally, *ubuntu* is a venerable African word at the core of Desmond Tutu's Truth and Reconciliation Commission, a concept word that recognizes the interconnection of all people, and which roughly translates as "I am human because you make me human, and you are human because I make you human."

URCHIN

A mischievous child, a brat, a kid with a prickly temperament. An eerily echoic word from the Middle English *yrichon* and *urchon*, hedgehog, and the Proto-Indo-European prefix *gers-*, "spiny, to prickle, to bristle." All told, our English word *urchin* is a visceral memory of how hedgehogs are forever poking their noses where they shouldn't be. The word has gone through two evolutions. First, *urchin* was used during the 16th century to describe people who were believed to resemble hedgehogs, including hunchbacks and goblins. Soon after, by 1556, *urchin* had lost its bristles but retained its sense of raggedness, as applied to the appearance of poor and bedraggled children living in the streets, nosing around in search of food or money or lodging. Companion words include *horripilation*, hair bristling and standing on end, as during a *horror movie.* Similarly, that spiny echinoderm the *sea urchin* has bristles reminiscent of a hedgehog's. Sea *urchins* were called "whore's eggs" in Newfoundland. "In Memory of Dylan Thomas," by poet Cecil Day-Lewis, features an inspired reference to the prickly creature: "The ribald, inspired *urchin* / Leaning over the lip / Of his world, / as over a rock pool / Or a lucky dip, / Found everything brilliant and virgin."

V

VANILLA

A neutrally flavored bean; a type of orchid; a euphemism for bland. A 17th-century word, from the Spanish *vainalla*, little pod, the diminutive of the vividly named *vaina*, sheath. The scabbardlike leaf that reminded Hernando Cortes's randy soldiers of a *vagina*, which happens to be Latin for anything sheath-shaped. That's what they named it, and the name stuck. Since the 1970s, *vanilla* has come full circle to suggest a nonflavor, anything neutral, common, or unimaginative, and by metaphoric extension, "conventional, ordinary sexual tastes." According to the International Ice Cream Association in 2008, 29 percent of those polled preferred *vanilla* to chocolate or strawberry. Nineteen-fifties heartthrob Pat Boone admits, in retrospect, "When you hear my records today, you hear a *vanilla* sounding artist with no black inflection, although I was trying to imitate what I heard."

VAUDEVILLE

Originally, variety entertainment from the French countryside; later a theatrical term for any performance in Tin Pan Alley. One of my proud French-Canadian father's favorite word origins. I remember him pointing out the wonderful fact that the word was rooted in the soil of Vaude-Vire, a Norman town in western France where the 15th-century poet Olivier Basser lived and wrote scores of popular folk songs. *Vaudeville* became shorthand for the music of the people, and in the 1920s the rage of Broadway, where it came to suggest "a slight dramatic sketch interspersed with songs and dances." My son's favorite dancer, Donald O'Connor, said, "I grew up in *vaudeville.* All the hoofers used to get together in a drugstore down the street from the theater, or what-have-you, and if they knew a new step they would teach it to you. I learned hoofing steps that way. But going into ballet didn't come until I made those pictures with [Gene] Kelly."

VENERATE

To worship, honor, respect utterly. For the old Romans, Venus (Greek Aphrodite) was such a beloved goddess they worshiped her in temples all across the Mediterranean and honored her in everyday life for myriad reasons, mainly her influence in matters of the heart. Given that she was the mother of Eros or Cupid, this was considered to be hedging your bets in the chancy game of ***love***.

Her followers, and lovers of art, made pilgrimages to sites like Knidos and Milos to view statues of her that were considered so preternaturally real that, surely, the goddess inhabited the marble. This devotion to Venus came to be known by the 15th century as *veneration*, from the Middle French *venerari*, to worship, revere, from *veneris*, beauty, love, desire. *Venus* lives on in *venerable*, worthy of reverence, often used to describe what is old, like ruins, art, and the elderly. Longfellow expresses this respect when he writes, "I *venerate* old age...." But unguarded, unprotected, untoward behavior under the influence of Venus brings problems: consider the malady also named after her, *venereal* disease, long considered a punishment for sexual misconduct. Companion words contributing to the language: *cupidity*, from Latin *cupido*, desire, but generally a frowned-upon longing bordering on coveting your neighbor's wife. Grosse's ***dictionary*** describes a "bawdy-house," a brothel, as a "School of Venus," and "clap" as "*venereal* taint." To illustrate the venereal connection he cites a lubricious couplet: "He went out by Had'em, and came round by Clapham home"—that is, he went out a-wenching, and got the clap.

VERBICIDE

Word killing; language torture. Victims include the pronunciation "nuke-you-lar" for *nuclear* and the stupefying belief that people in Latin America speak Latin. Derived from *verbum*, an action word, and *cide*, killing, from Latin *caedere*, to cut, hack, strike. Thus, *verbicide* can be used to describe both the deliberate misuse of a word and the obtuse, unintentional murder of its meaning. The consequences are not academic; they effect how—or even whether—we communicate. David W. Orr writes, in *The Nature of Design*, "We are losing the capacity to say what we really mean and ultimately to think about what we mean. We are losing the capacity for articulate intelligence about the things that matter most." Supreme Court Justice Oliver Wendell Holmes wrote, "Life and language are alike sacred. Homicide and *verbicide*—that is, violent treatment of a word with fatal results to its legitimate meaning, which is its life—are alike forbidden." Companions in word crime include the recently conjured *memoricide*, an officially recognized crime perpetrated through the intentional destruction of art or artifacts, which amounts to the murder of cultural memory, as in the destruction of the Sarajevo Library or the National Museum in Baghdad. *Tomecide* is "book killing," used to describe the crimes of book censors and book burners. Another powerful term is *logomachy*, fighting over words, from *logos*, word, and *machia*, fight or struggle.

W

WABI/SABI (JAPANESE)

The aesthetic flaw in art that reveals the soul of the work; the patina that only age can bring to it. Though usually regarded as separate words, as early as the 1940s D. T. Suzuki had linked them as *wabi-sabi*, defining the compound word as "an active aesthetical appreciation of poverty." According to Leonard Koren, roughly speaking, the nearest word in English is probably *rustic*, suggesting something earthy, primitive, unpretentious, unvarnished. Separately, *wabi* suggests a tough, humble spiritual attitude toward life and art, while *sabi* refers to the solitudinous, often ***melancholy*** quality in objects. The overlap between these often-hinged words is an affection and appreciation for imperfection. The old barn that was a little wobbly to begin with and has aged well with twenty coats of flaking red paint would be an example of *wabi-sabi*. If the barn was finally recognized as beautiful, perhaps after years of neglect and being taken for granted, then it could be said to illustrate *shibui*, "the beauty that ages beautifully."

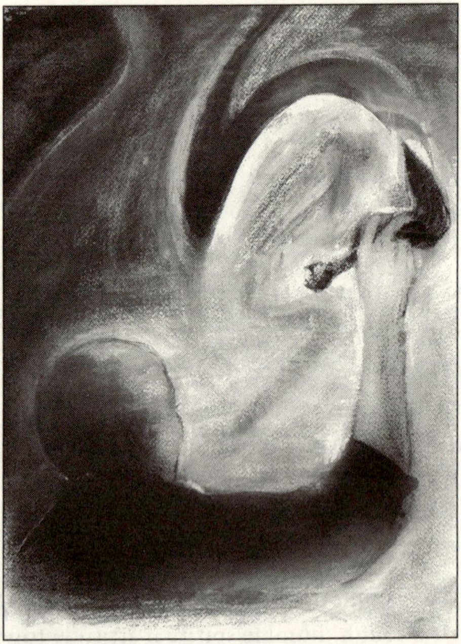

Wabi-Sabi

WEASEL WORD

An empty word, but a full story. This phrase is inspired by the folk memory of watching weasels pierce a small hole in an egg and suck all the life out of it, while leaving it apparently untouched and whole. Thus, weasel words give the appearance of fact but are empty of any real meaning since they don't include any proof or attribution. Examples include "It's commonly known…" "Everybody knows…" "They claim that…" "Contrary to popular belief…" and "Scientists say…" In February 2009, MSNBC's Keith Olbermann interviewed political analyst Richard Wolffe, who said, "Look, the truth is that when you see these kinds of *weasel words* coming from the office of an elected official, you know they've got something to hide."

WEIRD

Strange, curious, ominous. Weird's own peculiar roots reach back to the Old English *wyrd*, fate or destiny, literally "that which comes," and the Proto-Indo-European *wert-*, to turn, wind, bend. Together they suggest something eerie in the human condition, the sense that our fate is already known and that it is unwinding at every moment. The ***numinous*** power of *wyrd* has seen a revival in the recent spate of *Beowulf* ***translations***, as in the passage, "*Wyrd* was very near." As an adjective *weird* means ghastly, unearthly, witchlike; as a noun, fate or destiny, the sense that what will be will be. This haunting suspicion is personified in the Old Norse story of the Three Norns or Fates, who determined human destiny. Shakespeare made them out to be terrifying in *Macbeth*: "The *weird* sisters, hand in hand, / Posters of the sea and land." The phrase conjures up the mythic image of The Fates, the three goddesses presiding over mortals' destinies, who were known to the Scots as the *weirds*. During the 15th century, Scots repeated a legend that the Fates or *weird* sisters had appeared to Macbeth and lured him to his fate. By dint of Shakespeare's portrayal of them in *King Lear*, people came to believe that the *wyrd* in the *weird* sisters meant supernatural or uncanny. *Weird* assumes its modern sense of "odd, uncanny" in 1815, and this is how the novelist Barry Gifford used it: "The whole world is wild at heart and *weird* on top." Helen Keller wrote, "To keep our faces toward change and behave like free spirits in the presence of *fate* is strength undefeatable." Thus, *weird* describes "how strange it seems the way things turn out," or as is still heard in Scotland, "*Dree your weird*," which means "Put up with your lot in life!"

WHATCHAMACALLIT

The brother of thingabob, sister to jigamaree, second cousin to whipplesnizzit, and distant relative of widget. Whatchamacallit is one of scores of terms that refer to indescribable everyday items. It's an eccentric (from Greek *ekkentros*, out of center) family of words for things otherwise orphaned by their very namelessness, such as the stars you see when you're dizzy (*phosphenes*), the flap of leather in your shoe (the *tongue*), the flared grip of wood on the end of a baseball bat (the *knob*), the ridge above your lip (the *philtrum*), the slight column of cartilage that separates your nostrils (the *columella*), or the flap of skin on the outside of your ear (the *tragus*). More companions here than Garrison Keillor, including *doohickey, gizmo, jigger, thingamajig, doodad, thingummy, doodah,* and a gazillion more, such as *blivet*, a terrific onomatopoeic word to describe a useless contraption. You can imagine the eccentric basement inventor down the street asking you to see one. As one wag described it, a really useless invention would be a toothbrush for a chicken. Clever ***rhapsodies*** on the theme of gizmos you know but just can't name.

WHISTLE

To make a sometimes shrill, sometimes melodic sound by pushing the breath through the gap between the teeth or through the puckered lips. Whistle comes from the Old English *hwistilian*, which probably imitates nature's own *whistling* sounds, such as the wind, bird cries, the hissing of serpents, or the steam escaping from a teakettle. To *whistle* can mean to signal, like a train approaching a crossing; to summon, like the neighborhood call to kids for supper; to make music, like Otis Reading at the end of his song "Sittin' on the Dock of the Bay"; or to ***flirt***, as in the *wolf whistles* from construction workers when a pretty girl walks by. Over the centuries, inhabitants of a few remote sites around the world have developed sophisticated *whistling* languages. According to Charles Berlitz, people who live in the "Village of the Birds," nestled in the remote valleys of Kuskoy, in Eastern Turkey, "perfected a system of chirps, tweets, and twitters."

At least three other "whistling villages" are known: Silbo, on La Gamora, in the Canary Islands; Aas, in the Pyrenees; and the village of the Chepang tribe in Nepal. For further instructions, you need go no further than the movie *To Have or Have Not*, and the scene where the sultry Lauren Bacall purrs to the startled Humphrey Bogart, "You know how to *whistle*, right? Just put your lips together and blow."

WISDOM

Sagacity, prudence, the quality of being wise. From Old English *wis*, to see, and *dom*, quality or condition, hence, the quality of seeing; related to *witan*, to know, to wit. To "get *wise*" to Socrates meant to lead the well-lived life; to Dillinger it meant to "understand, learn something." "Wise up" suggests that someone has been on the dullard side and needs to "get smart." Companion words include *wiseacre*, a smart aleck, from the Middle Dutch *wijsseggheri*, soothsayer. *Wisdom tradition* has come to replace the loaded word *religion* for some scholars, such as Huston Smith. Figuratively, *wisdom* describes the capacity to act wisely, as in the famous couplet from the *Tao te Ching*: "A wise man has no extensive knowledge; He who has extensive knowledge is not a wise man." Companion words include the marvelous *waywiser*, an indicator of the way, an adaptation of the Dutch *wegwijzer*, one who shows the way. *Wisdom*, then, can be "way out," as hipsters chanted unwittingly over their bongos, or "way in," as that Taoist hippie, Lao-Tzu, might've said.

Wisdom

WIT

Inborn knowledge, natural or common sense, good humor, entertaining, lively intelligence. It is not being too *facetious* to say that there are myriad expressions pertaining to wit, especially since *facetious* itself originally meant "mirthfully witty," from Latin *facetiae*, and later meant "insincere." Among the witty companion words are *inwit*, knowledge from within, conscience, ***remorse***; and outwit, which first meant "knowledge from without, information," and only later "to outmaneuver." To be *fat-witted* is to be dull or stupid. A *flasher* is "one whose appearance of wit is an illusion." *The Five Wits* are "the five sensibilities, namely common wit, imagination, fantasy, estimation, and memory." *Unwit* means "ignorance"; *motherwit*, "natural talent"; *forewit*, "anticipation"; *gainbite/ayerbite*, the agenbite of inwit, "the backbiting of guilt." A *witworm* is someone who feeds on others' *wit*. According to Herbert Coleridge, in *A Dictionary of the First, or Oldest Words in the English Language* (1859), an *afterwit* is an afterthought. Coleridge registers *biwit* as someone "out of one's *wits*." To Johnson, a *witling* was "a pretender; a man of petty smartness. One with little understanding or grace but desire to be funny." In *Our Southern Highlanders,* Horace Kephart describes a *half-wit* as a silly or imbecilic person, writing, "Mountaineers never send their '*fitified* folks' or *half-wits*, or other unfortunates, to any institution in the lowlands." The witty Bill Bryson tracks *nitwit* down to the Americanization of the Dutch expression *Ik niet wiet,* "I don't know." The last (*witty*) word goes to John Florio, who translated Montaigne into English: "For he that hath not heard of Mountaigne yet / Is but a novice in the school of *wit*."

WORDFAST

True to one's word. What would a word book be without a few "word" words? Fellow words include *wordridden*, to be a slave to words you don't understand, and *wordwanton*, having a dirty mouth. A *wordmonger* is a show-off with words, rather than using them to express meaning, emotion, facts. A *witherword* is hostile language. One blessed with word dexterity is a *logodaedalus*, after the Greek *logo*, word, and *Daedalus*, the inventor of the ***labyrinth***, armor, and toys. Someone stricken with *logophilia* has caught the love of words; whereas *logomachy* is a fight or dispute over words. A *wordroom* is a place to indulge our passions for words, closely related to *lectory*, a place for reading. A *scriptorium* was a ***translation*** hall in medieval Ireland. A "lexicographical laboratory" was a backyard shed in London where James Murray and friends created *The Oxford English Dictionary* over the course of 49 years, comprising twelve volumes and 414,825 words, plus 1,827,306 citations to illuminate their meanings. "Words, words, words," cries Eliza Doolittle in *My Fair Lady,* "I'm so sick of words!" On the other hand, the Divine Sarah Bernhardt longed for them, as she wrote to her lover, Victorien Sardou, "Your *words* are my food, your breath my wine. You are everything to me."

WRITE

To make a mark; to record, communicate. "To trace symbols representing word(s)," says *The Concise Oxford Dictionary,* "especially with pen or pencil on paper or parchment." For as long as we have known, human beings have felt a compunction to record their thoughts, to reach out to one another using the magical letters of their respective alphabets. This effort began with a simple scratch on bark, or papyrus, which, incidentally, later gave us the word *paper.* It makes poetic sense, then, that the root of our word *write* is *writan*, Old English for "scratch." Ogden Nash's quip comes to mind: "Happiness is having a scratch for every itch." Look that up and you'll soon find "scratch" as a synonym for "money," though *writing* for "scratch" has eluded many a writer trying to "scratch out a living." Incidentally, "starting from scratch" refers to making a mark in the dirt for the start of a race, which is often then *written* about. And what do we *write* with? A *ballpoint pen*, which was originally called a "non-leaking, high-altitude *writing* stick." When I first read that, I had to scratch my head before *writing* it down. As for the *secret* of *writing*, I was taught that *writing* is rewriting is rewriting. When an interviewer asked S. J. Perelman how many drafts of a story he was used to *writing*, the gag man for the Marx Brothers and others replied: "Thirty-seven. I once tried doing thirty-three, but something was lacking, a certain—how shall I say?—*Je ne sais quoi.*"

WRITHE

To twist and turn in acute pain. One of J. R. R. Tolkien's favorite words, a 12th-century one from Middle English, from Old English *wruthan*; akin to Old Norse *rutha*, to twist into coils or folds or twist into distortion. Tolkien's avid studies in Anglo-Saxon (he was the world expert on *Beowulf*) provided the inspiration for his famously evil *wraiths* in *The Lord of the Rings*, which are the very embodiment—or enspiritment—of *wrenching, wrangling, and writhing.* Companion words include *wraith*, vividly defined by Mackay as "the supposed apparition of the soul about to quit the body of a dying person." Curiously related is *twistification*, cited in *Southern Appalachian Slang* as a "pejorative term for dancing used by churchmen. Wherever the church has not put its ban on twistifications the country dance is the chief amusement of young and old."

X

XENOGENESIS

Creation of offspring with different characteristics than their parents'. Technically, *xenogenesis* is defined as "the supposed production of offspring markedly different from either parent," according to *The American Heritage Dictionary.* Sometimes it's distinguished from *metagenesis*, altered generation, or *abiogenesis*, spontaneous generation. Figuratively, it describes a certain fear and terror about the identity of your offspring, your own kids, as in, Are they really ours, honey? Are you sure they weren't switched in the hospital nursery? The feeling arises at the age—teens—when your kids just seem *alien* to you (and you to them, by the way); this is just the word to describe that ***weirdness***. But the technical definition doesn't begin to capture the *otherness* of the situation. Better to evoke Sigourney Weaver's cry of surprise and horror in *Alien* when the creature leaps out of the chest of one of her crew. *Xenogenesis* or not, we still ***love*** 'em, right?

XENOPHILIA

Admiration for, attraction to, or outright love for unknown, even strange, objects, peculiar experiences, or exotic people. Often, we remember negative words because of their *sonicky* power, words such as *xenophobia*, "fear or suspicion of strangers." Not often enough do we explore their opposites, such as this obscure but still valuable word, from *xeno*s, unknown or foreign, and *philos*, ***love*** or affection. This word could help you describe someone's otherwise indescribable compulsive collecting, let's say, or Joseph Cornell's lifelong search for the oddments he placed in his shadow boxes, or Peter the Great's secretive ***travels*** around Europe in search of the exotic for his Curiosity Cabinets. My 13-year-old son, Jack, reminds me of a character named Xenophilius Lovegood, in *Harry Potter and the Deathly Hallows*, who is known for his peculiar interest in "unusual or unknown objects, animals, and concepts." Companion words include the even more intense *philoxenia*, the ancient belief that a stranger who knocks on your door might be a god or goddess in disguise, a motif explored in such beloved myths as the story of Philemon and Baucis. This core belief persisted through the centuries in Greece, producing one of the most hospitable cultures in the world. When I went to Athens for the 2004 Olympics I was hosted by a series of Greek friends—and total strangers—who took me in because I'd written a book about their country. One of them, George Tsakorias, explained, "Why am I hosting you? Because I am Greek and I believe, like my ancestors, in *xenophilia*."

Y

YEARN

To tremble with desire, be filled with longing. More than the vaporous *wishing* and less literal than the possessive *wanting*, *yearning* goes to the bone. Since its origins in the 11th-century Old English *geoman* and Middle English *yemen,* German *geron*, desire, it has meant "a strong, often ***melancholic*** desire, a persistent and wistful longing," tinged with something missing in sheer longing—namely, deep pity, sympathy, as in the *yearning* for your child to make it safely home from school, or for the shooting to stop in the war-torn inner city. All these influences go into understanding the depth of Stephen Jay Gould's reflection, "We are glorious accidents of an unpredictable process with no drive to complexity, not the expected results of evolutionary principles that yearn to produce a creature capable of understanding the mode of its own necessary construction." As usual, Goethe's commentary is hard to improve upon: "I love those who *yearn* for the impossible."

YELLOW DOG CONTRACT

Any contract that forbids employees to join a union. This cute and colorful term belies the red-faced American labor disputes that date back to the mid-19th century. The phrase *yellow dog* first surfaces in the spring of 1921 during a time when editorials began appearing, especially in the labor presses. Exemplary of the stance and of the folk etymology of the term is this excerpt from an editorial in the *United Mine Workers* newsletter: "This agreement has been well named. It is *yellow dog* for sure. It reduces to the level of a *yellow dog* any man that signs it, for he signs away every right he possesses under the Constitution and laws of the land and makes himself the truckling, helpless slave of the employer." According to the *Dictionary of Color*, yellow is symbolic because "If someone is *yellow* it means they are a coward, so yellow can have a negative meaning in some cultures. Yellow is for mourning in Egypt, and actors of the Middle Ages wore yellow to signify the dead. Yet yellow has also represented courage (Japan), merchants (India), and peace." A yellow ribbon stands for hope, as we saw with the mothers of soldiers stationed in Iraq; "mellow yellow" was the singer Donovan's way of saying laid-back; "yellow-bellied sapsucker," a species of bird, was an insult in Ireland; *yellow journalism*, reportage that is biased and sensationalized, was practiced by Hearst. "Y'er *yellah*" was one of the worst insults imaginable in the old John Ford Westerns. And here's why the Simpsons characters were drawn *yellow*—to catch the eye of channel-surfers.

YOUTHY

Sort of youthful; not quite adulty. Samuel Pepys preferred *youthsome*, but *youthy* is an actual word, not from Stephen Colbert, but from the great Scot James Halliwell, who included it in his word list from 1611. This corner believes it is a MNW (much needed word), if not an indispensable word, because it captures in a catchy way the essence of the obsession with staying young at all costs or worshipping at the altar of youth. Epitomizing this phenomenon are Hollywood, Paris, and Monaco, among other places, where naturally aging people do unnatural things to themselves in an attempt to appear younger than they are. Compare this monomaniacal behavior to the philosophy championed by the immortal Satchel Paige, who once said: "How old would you be if you didn't know how old you were?" Companion words obsessed with youth include *youth culture*, *youth-oriented*, and *fountain of youth*. Of the concern with youthfulness, Mae West said, "You're never too old to become younger," and the youthsome Oscar Wilde uttered, "An inordinate passion for pleasure is the secret of remaining young." At least he didn't say *youthy*.

YUMA (CUBAN-SPANISH)

Cuban street slang for "foreigner," especially those from Europe or North America. The word was all the vogue for young Cubans after Castro's coup in 1959, and was spontaneously revived after the 1980s surge of asylum-seeking abroad. In the expression "I want to go to *La Yuma*" it became shorthand for "Stateside." To this day, it's a word or phrase relatively unknown in Mexico or Spain, and despite the fact that few Cubans would be able to locate Yuma on a map, it remains popular. The folk etymology traces it back to the 1957 movie version of Elmore Leonard's short story, *3:10 to Yuma,* which mythologized "cowboy honor." To Cubans, the flick became the Hollywood equivalent of a "cherried-out" '63 Impala or the innumerable cowboy dime novels seen around Cuba, which have become emblematic of "honor and obligation." In the movie, a struggling rancher agrees, for the price of a bounty, to take a captured outlaw into custody until the train arrives that will take him to court in *Yuma*, Arizona. While they wait, the outlaw tries to sway the rancher to let him escape. What was in the movie that caught the Cubans' attention and affection? When I viewed the 2007 remake, the lines leapt out at me. The rancher, Dan Evans (Van Heflin/Christian Bale), is stupefied that the outlaw, Ben Wade (Glenn Ford/Russell Crowe), rescued him when he could've escaped: Evans: "Why did you do it, Ben?" Wade: "I don't like owing anybody any favors. You saved my life back at the hotel. That's all right, I've broken out of Yuma before." *3:10 to Yuma* is a cry for freedom.

Z

ZAFTIG (YIDDISH)

Pleasingly, plumply pulchritudinous; alluringly curvaceous. My now nearly forty-year-old going-to-college gift from my parents, the wheel-stop-worthy *Random House Dictionary*, simply and safely defines *zaftig* as "sexually attractive." That hardly does justice to the sizzling *z*, the long-sighing *a,* and the suggestive "tig." We come closer if we think *full-bodied, full-bosomed,* or if we consult a Yiddish dictionary or a Yiddish-speaking friend. *Zaftig* comes from the Yiddish *zaftik*, which means "juicy," from *zaft*, juice. So, properly speaking, a *zaftig* woman is a *juicy Lucy*, full of life, *saucy*, full of sass, *ripe* and *luscious*. To further appreciate *zaftig*, look at Rembrandt's *Delilah*, Titian's *Venus of Urbina*, or Diego Rivera's portrait of his wife, Frida Kahlo. Woody Allen writes, in *Mere Anarchy*, "I never once in forty years looked at another woman except for Elsie, which candidly was not so easy as I'm the first to admit she's not a dish like those *zaftig* courvers who pose in God knows what positions in magazines you probably wait drooling on the docks for as the boats arrive from Copenhagen."

ZEMBLANITY

An unhappy accident or unfortunate encounter; the opposite of serendipity. Coined by novelist William Boyd, in *Armadillo*, after reading of the unfortunate fate of the Arctic island Novaya Zemlya, north of mainland Russia, which was riddled with atomic blasts set off by the Russians. Boyd figured it was news he could live without, but he couldn't quite find the word to say that, so he plucked the word right out of the paper. *Zemblanity* is an experience you didn't want to happen and no one wants to hear about. While researching my book *Once and Future Myths*, in 2000, I came across a column by one of my favorite word virtuosos, William Safire, on "Zemblanity." The word caught my eye because it didn't remotely resemble any word I'd ever seen before. I clipped the column for future reference and recently dug it out. Safire wrote, "The novel's hero … is undone by an outbreak of *zemblanity*, the opposite of serendipity. … Think of another world in the far north, barren, icebound—Zembla. Ergo: *zemblanity*, the opposite of serendipity, the faculty of making unhappy, unlucky and expected discoveries by design." Writers from Jonathan Swift and Alexander Pope to Jules Verne and Salman Rushdie have used Novaya Zemlya's arctic wastes as symbolic of what Charlotte Brontë called "forlorn regions of dreary space." Now this site for testing non-nuclear explosives at a nuclear facility has given birth to *zemblanity*, the discovery of what we don't want to know.

ZEPHYR

One of the eight gods of the winds in classical times; a soft breeze in ours. A refreshing breeze from the West, a gentle wind. *Zephyr* is from *Zephyrus*, the West Wind. While traveling in Taiwan for work on a film and book about tea, I carried with me a ***translation*** of the first known book on the subject, the 8th-century *Classic Book of Tea*, by Lu Yu. There, he writes, with metaphors as rich as the finest mountain Oolong, "The best quality tea must have creases like the leathern boot of Tartar horsemen, curl like the dewlap of a mighty bullock, unfold like a mist rising out of a ravine, gleam like a lake touched by a *zephyr*, and be wet and soft like a fine earth newly swept by rain." Thomas Gray wrote liltingly, in "The Bard," "Fair laughs the morn, and soft the *zephyrs*." Tenderly, Emily Dickinson wrote, "Good Night! Which put the Candle out? / A jealous *Zephyr*—not a doubt—" In August 2009 Leah Garchik wrote in the *San Francisco Chronicle,* "It had been a rare warm day in San Francisco, and I'd pictured after-show lounging on the veranda, with *zephyrs* gently fanning the flames of the nearby fire pit." And this just in from the curiosity department: a *zephyr* is also a lightweight garment worn by rowing crews.

ZITCOM

A sitcom for teens. One of the more colorful of the bountiful examples of newly slung slang. In all *truthiness,* as Stephen Colbert calls slippery talk, it takes a *staminac,* a sleep-starved overachiever, or a *sleep camel,* a power-sleeping workaholic who slaves away for a few days, then draws on those stored *z*'s for the long trek across a week of nineteen-hour workdays, to keep up with the slang. Other eclectic examples: *Spendorphins* is the curious boost of shopping endorphins released upon entrance into the local mall. *Banalysis* is a trivial recap of complex material; *blamestorming* is faultfinding among co-workers. *Chipmunking* is looking all scrunched up while typing out text messages. *Digitalia* refers to indispensable gadgets from the wired world. *Infonesia* is amnesia about information, possibly due to being overwhelmed by *infoglut.* And for me the most stirring neologism of all, *tankmanning*: standing up to authority, after the anonymous man who defied the tanks in Beijing's Tiananmen Square in 1989, providing the world with a modern equivalent of Gandhi's Salt March, King's Selma March, and the actions of the current titan of courageous protest, the pro-democracy figure Aung San Suu Kyi, who has been calmly defying Burmese authorities for the last nineteen years.

ZOMBIFICATION

Turning the living into the walking dead by administering the evil potion of consumerism. Coined by the court jester of NPR, poet-satirist Andrei Codrescu, who based an essay on the word *zombie*. From Haitian, actually a 19th-century word from West African Kikongo, *zumbi*, and *Kimbundu nzambi*, god, a snake god. In the Caribbean it evolved to mean a corpse that's come back to life, as depicted in the *vodou* cult of Haiti and in the American cult of horror films such as *Night of the Living Dead*. Codrescu's revival of the word promises to be even more lethal, suggesting a culture of the walking dead, people deadened by a culture of consumerism and soul-sapping popular culture. By the 1930s *zombie* had also come to suggest a "slow-witted" person. With no little irony, Codrescu writes, "The world is undergoing *zombification*. It was gradual a while, a few *zombies* here and there, mostly in high office, where being a corpse in a suit was de rigueur. ... The worst part about zombies raging unchecked is the slow paralysis they induce in people who aren't quite *zombies* yet." A curious–to-strange companion word is *cad*, from *cadaver*, a corpse or dead body, an example of campus black humor, according to Brewer, meaning anyone not enrolled in a university, thus, uneducated, a deadhead. And who can forget the *Zombies*, the '60s rock group from England, with hits like "She's Not There," "Tell Her No," and "Time of the Season." You see, there's still some life in those old dead words.

THE TEN MOST BEAUTIFUL WORDS

(Source: The British Council, 2004; based on a poll of 40,000 people in 102 countries)

1. mother
2. passion
3. smile
4. love
5. eternity
6. fantastic
7. destiny
8. freedom
9. liberty
10. tranquility

SOURCES AND RECOMMENDED READING

American Heritage Dictionaries, eds. *Word Histories and Mysteries: From Abracadabra to Zeus*. New York: Houghton Mifflin, 2004.

American Psychiatric Association. *A Psychiatric Glossary*. Washington, DC: American Psychiatric Association, 1964.

Asimov, Isaac. *Words from the Myths*. New York: Signet Books, 1961.

Ayto, John. *Dictionary of Word Origins: The Histories of More Than 8,000 English-Language Words*. New York: Arcade Publishing, 1980.

Barfield, Owen. *The History in English Words*. Foreword by W. H. Auden. Great Barrington, Mass.: Lindisfarne Press, 1985.

Bartlett, John. *Bartlett's Shakespeare Quotations*. New York and Boston: Little, Brown, 2005.

Basbane, Nicholas. *A Gentle Madness*. New York: Henry Holt, 1996.

Berlitz, Charles. *Native Tongues: A Book of Captivating Facts on*

Languages and Their Origins. New York: Grossett & Dunlap, 1982.

Bierce, Ambrose. *The Devil's Dictionary*. Cleveland and New York: World Publishing, 1941.

Black, Donald Chain. *Spoonerisms, Sycophants and Sops: A Celebration of Fascinating Facts About Words*. New York: Harper & Row, 1988.

Blount, Roy Jr. *Alphabet Juice: The Energies, Gists, and Spirits of Letters, Words, and Combinations Thereof; Their Roots, Bones, Innards, Piths, Pips, and Secret Parts, Tinctures, Tonics, and Essences; With Examples of Their Usage Foul and Savory*. New York: Farrar, Strauss, and Giroux, 2008.

Blount, Thomas. *Glossographia*. 1656.

Bowler, Peter. *The Superior Person's Book of Words*. Boston: David R. Godine, 1977.

______. *The Superior Person's Second Book of Words*. Boston: David R. Godine, 1987.

______. *The Superior Person's Third Book of Words*. Boston: David R. Godine, 1997.

Brewer, E. Cobham. *Brewer's Dictionary of Phrase & Fable*. Centenary edition, revised. Edited by Ivor H. Evans. New York: Harper & Row, 1981.

Bryson, Bill. *Made in America: An Informal History of the English Language in the United States*. New York: William Morrow, 1994.

Cassidy, Daniel. *How the Irish Invented Slang: The Secret Language at the Crossroads*. Petrolia, Calif.: CounterPunch/AK Press, 2007.

Cawdrey, Robert. *The First English Dictionary: 1604.* John Simpson, ed. Oxford: Bodleian Library, University of Oxford Press, 2007.

Ciardi, John. *A Browser's Dictionary: A Compendium of Curious Expressions & Intriguing Facts.* New York: Harper & Row, 1980.

Coleridge, Herbert. *A Dictionary of the First or Oldest Words in the English Language: From the Semi-Saxon Period of AD 1250–1300: Consisting of an Alphabetical Inventory of Every Word Found in the Printed English Literature of the 13th Century.* London: John Camden Hotten, Piccadilly, 1862.

Concise Oxford Dictionary of Current English. H. W. Fowler, ed. Fourth Edition. Oxford at the Clarendon Press, 1956.

Crabb's English Synonyms. Revised and enlarged. New York and London: Harper and Brothers, 1917.

Danziger, Danny. *The Watchamacallit: Those Everyday Objects You Just Can't Name (And Things You Think You Know About, but Don't).* New York: Hyperion, 2009.

Decharne, Max. *Straight from the Fridge, Dad: A Dictionary of Hipster Slang.* New York: Broadway Books, 2001.

Ernst, Margaret S. *More About Words.* New York: Alfred A. Knopf, 1951.

Farwell, Harold F. Jr., and J. Karl Nicholas, eds. *Smoky Mountain Voices: A Lexicon of Southern Appalachian Speech.* Lexington, Ky.: University of Kentucky Press, 1993.

Florio, John. *A Worlde of Wordes, Or Most copious, and exact Dictionairie in Italian and English.* First published in 1598. Republished in 1611 as *Queen Anne's New Worlde of Wordes.*

Funk, Charles Earle, and Charles Earle Funk Jr. *Horsefeathers & Other Curious Words*. New York: Harper & Row, 1958.

Funk, Wilfred. *Word Origins and Their Romantic Stories*. New York: Bell Publishing, 1978.

Garrison, Webb. *Why You Say It*. New York and Nashville: Abingdon Press, 1955.

Gifis, Steven H. *Law Dictionary*. Woodbury, N.Y.: Barron's Educational Series, 1975.

Green, Jonathon. *Chasing the Sun: Dictionary Makers and the Dictionaries They Made*. New York: Henry Holt, 1996.

Grose, Francis, Captain. *Dictionary of the Vulgar Tongue: A Dictionary of Buckish Slang, University Wit, and Pickpocket Eloquence*. Unabridged, from the original 1811 edition. Nu-Vision Publications, 2007.

Halliwell, James Orchard. *Dictionary of Archaic Words*. London: Bracken Books, 1989. Originally published in London, 1850.

Heifetz, Josepha (Mrs. Byrne). *Mrs. Byrne's Dictionary*. Secaucus, N.J.: Citadel Books, 1974.

Hellweg, Paul. *The Insomniac's Dictionary: The Last Word on the Odd Word*. New York: Ballantine Books, 1986.

Hitchings, Henry. *Dr. Johnson's Dictionary: The Extraordinary Story of the Book That Defined the World*. London: John Murray Publishers, 2005.

Hook, J. N. *The Grand Panjandrum: And 1,999 Other Rare, Useful, and Delightful Words and Expressions*. New York: MacMillan Publishing, 1980.

Hoyt's New Cyclopedia of Practical Quotations. Completely revised and greatly enlarged by Kate Louise Roberts. New York and London: Funk & Wagnalls, 1922.

Johnson, Samuel. *A Dictionary of the English Language.* First published 1755. New edition, edited, compiled by David Crystal. London: Penguin Books, 2002.

______. *Johnson's Insults.* Jack Lynch, ed. New York: Walker Publishing, 2004.

Kacirk, Jeffrey. *Altered English: Surprising Meanings of Familiar Words.* Petaluma, Calif.: Pomegranate Books, 2002.

Kinneally, Christine. *The First Word: The Search for the Origins of Language.* New York: Penguin Books, 2007.

Lempriere, J. *Lempriere's Classical Dictionary of Proper Names mentioned in Ancient Authors.* London: Routledge & Kegan Paul, reprinted 1958. First published 1788.

Lepore, Jill. *A Is for American: Letters and Other Characters in the Newly United States.* New York: Vintage Books, 2003.

Mackay, Charles. *Lost Beauties of the English Language.* London: Bibliophile Books, 1987. Originally published 1874.

MacNeil, Robert. *The Story of English.* (Revised edition.) New York: Penguin Books, 1993.

Mencken, H. L. *The American Language.* Volumes 1–4, plus Supplements 1–2. New York: Alfred A. Knopf, 1936, 1945, 1977.

Moore, Christopher J. *In Other Words: A Language Lover's Guide to the Most Intriguing Words Around the World.* New York: Walker & Company, 2004.

Mugglestone, Lynda. *Lost for Words: The Hidden History of the Oxford English Dictionary.* New Haven and London: Yale

University Press, 2005.

Novobatzky, Peter, and Ammon Shea. *Depraved and Insulting English: Words to Offend and Amuse.* New York, London, Sydney: Harcourt, 1999.

Olive, David. *A Devil's Dictionary of Business Jargon.* Toronto: Key Porter Books, 2001.

Patterson, Ian. *A Dictionary of Color.* London: Thorogood Publishers, 2003.

Payack, Paul J. J. *A Million Words and Counting: How Global English Is Rewriting the World.* New York: Citadel Press, 2008.

Polastron, Lucien X. *Books on Fire: The Destruction of Libraries throughout History.* Rochester, Vt.: Inner Traditions, 2004.

Random House Dictionary of the English Language: The Unabridged Edition. Jess Stein, ed. New York: Random House, 1967.

Reisner, Robert. *Graffiti: Two Thousand Years of Wall Writing.* Chicago: Cowles Book Company, 1971.

Rheingold, Howard. *They Have a Word For It: A Lighthearted Lexicon of Untranslatable Words and Phrases.* Los Angeles: Jeremy P. Tarcher, 1988.

Rosten, Leo. *Hooray for Yiddish: A Book about English.* New York: Galahad Books, 1998.

Salny, Abbie F. *The Mensa Book of Words, Word Games, Puzzles & Oddities.* New York: HarperCollins, 1988.

Schuster, M. Lincoln. *A Treasury of the World's Greatest Letters: From Alexander the Great to Thomas Mann.* New York: Simon & Schuster, 1940.

Shea, Ammon. *Reading the OED: One Man, One Year, 21,430 Pages.* New York: Perigee Books, 2008.

Skeat, Walter W. *Concise Dictionary of English Etymology.* Hertfordshire, UK: Wordsworth Editions, 1993. First published 1882.

Sperling, Susan Kelz. *Lollibones.* New York: Penguin Books, 1977.

Stevenson, James A. C. *Dictionary of Scots Words & Phrases in Current Use.* London: Athlone Press, 1989.

Taylor, Joseph. *Antiquitates Curiosae: The Etymology of Many Remarkable Old Sayings, Proverbs, and Singular Customs.* Originally published 1820. Reprinted, San Francisco: Familiar Productions, 1995.

Wilton, David. *Word Myths: Debunking Linguistic Urban Legends.* New York: Oxford University Press, 2008

Winchester, Simon. *The Meaning of Everything: The Story of the Oxford English Dictionary.* New York and Oxford: Oxford University Press, 2004.

______. *The Professor and the Madman: A Tale of Murder, Insanity, and the Making of the Oxford English Dictionary.* New York: HarperCollins, 1998.

AFTER TALE

There is a coda at the end of George Plimpton's wonderful posthumous collection of essays, *The Man in the Flying Lawn Chair*, titled "Wish List," in which he lists the many things he would like to do before he dies. In that spirit of wishful thinking I offer here a final section of words, some untranslatable but indispensable, that I wish could be revived, used, and enjoyed for their sheer delight.

Charles Mackay titled his 19th-century dictionary *Lost Beauties*, to describe unfortunately abandoned, deleted, or misplaced words or derivations. Edifying examples abound, such as *emersal*, what a light wood does when released as it bops to the water's surface, perhaps inspired by *emerge*. Also *hurkle*, to shrug shoulders. *Acnestis* refers to the part of an animal's back that it just... can't...reach to scratch. Brewer defines *merry-thoughts* as "the *furcula* or wishing-bone in the breast of a fowl; sometimes pulled asunder by two persons, the one holding the larger portion being supposed to have his wish." Fellow words include *merry-go-sorry,* a story that conveys joy and sorrow, happiness and sadness, at same time: good news and bad news. If Mackay can immortalize a raft full of "lost beauties," I can rescue a handful of "lost lovelies," such as *skyme*, a glimmer of light, and *spoffle*, to look busy while trifling over little matters. Stevenson's Scottish dictionary lists the wonderful mouthful *clishmaclaver*, idle talk, gossip—a word Scotland's Radio Three describes as having built into it "a feeling of tongues wagging endlessly." The OED provides us with the pugnacious *bully-scribbler,* a nasty writer. And one of the most charming derivations of all is Diane Ackerman's discovery of the Aramaic origins of the word *poet*, which denotes, says she, the sound of water rushing over pebbles.

The Scottish *tartle* means "to hesitate in recognizing someone or something." Far more fun—and forgivable—to say than that we've gone "brain-dead" when we meet somebody and can't conjure up their name. An eye-popping illustration of this comes from the old Scottish term *groping*, which, according to Cox, 1828, was "a mode of catching trout by tickling them with the hands under rocks or banks." Stevenson calls this Highlands and Borderlands practice *guddling*, "to catch fish with hands by feeling way into places in a stream where they may lurk. The ability to guddle trout is an admired skill." Stevenson reports that in 1987 one Glasgow hospital averaged 21 soccer and rugby players "*hirpling* through the doors every week." I can personally attest to the still widespread Scottish use of the hilarious-sounding *hirple*, to walk with a limp, to hobble. When I was hospitalized for pneumonia in northern Scotland in the summer of 2007, I overheard one nurse joking to another,

"Did ye see the Yank *hirpling* in here this afternoon?"

And finally, a last word to consider reviving: the Greek *aposiopesis*, which means "becoming silent." Remember the old radio comedy *Fibber McGee and Molly*? Each show ended with Fibber saying , "I'll just look here in the hall closet, and—" followed by crashing sounds and then pure, golden, cleansing silence.

Photo by Jo Beaton

ABOUT THE AUTHOR

Phil Cousineau has been a wordcatcher since he was a boy growing up in Wayne, Michigan, a little Civil War–era town outside Detroit and reading Homer, Mark Twain, Ray Bradbury, *Superman* comics, and baseball biographies. From the age of 16 he has been a freelance writer, and for the past twenty years a filmmaker, creativity consultant, and youth sports coach. He has published over twenty-five books, written or co-written eighteen documentary films, and contributed to forty-two other books. Currently, he is the host and co-writer of the nationally broadcast television series *Global Spirit*, on LINK TV.